C++ System Programming Cookbook

Practical recipes for Linux system-level programming using the latest C++ features

Onorato Vaticone

BIRMINGHAM - MUMBAI

C++ System Programming Cookbook

Copyright © 2020 Packt Publishing

Commissioning Editor: Richa Tripathi
Acquisition Editor: Karan Gupta
Content Development Editor: Pathikrit Roy
Senior Editor: Rohit Singh
Technical Editor: Gaurav Gala
Copy Editor: Safis Editing
Project Coordinator: Francy Puthiry
Proofreader: Safis Editing
Indexer: Rekha Nair
Production Designer: Jyoti Chauhan

First published: February 2020

Production reference: 1210220

Published by Packt Publishing Ltd.
Livery Place
35 Livery Street
Birmingham
B3 2PB, UK.

ISBN 978-1-83864-655-4

www.packt.com

Pack‹t›

Packt.com

Subscribe to our online digital library for full access to over 7,000 books and videos, as well as industry leading tools to help you plan your personal development and advance your career. For more information, please visit our website.

Why subscribe?

- Spend less time learning and more time coding with practical eBooks and Videos from over 4,000 industry professionals

- Improve your learning with Skill Plans built especially for you

- Get a free eBook or video every month

- Fully searchable for easy access to vital information

- Copy and paste, print, and bookmark content

Did you know that Packt offers eBook versions of every book published, with PDF and ePub files available? You can upgrade to the eBook version at www.packt.com and as a print book customer, you are entitled to a discount on the eBook copy. Get in touch with us at customercare@packtpub.com for more details.

At www.packt.com, you can also read a collection of free technical articles, sign up for a range of free newsletters, and receive exclusive discounts and offers on Packt books and eBooks.

Contributors

About the author

Onorato Vaticone is a software engineer with over 18 years of experience. A C++ expert, he has deep, system-level programming experience. An Agile coach and XP advocate, TDD and Simple Design are his everyday tools. He has worked on real-time systems (defense and energy transmission) with C++. During this time, he learned to write multiplatform code. Early in his career, he realized that a form of agility was needed. He holds an MSc in cloud computing and a BSc in computer engineering and software. He finds learning how things work under the hood to be fascinating!

About the reviewers

Scott Hutchinson leads a team of C++ and F# developers in Oxnard, California. After a few years as a VB/VBA developer, he started developing with .NET Framework immediately after its launch in 2002. Since 2016, he has done most of his development in C++. He is a mentor for the F# track on Exercism, and teaches functional programming in F# to his team at work. His main professional interests are functional programming and machine learning. When he's not learning some new software development skill, he's usually hiking in the mountains of Southern California.

Daniel Durante is an author and technical editor for Packt Publishing, a consultant and strategist for multiple Fortune 100 companies, and has been a full-stack developer since the age of 12. His code exists in infrastructures such as Hubcash, Stripe, and Walmart.

He has worked on text-based browser games that have reached over 1,000,000 active players, created bin-packing software for CNC machines, embedded programming with Cortex-M and PIC circuits, built high-frequency trading applications, and helped contribute to and maintain one of the oldest ORMs of Node.js (SequelizeJS). He has worked on various books such as *Rust Standard Library Cookbook*, *PostgreSQL Developer's Guide*, and *Rust Programming By Example*, among many others.

I would like to thank my parents, my brother, my mentors, and friends who have all put up with my insanity sitting in front of a computer day in and day out. I would not be here today if it wasn't for their patience, guidance, and love.

Packt is searching for authors like you

If you're interested in becoming an author for Packt, please visit `authors.packtpub.com` and apply today. We have worked with thousands of developers and tech professionals, just like you, to help them share their insight with the global tech community. You can make a general application, apply for a specific hot topic that we are recruiting an author for, or submit your own idea.

Table of Contents

Preface

This book aims to provide ready-to-use solutions (to developers) for the essential aspects of system programming, using the latest C++ standards wherever possible. System programming deals with structuring computer programs that closely interact with the operating system and allow computer hardware to interface with the programmer and the user. Due to its efficient features, namely, low-level computation, data abstraction, and object-oriented features, C++ is the preferred language for system programming. You will learn how to create robust and concurrent systems, and you will also understand the inter-process communication mechanism with shared memory and pipe. Moving forward, you will deep dive into the C++ built-in libraries and frameworks in order to design robust systems as per your requirements.

Who this book is for

This book is for C++ developers who want to gain practical knowledge of systems programming. Though no experience of Linux system programming is assumed, intermediate knowledge of C++ is necessary.

What this book covers

Chapter 1, *Getting Started with System Programming*, introduces you to the fundamentals such as learning about the shell, users and groups, process IDs, and thread IDs to be able to use a Linux system proficiently and so on that you must know for the rest of the book. For example you will learn how Linux is designed, the shell, users and groups, process ID and thread IDs. Furthermore, you will learn how to develop a simple Hello World program, write its makefile, execute it, and debug it. This knowledge, although basic, is fundamental for the more advanced topics that will appear in later chapters.

Chapter 2, *Revisiting C++*, refreshes your understanding of C++17, which will be used throughout the entire book. It'll show why C++ represents a great opportunity for writing good quality code that is concise and more portable than ever. This chapter contains all the new features introduced by C++11/17/20 that you will find useful in this book.

Chapter 3, *Dealing with Processes and Threads*, introduces you to processes and threads that are the foundation of any elaboration. A program is rarely ever made of just one process. This chapter reveals the techniques for dealing with threads and processes in C++. The chapter will demonstrate how easy and convenient it is to deal with threads (and tasks) compared to POSIX. Although C++ does not have a formal way of creating a process, there are rare cases in which a thread cannot do the job.

Chapter 4, *Deep Dive into Memory Management*, introduces you to memory, which is one of the core concepts of dealing with system development. Allocating, freeing, and learning how memory is managed and what C++ can offer to simplify and manage memory is crucial. Furthermore, this chapter presents recipes on how to check and allocate aligned memory and how to deal with memory-mapped I/O.

Chapter 5, *Using Mutexes, Semaphores, and Condition Variables*, shows us the POSIX mechanism solutions and the ones offered by C++ to synchronize threads and processes.

Chapter 6, *Pipes, First-In First-Out (FIFO), Message Queues, and Shared Memory*, focuses on making the processes communicate with each other. There are different solutions available – pipes, FIFO, message queues, and shared memory. For each inter-process communication mechanism, a recipe is provided.

Chapter 7, *Network Programming*, demonstrates how communication takes place from the connection to the end. Communication between processes on different machines is the foundation of the internet today, and TCP/IP is the standard de facto. Both **TCP** (short for **Transmission Control Protocol**) and **UDP** (short for **User Datagram Protocol**) will be described in detail, as the first represents connection-oriented and the latter represents connectionless-oriented. This is quite important these days, especially with the video streaming services that are available online.

Chapter 8, *Dealing with Console I/O and Files*, presents you with useful recipes for dealing with files, I/O to and from the console, and streams of strings.

Chapter 9, *Dealing with Time Interfaces*, provides you with a deep understanding of how to deal with and measure time with the features that are provided by both C++ and POSIX. The chapter will offer ready-to-use recipes for each method.

Chapter 10, *Managing Signals*, introduces us to signals that are software interrupts. They provide a way of managing asynchronous events. For example, a user typing the interrupt key from the terminal, or another process sending a signal that must be managed. Every signal has a name starting with SIG (for example, SIGABRT). This chapter will show the reader how to write code to properly manage software interrupts, what the default actions defined by Linux for each signal are, and how to override them.

Chapter 11, *Scheduling,* shows you how to use POSIX (the C++ standard does not provide this) to set scheduler parameters, the scheduler policy, and the scheduler priorities. System programming is about interacting with the underlying OS as seen so far. The scheduler is one of the main components of every OS and impacts the way processes are allocated on CPUs. There are cases where the developer needs control over this or, at least, tries to influence the scheduler.

To get the most out of this book

Here is a list of requirements for this book:

- Intermediate knowledge of C++.
- Any additional requirements are mentioned in the *Technical requirements* section of each chapter.
- Disclaimer: The C++20 standard has been approved (that is, technically finalized) by WG21 in a meeting in Prague at the end of February. This means that the GCC compiler version that this book uses, 8.3.0, does not include (or has very, very limited support for) the new and cool C++20 features. For this reason, the Docker image does not include the C++20 recipe code.
  GCC keeps the development of the newest features in branches (you have to use appropriate flags for that, for example, -std=c++2a); therefore, you are encouraged to experiment with them by yourself. So, clone and explore the GCC contracts and module branches and have fun.
- Some recipes (especially in Chapter 11, *Scheduling*) require the Docker image running with admin privileges to execute properly. Depending on your Docker configuration, you may be required to run the Docker with sudo. To avoid that you can create a Linux group (for example, docker) and add users to it.

Download the example code files

You can download the example code files for this book from your account at www.packt.com. If you purchased this book elsewhere, you can visit www.packtpub.com/support and register to have the files emailed directly to you.

You can download the code files by following these steps:

1. Log in or register at www.packt.com.
2. Select the **Support** tab.
3. Click on **Code Downloads**.
4. Enter the name of the book in the **Search** box and follow the onscreen instructions.

Once the file is downloaded, please make sure that you unzip or extract the folder using the latest version of:

- WinRAR/7-Zip for Windows
- Zipeg/iZip/UnRarX for Mac
- 7-Zip/PeaZip for Linux

The code bundle for the book is also hosted on GitHub at https://github.com/PacktPublishing/C-System-Programming-Cookbook. In case there's an update to the code, it will be updated on the existing GitHub repository.

We also have other code bundles from our rich catalog of books and videos available at https://github.com/PacktPublishing/. Check them out!

Download the color images

We also provide a PDF file that has color images of the screenshots/diagrams used in this book. You can download it here: https://static.packt-cdn.com/downloads/9781838646554_ColorImages.pdf.

Code in Action

Please visit the following link to check out the CiA videos: http://bit.ly/2uXftdA

Conventions used

There are a number of text conventions used throughout this book.

CodeInText: Indicates code words in text, database table names, folder names, filenames, file extensions, pathnames, dummy URLs, user input, and Twitter handles. Here is an example: "In the second step, we started developing the main method."

A block of code is set as follows:

```
std::cout << "Start ... " << std::endl;
    {
        User* developer = new User();
        developer->cheers();
        delete developer;
    }
```

When we wish to draw your attention to a particular part of a code block, the relevant lines or items are set in bold:

```
auto* mapPtr = static_cast<T*> (mmap(0, sizeof(T) * n,
                                PROT_READ | PROT_WRITE,
```

Any command-line input or output is written as follows:

```
$ grep "text" filename
$ ls -l | grep filename
```

Bold: Indicates a new term, an important word, or words that you see on screen. For example, words in menus or dialog boxes appear in the text like this. Here is an example: "Select **System info** from the **Administration** panel."

Warnings or important notes appear like this.

Tips and tricks appear like this.

Sections

In this book, you will find several headings that appear frequently (*Getting ready*, *How to do it...*, *How it works...*, *There's more...*, and *See also*).

To give clear instructions on how to complete a recipe, use these sections as follows.

Getting ready

This section tells you what to expect in the recipe and describes how to set up any software or any preliminary settings required for the recipe.

How to do it...

This section contains the steps required to follow the recipe.

How it works...

This section usually consists of a detailed explanation of what happened in the previous section.

There's more...

This section consists of additional information about the recipe in order to make you more knowledgeable about the recipe.

See also

This section provides helpful links to other useful information for the recipe.

Get in touch

Feedback from our readers is always welcome.

General feedback: If you have questions about any aspect of this book, mention the book title in the subject of your message and email us at `customercare@packtpub.com`.

Errata: Although we have taken every care to ensure the accuracy of our content, mistakes do happen. If you have found a mistake in this book, we would be grateful if you would report this to us. Please visit `www.packtpub.com/support/errata`, selecting your book, clicking on the Errata Submission Form link, and entering the details.

Piracy: If you come across any illegal copies of our works in any form on the internet, we would be grateful if you would provide us with the location address or website name. Please contact us at `copyright@packt.com` with a link to the material.

If you are interested in becoming an author: If there is a topic that you have expertise in and you are interested in either writing or contributing to a book, please visit `authors.packtpub.com`.

Reviews

Please leave a review. Once you have read and used this book, why not leave a review on the site that you purchased it from? Potential readers can then see and use your unbiased opinion to make purchase decisions, we at Packt can understand what you think about our products, and our authors can see your feedback on their book. Thank you!

For more information about Packt, please visit `packt.com`.

1
Getting Started with System Programming

In this chapter, you will be introduced to the foundations on which the entire book is framed. You will learn (or refresh your knowledge of) how Linux is designed, and you will also learn about the shell, users and groups, process IDs, and thread IDs to be able to use a Linux system proficiently and get prepared for the next chapters. Furthermore, you will also learn how to develop a simple `hello world` program, and find out about its makefile, and also how to execute and debug it. Another important aspect of this chapter is to learn how Linux deals with errors, from both a shell and a source code point of view. This foundational knowledge is important to understand other advanced topics in the following chapters. You can safely skip this and the next chapters if this refresher is not needed.

This chapter will cover the following recipes:

- Learning the Linux fundamentals – architecture
- Learning the Linux fundamentals – shell
- Learning the Linux fundamentals – users
- Using a makefile to compile and link a program
- Using the **GNU Project Debugger** (**GDB**) to debug a program
- Learning the Linux fundamentals – processes and threads
- Handling a Linux bash error
- Handling Linux code error

Technical requirements

In order to let you try the programs immediately, we've set up a Docker image that has all the tools and libraries we'll need throughout the book. This is based on Ubuntu 19.04.

In order to set this up, follow these steps:

1. Download and install the Docker Engine from `www.docker.com`.
2. Pull the image from Docker Hub: `docker pull kasperondocker/system_programming_cookbook:latest`.
3. The image should now be available. Type in the following command to view the image: `docker images`.
4. You should have at least this image now: `kasperondocker/system_programming_cookbook`.
5. Run the Docker image with an interactive shell, with the help of the following command: `docker run -it --cap-add sys_ptrace kasperondocker/system_programming_cookbook:latest /bin/bash`.
6. The shell on the running container is now available.
   Run `root@39a5a8934370/# cd /BOOK/` to get all the programs developed, by chapters.

The `--cap-add sys_ptrace` argument is needed to allow GDB in the Docker container to set breakpoints, which, by default, Docker does not allow.

Learning the Linux fundamentals - architecture

Linux is a clone of the Unix operating system, developed by Linus Torvalds in the early '90s. It is a multiuser, multitasking operating system that runs on a wide variety of platforms. The Linux kernel has a monolithic architecture for performance reasons. This means that it is self-contained in one binary, and all its **services** run in kernel space. This was one of the most controversial topics at the beginning. Andy Tanenbaum (professor at the Vrije Universiteit, Amsterdam) argued against its monolithic system, saying: *This is a giant step back into the 1970s.* He also argued against its portability, saying: *LINUX is tied fairly closely to the 80 x 86. Not the way to go.* In the *minix* user group, there still is the thread of full chat involving Torvalds, Tanenbaum, and others.

The following diagram shows the main Linux building blocks:

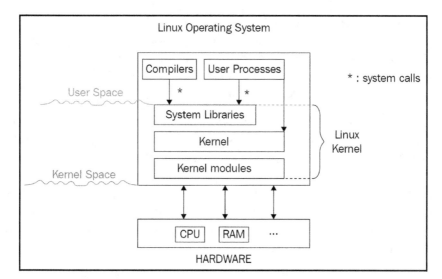

Let's describe the layers we see in the diagram:

- On the top layer, there are user applications, processes, compilers, and tools. This layer (which runs in a user space) communicates with the Linux kernel (which runs in kernel space) through system calls.
- **System libraries**: These are a set of functions through which an application can interact with the kernel.
- **Kernel**: This component contains the core of the Linux system. Among other things, it has the scheduler, networking, memory management, and filesystems.
- **Kernel modules**: These contain pieces of kernel code that still run in kernel space but are fully dynamic (in the sense that they can be loaded and unloaded with the running system). They typically contain device drivers, kernel code that is specific to a particular hardware module implementing a protocol, and so on. One huge advantage of the kernel modules is that users can load them without rebuilding the kernel.

GNU is a recursive acronym that stands for **GNU is Not Unix**. GNU is an operating system that is free software. Note the term *operating system* here. Indeed, GNU used alone is meant to represent a full set of tools, software, and kernel parts that an operating system needs. The GNU operating system kernel is called the **Hurd**. As the Hurd was not production-ready, GNU typically uses the Linux kernel, and this combination is called the **GNU/Linux operating system**.

So, what are the GNU components on a GNU/Linux operating system? Packages* such as the **GNU Compiler Collection (GCC)**, the **GNU C library**, GDB, the GNU Bash shell, and the **GNU Network Object Model Environment (GNOME)** desktop environment, to mention just a few. Richard Stallman and the **Free Software Foundation (FSF)**—of which Stallman is the founder—authored the **free software definition** to help respect users' freedom. *Free software* is considered any package that grants users the following four types of freedoms (so-called **essential freedoms**: https://isocpp.org/std/the-standard):

1. The freedom to run the program as you wish, for any purpose (Freedom *0*).
2. The freedom to study how the program works and to change it, so it does your computing as you wish (Freedom *1*). Access to the source code is a precondition for this.
3. The freedom to redistribute copies so that you can help others (Freedom *2*).
4. The freedom to distribute copies of your modified versions to others (Freedom *3*). By doing this, you can give the whole community a chance to benefit from your changes. Access to the source code is a precondition for this.

The concrete instantiation of these principles is in the GNU/GPL license, which FSF authored. All of the GNU packages are released under the GNU/GPL license.

How to do it...

Linux has a pretty standard folder structure across the distributions, so knowing this would allow you to easily find programs and install them in the correct place. Let's have a look at it as follows:

1. Open a Terminal on the Docker image.
2. Type the command `ls -l /`.

How it works...

The output of the command will contain the following folders:

```
root@620b2c88b4c2:/# ls -l /
total 52
drwxr-xr-x   1 root root 4096 Jun 24 23:40 BOOK
lrwxrwxrwx   1 root root    7 Apr 23 06:57 bin -> usr/bin
drwxr-xr-x   2 root root 4096 Apr 16 07:36 boot
drwxr-xr-x   5 root root  360 Jul 25 19:54 dev
drwxr-xr-x   1 root root 4096 Jul 25 19:54 etc
drwxr-xr-x   2 root root 4096 Apr 16 07:36 home
lrwxrwxrwx   1 root root    7 Apr 23 06:57 lib -> usr/lib
lrwxrwxrwx   1 root root    9 Apr 23 06:57 lib32 -> usr/lib32
lrwxrwxrwx   1 root root    9 Apr 23 06:57 lib64 -> usr/lib64
lrwxrwxrwx   1 root root   10 Apr 23 06:57 libx32 -> usr/libx32
drwxr-xr-x   2 root root 4096 Apr 23 06:57 media
drwxr-xr-x   2 root root 4096 Apr 23 06:57 mnt
drwxr-xr-x   2 root root 4096 Apr 23 06:57 opt
dr-xr-xr-x 198 root root    0 Jul 25 19:54 proc
drwx------   1 root root 4096 Jul 23 20:16 root
drwxr-xr-x   1 root root 4096 May 12 15:36 run
lrwxrwxrwx   1 root root    8 Apr 23 06:57 sbin -> usr/sbin
drwxr-xr-x   2 root root 4096 Apr 23 06:57 srv
dr-xr-xr-x  13 root root    0 Jul 25 19:54 sys
drwxrwxrwt   1 root root 4096 Jul 23 20:16 tmp
drwxr-xr-x   1 root root 4096 Apr 23 06:57 usr
drwxr-xr-x   1 root root 4096 Apr 23 06:58 var
```

As you can see this folder structure is pretty organized and consistent across all the distributions. Under the hood, the Linux filesystem is quite modular and flexible. A user application can interact with the GNU C library (which provides interfaces such as open, read, write, and close) or the Linux system call directly. The system call interface, in this case, talks to the **Virtual Filesystem** (often referred to as the **VFS**). The VFS is the abstraction on top of the concrete filesystem implementations (for example, ext3, **Journaled File System** (**JFS**), and more). This architecture, as we can imagine, gives a high level of flexibility.

Learning the Linux fundamentals - shell

A shell is a command interpreter that receives commands in an input, redirects them to GNU/Linux, and returns back the output. It is the most common interface between a user and GNU/Linux. There are different shell programs available. The most used ones are Bash shell (part of the GNU Project), tcsh shell, ksh shell, and zsh shell (this is basically an extended Bash shell).

Why would you need a shell? A user needs a shell if they need to interact with the operating system through the **command line**. In this recipe, we'll show some of the most common shell commands. Quite often, the terms *shell* and *Terminal* are used interchangeably, even though, strictly speaking, they are not exactly the same thing.

How to do it...

In this section, we will learn the basic commands to run on the shell—for example, to find a file, grep a text into a file, copy, and delete:

1. Opening a shell: Depending on the GNU/Linux distribution, opening a new shell command has different shortcuts. On Ubuntu, press *Ctrl + Alt + T*, or press *Alt + F2*, then type gnome-terminal.
2. Closing a shell: To close Terminal, just type exit and press *Enter*.
3. The find command: This is used to search files in a directory hierarchy. In its simplest form, it appears like this:

```
find . -name file
```

It supports wildcards, too:

```
$ find /usr/local "python*"
```

4. The grep command prints the lines by matching a pattern:

```
$ grep "text" filename
```

grep also supports recursive search:

```
$ grep "text" -R /usr/share
```

5. Pipe commands: Commands running on the shell can be concatenated, to make the output of one command the input for another. The concatenation is done with the | (pipe) operator:

```
$ ls -l | grep filename
```

6. Editing a file: The most two common tools to edit a file on Linux are vi and emacs (if you're not interested in editing the file, cat filename will print the file to the standard output). While the first is inherited by the Unix operating system, the latter is part of the GNU Project. This book will extensively use vi:

```
$ vi filename
```

Next, we will look at shell commands related to file manipulation.

7. This is the command to remove files:

```
$ rm filename
```

8. This is the command to remove directories:

   ```
   $ rm -r directoryName
   ```

9. This is the command to clone a file:

   ```
   $ cp file1 file2
   ```

10. This is the command to clone a folder:

    ```
    $ cp -r folder1 folder2
    ```

11. This is the command to clone a folder using a relative and absolute path:

    ```
    $ cp -r /usr/local/folder1 relative/folder2
    ```

The next section will describe these commands.

How it works...

Let's have a look at the commands discussed in the *How to do it...* section, in detail:

1. The first command searches (`.`) from the current folder and can contain absolute paths (for example, `/usr/local`) or relative paths (for example, `tmp/binaries`). For example, here, `-name` is the file to search.
2. The second command searches from the `/usr/local` folder any file or folder that starts with `python`. The `find` command offers huge flexibility and a wide variety of options. For more information, refer to `man page` through the `man find` command.
3. The `grep` command searches and prints any line that contains the word `text` in the `filename` file.
4. The `grep` recursive search command searches and prints any line that contains the word `text` in any file recursively from the `/usr/share` folder.
5. Pipe command (`|`): The output of the first command is shown in the following screenshot. A list of all the files and directories is passed as input to the second command (`grep`), which will be used to `grep` the filename:

```
root@229a73ca4c0e:/usr/share# ls -l | grep readline
drwxr-xr-x  2 root root 4096 May 12 15:36 readline
root@229a73ca4c0e:/usr/share#
```

Now, let's look at the commands that perform actions such as editing a file, and adding/removing files and directories.

Editing a file:

- The `vi` command will open the filename in edit mode, assuming the current user has writing permissions on it (we will discuss permissions in more detail later). The following is a short summary of the most used commands in `vi`:
    - *Shift* + *:* (that is, the *Shift* key + colon) to switch in edit mode.
    - *Shift* + *:i* to insert.
    - *Shift* + *:a* to append.
    - *Shift* + *:q!* to quit the current session without saving.
    - *Shift* + *:wq* to save and quit the current session.
    - *Shift* + *:set nu* to show the line numbers on the file.
    - *Shift* + *:23* (*Enter*) goes at line 23.
    - Press the (*Esc*) key to switch to command mode.
    - *.* to repeat the last command.
    - *cw* to change the word, or do this by pointing the cursor at the beginning of the word.
    - *dd* to remove the current line.
    - *yy* to copy the current line. If a number *N* is selected before the *yy* command, the *N* line will be copied.
    - *p* to paste the copied line with the *yy* command.
    - *u* to undo.

Adding and removing files and directories:

1. The first command removes the file named `filename`.
2. The second command removes `directoryName` and its content, recursively.
3. The third command creates `file2`, which is an exact copy of `file1`.
4. The fourth command creates `folder2` as a clone of `folder1`:

```
root@620b2c88b4c2:/BOOK/chapter1# rm filename
root@620b2c88b4c2:/BOOK/chapter1# rm -r directoryName
root@620b2c88b4c2:/BOOK/chapter1# cp file1 file2
root@620b2c88b4c2:/BOOK/chapter1# cp -r folder1 folder2
```

There is a common pattern in the execution of the commands shown in this recipe. They are listed as follows:

1. The user types a command and hits *Enter*.
2. The command is interpreted by Linux.
3. Linux interacts with its different parts (memory management, networking, filesystem, and more) to execute the command. This happens in kernel space.
4. The results are returned to the user.

There's more...

This recipe showed some of the most recurrent commands. Mastering all the options, even just for the most common shell commands, is tricky, and that is why man pages were created. They contain a solid and clear reference for the Linux user.

See also

Chapter 8, *Dealing with Console I/O and Files*, will go deeper into console I/O and file management.

Learning the Linux fundamentals - users

Linux is a multiuser and multitasking operating system, so basic user administration skills are a must. This recipe will show you how permissions for files and directories are structured, how to add and remove a user, how to change a user's password, and how to assign a user to a group.

How to do it...

The following series of steps shows useful commands for basic user administration activities:

1. **Creating a user**: Having one user configured for each individual using Linux is not just a best practice, it is also recommended. Creating a user is quite simple:

```
root@90f5b4545a54:~# adduser spacex --ingroup developers
Adding user `spacex' ...
Adding new user `spacex' (1001) with group `developers' ...
```

```
Creating home directory `/home/spacex' ...
Copying files from `/etc/skel' ...
New password:
Retype new password:
passwd: password updated successfully
Changing the user information for spacex
Enter the new value, or press ENTER for the default
Full Name []: Onorato
Room Number []:
Work Phone []:
Home Phone []:
Other []:
Is the information correct? [Y/n] Y
```

The spacex user has been created and assigned to the existing developers group. To switch to the newly created user, log in using the new user's credentials:

```
root@90f5b4545a54:~# login spacex
Password:
Welcome to Ubuntu 19.04 (GNU/Linux 4.9.125-linuxkit x86_64)
* Documentation: https://help.ubuntu.com
* Management: https://landscape.canonical.com
* Support: https://ubuntu.com/advantage
This system has been minimized by removing packages and content
that are
not required on a system that users do not log into.
To restore this content, you can run the 'unminimize' command.
The programs included with the Ubuntu system are free software;
the exact distribution terms for each program are described in the
individual files in /usr/share/doc/*/copyright.
Ubuntu comes with ABSOLUTELY NO WARRANTY, to the extent permitted
by
applicable law.
spacex@90f5b4545a54:~$
```

2. **Updating a user's password**: Periodically, the password must be changed. Here is the command to do this:

```
spacex@90f5b4545a54:~$ passwd
Changing password for spacex.
 Current password:
 New password:
 Retype new password:
 passwd: password updated successfully
 spacex@90f5b4545a54:~$
```

3. **Assigning a user to a group**: As shown, a user can be assigned to a group when created. Alternatively, a user can be assigned to a group at any time, by running the following command:

```
root@90f5b4545a54:~# usermod -a -G testers spacex
here spacex is added to the testers group
```

4. **Removing a user**: Likewise, removing a user is pretty simple:

```
root@90f5b4545a54:~# userdel -r spacex
userdel: spacex mail spool (/var/mail/spacex) not found
root@90f5b4545a54:~#
```

The -r option indicates to remove the spacex home directory and mail spool.

5. Now, let's have a look at the final command, which shows a list of the groups to which the current user (spacex) belongs:

```
spacex@90f5b4545a54:~$ groups
developers testers
spacex@90f5b4545a54:~$
```

As you can see, the spacex user belongs to the developers and testers groups.

How it works...

In *step 1*, we used the adduser command to add the spacex user and, contextually, added the user to the developers group.

Step 2 shows how to change the password of the current user. To change the password, the previous password must be provided. It is a good practice to change the password periodically.

If we want to assign a user to a group, it can be done with the usermod command. In *step 3*, we have added the spacex user to the testers group. The -a and -G parameters just indicate that the new groups (-G) will be appended to the current groups (-a) of the user. That is, the spacex user will be assigned to the testers group, which will be contextually created. The groups command, in the same step, shows which groups the current user belongs to. If you only want to create a group, then groupadd group-name is the command you need.

Step 4 shows how to remove a user with the `userdel` command, passing the `-r` parameter. This parameter ensures that all the files of the user we're removing will be deleted.

There's more...

On a Linux filesystem, each file and directory has a set of information defining who can do what. The mechanism is simple, as well as powerful. The operations allowed on a file (or directory) are read, write, and execute (`r`, `w`, and `x`, respectively). These operations can be done by the owner of the file or directory, by a group of users, or by all users. Linux represents this information with Owner: `rwx`; Group: `rwx`; All Users: `rwx`; or, more simply: `rwx-rwx-rwx` (9 in total). Actually, Linux has one more flag on top of these ones that represents the type of file. It can be a folder (`d`), a symbolic link to another file (`l`), a regular file (`-`), a named pipe (`p`), a socket (`s`), a character device file (`c`), and a block device (`b`). Typical permissions for a file look like this:

```
root@90f5b4545a54:/# ls -l
 -rwxr-xr-x 1 root root 13 May 8 20:11 conf.json
```

Let's see this in detail:

- Reading from the left-hand side, the first character, `-`, informs us that `conf.json` is a regular file.
- The next three characters are about the current user, `rwx`. The user has full **read (r)**, **write (w)**, and **execution (x)** permissions over the file.
- The next three chars are about the group to which the user belongs, `r-x`. All the users belonging to the group can read and execute the file, but cannot modify it (`w` is not selected, marked as `-`).
- The last three characters are about all the other users, `r-x`. All other users can just read and execute the file (`r` and `x` are marked, but `w` is not).

The owner (or the root user) can change the permissions of the file. The easiest way to achieve this is through the `chmod` command:

```
$ chmod g+w conf.json
```

Here, we're asking the Linux kernel to add the write permission (w) to the group user type (g). The types of users are as follows: u (for user), o (for others), a (for all), and g (for group), and the permissions flag can be x, w, and r, as explained previously. chmod can also accept an integer:

```
$ chmod 751 conf.json
```

There is a binary-to-decimal conversion on permission flags for each group type, for example:

wxr: 111 = 7
w-r: 101 = 5
--r: 001 = 1

It could be a little cryptic at the beginning, but it is very practical and handy for everyday use.

See also

The man pages are an infinite resource of information and should be the first thing you look at. Commands such as man groups, man userdel, or man adduser will help with this.

Using a makefile to compile and link a program

A makefile is a file that describes the relationship among the sources of a program used by the make utility to build (compile and link) the target goal (executable, shared object, and more). Makefiles are really important as they help to keep sources organized and easy to maintain. A program, to become executable, must be compiled and linked with other libraries. GCC is the most widely used collection of compilers. The two compilers used in the C and C++ world are GCC and g++ (for the C and C++ programs, respectively). This book will use g++.

How to do it...

This section will show how a makefile is written, to compile and run a simple C++ program. We'll develop a simple program, and create its makefile to learn its rules:

1. Let's start by developing the program by opening the `hello.cpp` file:

   $vi hello.cpp

2. Type in the following code (refer to the *Learning the Linux fundamentals - shell* recipe to review the `vi` commands):

   ```
   #include <iostream>
   int main()
   {
       std::cout << "Hello World!" << std::endl;
       return 0;
   }
   ```

3. Save and exit: in `vi`, from the command mode, type `:wq`, which means write and quit. The `:x` command has the same effect.

4. From the shell, create a new file called `Makefile`:

   $ vi Makefile

5. Type in the following code:

   ```
   CC = g++
   all: hello
   hello: hello.o
           ${CC} -o hello hello.o
   hello.o: hello.cpp
           ${CC} -c hello.cpp
   clean:
           rm hello.o hello
   ```

Although this is a typical `Hello World!` program, it is useful to show how a makefile is structured.

How it works...

Simply, a makefile consists of a set of rules. A rule consists of a target, a list of prerequisites, and a command.

In the first step, we opened the file (`hello.cpp`) and typed the program listed in *step 2*. Likewise, we opened another file, `Makefile`, in the same folder of the `hello.cpp` program, and typed the specific makefile commands. Let's now dive into the makefile internals. A typical makefile has the following content:

1. The first rule consists of a target called `all`, and a prerequisite called `hello`. There is no command for this rule.
2. The second rule consists of a target called `hello`. It has a prerequisite on `hello.o` and a command to link: `g++`.
3. The third rule has a target called `hello.o`, a prerequisite on `hello.cpp`, and a command to compile: `g++ -c hello.cpp`.
4. The last rule has a `clean` target with a command to remove all the `hello` and `hello.o` executables. This forces the recompilation of the files.
5. For any rule, if any of the source files change, then the command defined is executed.

We're now able to compile the program using the makefile we created:

```
$ make
```

We're also able to execute the program, whose output is as follows:

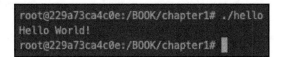

```
root@229a73ca4c0e:/BOOK/chapter1# ./hello
Hello World!
root@229a73ca4c0e:/BOOK/chapter1#
```

The process of generating a binary executable from a source file includes the phase of compilation and linking, which here is compressed inside a single command; it'll be like this in most cases. In general, a large system code base relies on more sophisticated mechanisms but the steps are still the same: source file editing, compilation, and linking.

There's more...

This simple example just showed us the very basic concepts of a makefile and its `make` command. There is much more to it than that. Here are a few examples:

1. Use of macros: A makefile allows the use of macros, which can be seen as **variables**. These can be used to organize the makefile to be more modular, for example:

   - A macro for all the dynamic libraries used in the program: `LIBS = -lxyz -labc`.
   - A macro for the compiler itself (in case you want to change to another compiler): `COMPILER = GCC`.
   - Reference these macros over all the makefile: `$(CC)`. This gives us the freedom to make changes in just one place.

2. By just typing `make` on a shell, the first rule defined in the makefile will run. In our case, the first rule is `all`. If we changed the makefile by putting `clean` as a first rule, running `make` without parameters would execute the `clean` rule. In general, you'll always pass some parameters—for example, `make clean`.

Using GDB to debug a program

Debugging is the process of identifying and removing errors from software systems. The GNU/Linux operating system has a **standard** *de facto* tool (that is, not part of any standard, but used by almost anybody in the Linux world) called GDB. The GDB version installed on this book's Docker is version 8.2.91. Of course, there are graphical tools that can use GDB under the hood, but GDB on Linux is the way to go for its reliability, simplicity, and speed. In this recipe, we will debug the software we've written in the previous recipe.

How to do it...

In order to use some of the GDB commands, we need to modify the previous program and add some variables in it:

1. Open a shell and modify the `hello.cpp` file by typing in the following code:

```
#include <iostream>
int main()
{
    int x = 10;
```

```
    x += 2;
    std::cout << "Hello World! x = " << x << std::endl;
    return 0;
}
```

This is a very simple program: take a variable, add 2 to it, and print the result.

2. Let's make sure that the program is compiled by typing the following command:

```
root@bffd758254f8:~/Chapter1# make
g++ -c hello.cpp
g++ -o hello hello.o
```

3. Now that we have the executable, we will debug it. From the command line, type gdb hello:

```
root@bffd758254f8:~/Chapter1# gdb hello
GNU gdb (Ubuntu 8.2.91.20190405-0ubuntu3) 8.2.91.20190405-git
Copyright (C) 2019 Free Software Foundation, Inc.
License GPLv3+: GNU GPL version 3 or later
<http://gnu.org/licenses/gpl.html>
This is free software: you are free to change and redistribute it.
There is NO WARRANTY, to the extent permitted by law.
Type "show copying" and "show warranty" for details.
This GDB was configured as "x86_64-linux-gnu".
Type "show configuration" for configuration details.
For bug reporting instructions, please see:
<http://www.gnu.org/software/gdb/bugs/>.
Find the GDB manual and other documentation resources online at:
<http://www.gnu.org/software/gdb/documentation/>.
For help, type "help".
Type "apropos word" to search for commands related to "word"...
Reading symbols from hello...
(No debugging symbols found in hello)
(gdb)
```

4. As you can see, the last line says (No debugging symbols found in hello). GDB doesn't have to debug symbols to debug the program, so we have to communicate to the compiler that the debug symbols are to be included during the compilation. We have to quit the current session; to do this, type q (*Enter*). Then, edit the makefile, and add the -g option to the g++ compiler section (the hello.o target):

```
CC = g++
all: hello
hello: hello.o
    ${CC} -o hello hello.o
```

```
hello.o: hello.cpp
    $(CC) -c -g hello.cpp
clean:
    rm hello.o hello
```

5. Let's run it again, but, first, we have to rebuild the application with the `make` command:

```
root@bcec6ff72b3c:/BOOK/chapter1# gdb hello
GNU gdb (Ubuntu 8.2.91.20190405-0ubuntu3) 8.2.91.20190405-git
Copyright (C) 2019 Free Software Foundation, Inc.
License GPLv3+: GNU GPL version 3 or later
<http://gnu.org/licenses/gpl.html>
This is free software: you are free to change and redistribute it.
There is NO WARRANTY, to the extent permitted by law.
Type "show copying" and "show warranty" for details.
This GDB was configured as "x86_64-linux-gnu".
Type "show configuration" for configuration details.
For bug reporting instructions, please see:
<http://www.gnu.org/software/gdb/bugs/>.
Find the GDB manual and other documentation resources online at:
 <http://www.gnu.org/software/gdb/documentation/>.
For help, type "help".
Type "apropos word" to search for commands related to "word"...
Reading symbols from hello...
(No debugging symbols found in hello)
(gdb)
```

We're ready to debug it. A debug session typically includes setting breakpoints, watching the content of variables, setting watchpoints, and many others. The next section will show the most common debug commands.

How it works...

In the previous section, we have seen the steps necessary to create a program and a makefile. In this section, we'll learn how to debug the `Hello World!` program we developed.

Let's start by visualizing the code we're going to debug. We do this by running the `l` command (short for list):

```
(gdb) l
1 #include <iostream>
2 int main()
3 {
4     int x = 10;
5     x += 2;
6     std::cout << "Hello World! x = " << x << std::endl;
7     return 0;
8 }
```

We have to set a breakpoint. To set a breakpoint, we run the `b 5` command. This sets a breakpoint to the code line number 5 in the current module:

```
(gdb) b 5
Breakpoint 1 at 0x1169: file hello.cpp, line 5.
(gdb)
```

It's time to run the program now. To run a program, we type the `r` command. This runs the `hello` program we started with GDB:

```
(gdb) r
Starting program: /root/Chapter1/hello
```

Once started, GDB will automatically stop at any breakpoint hit by the process flow. In this case, the process runs, and then stops at line 5 of the `hello.cpp` file:

```
Breakpoint 1, main () at hello.cpp:5
5 x += 2;
```

To proceed step by step, we run the `n` command (that is, step over) on GDB. This executes the current visualized line of code. A similar command is `s` (step into). If the current command is a function, it steps into the function:

```
(gdb) n
6 std::cout << "Hello World! x = " << x << std::endl;
the 'n' command (short for next) execute one line. Now we may want to check
the content of the variable x after the increment:
```

If we need to know the content of a variable, we run the `p` command (short for print), which prints the content of a variable. In this case, as expected, `x = 12` gets printed:

```
(gdb) p x
$1 = 12
```

Now, let's run the program until the end (or until the next breakpoint, if set). This is done with the c command (short for continue):

```
(gdb) c
Continuing.
Hello World! x = 12
[Inferior 1 (process 101) exited normally]
(gdb)
```

GDB really acts as an interpreter by letting the programmer step the program line by line. This helps the developer to troubleshoot problems, see the content of variables at runtime, change the status of variables, and more.

There's more...

GDB has a lot of very useful commands. In the following chapters, GDB will be explored more. There are four more commands to show here:

1. s: Short for step. If called on a method, it steps into it.
2. bt: Short for backtrace. Prints the call stack.
3. q: Short for quit. Use to exit GDB.
4. d: Short for delete. It removes a breakpoint. For example, d 1 removes the first breakpoint set.

> The main page of the GNU GDB Project can be found here: https://www.gnu.org/software/gdb. More detailed information can be found on the man dbg man pages and online. You can also refer to *Using GDB: A Guide to the GNU Source-Level Debugger*, by Richard M. Stallman and Roland H. Pesch.

Learning the Linux fundamentals - processes and threads

Processes and threads are the execution units of any operating system. In this recipe, you'll learn how to deal with processes and threads on GNU/Linux on the command line. A process is a running instance of a program with a well-defined set of resources such as files, processor state, and threads of execution allocated to it.

A process in Linux is defined by the `task_struct` structure defined in the `sched.h` header file. On the other hand, a thread is defined by the `thread_info` structure in the `thread_info.h` header file. A thread is one possible flow of execution of the main process. A process has at least one thread (the main thread). All the threads of a process run concurrently on a system.

One aspect to keep in mind on Linux is that it doesn't differentiate between processes and threads. A thread is just like a process that shares some resources with some other processes. For this reason, in Linux, threads are often referred to as a **lightweight process (LWP)**.

How to do it...

In this section, we'll learn, step by step, all the most common commands to control processes and threads on a GNU/Linux distribution:

1. The `ps` command shows the processes, attributes, and other parameters in the current system:

   ```
   root@5fd725701f0f:/# ps u
   USER PID %CPU %MEM VSZ RSS TTY STAT START TIME COMMAND
   root 1 0.0 0.1 4184 3396 pts/0 Ss 17:20 0:00 bash
   root 18 0.0 0.1 5832 2856 pts/0 R+ 17:22 0:00 ps u
   ```

2. Another way to get info on a process (and its threads) is to look in the `/process/PID` folder. This folder contains all the process info, threads of the process (in the form of subfolders with **process identifiers (PIDs)**), memory, and much more:

   ```
   root@e9ebbdbe3899:/# ps aux
   USER PID %CPU %MEM VSZ RSS TTY STAT START TIME COMMAND
   root 1 0.0 0.1 4184 3344 pts/0 Ss 16:24 0:00 bash
   root 149 0.0 0.1 4184 3348 pts/1 Ss 17:40 0:00 bash
   root 172 85.0 0.0 5832 1708 pts/0 R+ 18:02 0:04 ./hello
   root 173 0.0 0.1 5832 2804 pts/1 R+ 18:02 0:00 ps aux
   root@e9ebbdbe3899:/# ll /proc/172/
   total 0
   dr-xr-xr-x 9 root root 0 May 12 18:02 ./
   dr-xr-xr-x 200 root root 0 May 12 16:24 ../
   dr-xr-xr-x 2 root root 0 May 12 18:02 attr/
   -rw-r--r-- 1 root root 0 May 12 18:02 autogroup
   -r-------- 1 root root 0 May 12 18:02 auxv
   -r--r--r-- 1 root root 0 May 12 18:02 cgroup
   --w------- 1 root root 0 May 12 18:02 clear_refs
   ```

```
-r--r--r-- 1 root  root  0 May 12 18:02 cmdline
-rw-r--r-- 1 root  root  0 May 12 18:02 comm
-rw-r--r-- 1 root  root  0 May 12 18:02 coredump_filter
-r--r--r-- 1 root  root  0 May 12 18:02 cpuset
lrwxrwxrwx 1 root  root  0 May 12 18:02 cwd -> /root/Chapter1/
-r-------- 1 root  root  0 May 12 18:02 environ
lrwxrwxrwx 1 root  root  0 May 12 18:02 exe -> /root/Chapter1/hello*
dr-x------ 2 root  root  0 May 12 18:02 fd/
dr-x------ 2 root  root  0 May 12 18:02 fdinfo/
-rw-r--r-- 1 root  root  0 May 12 18:02 gid_map
-r-------- 1 root  root  0 May 12 18:02 io
-r--r--r-- 1 root  root  0 May 12 18:02 limits
...
```

3. A process can be killed, too. Technically, killing a process means stopping its execution:

   root@5fd725701f0f:/# kill -9 PID

This command sends the `kill` signal (9) to the process identified with the PID. Other signals can be sent to processes—for example, HUP (hangup) and INT (interrupt).

How it works...

In *step 1* for each process, we can see the following:

- The user to whom the process belongs
- The PID
- The percentage of CPU and memory in a specific moment
- When the process started, and its running time
- The command used to run the process

Through the `ps aux` command, we can grab the PID of the `hello` process, which is 172. We can now look into the /proc/172 folder.

Processes and threads are building blocks of an operating system. In this recipe, we've seen how to interact with the kernel on the command line to get info on processes through a command (for example, `ps`), and by looking into a specific folder that Linux updates as the process runs. Again, every time we invoke a command (to get info on a process, in this case), the command must enter in kernel space to get valid and updated info on it.

There's more...

The ps command has many more parameters than the basic one seen in this recipe. A complete list is available on its Linux man page, man ps.

A more advanced and interactive command to consider as an alternative to ps is the top command, man top.

Handling a Linux bash error

We've seen that one way to interact with the Linux kernel is through the shell, by invoking commands. A command can fail, as we can imagine, and a way to communicate a failure is to return a non-negative integer value. 0, in most cases, means success. This recipe will show you how to deal with error handling on the shell.

How to do it...

This section will show you how to get errors directly from the shell and via a script, which is a fundamental aspect of script development:

1. First, run the following command:

```
root@e9ebbdbe3899:/# cp file file2
cp: cannot stat 'file': No such file or directory
root@e9ebbdbe3899:/# echo $?
1
```

2. Create a new file called first_script.sh and type in the following code:

```
#!/bin/bash
cat does_not_exists.txt
if [ $? -eq 0 ]
then
    echo "All good, does_not_exist.txt exists!"
    exit 0
else
    echo "does_not_exist.txt really DOES NOT exists!!" >&2
    exit 11
fi
```

3. Save the file, and exit (`:wq` or `:x`).

4. Give execution permission (the `x` flag) to the current user for the `first_script.sh` file:

```
root@e9ebbdbe3899:~# chmod u+x first_script.sh
```

These steps are detailed in the next section.

How it works...

In *step 1*, the `cp` command failed, as `file` and `file2` don't exist. By querying `echo $?`, we get the error code; in this case, it is `1`. This is particularly useful when writing bash scripts where we might need to check for a particular condition.

In *step 2*, the script just lists the `does_not_exist.txt` file and reads the error code returned. If all goes fine, it prints an acknowledgment message and returns `0`. Otherwise, it returns the error code `11`.

By running the script, we get the output as follows:

```
root@229a73ca4c0e:/BOOK/chapter1# ./first_script.sh
cat: does_not_exists.txt: No such file or directory
does_not_exists.txt really DOES NOT exists!!
root@229a73ca4c0e:/BOOK/chapter1#
```

Here, we notice a couple of things:

- We logged our error string.
- The error code is the one we had set in the script.

Under the hood, every time a command is invoked, it enters into kernel space. The command is executed, and a return status is sent back to the user in the form of an integer. It's really important to consider this return status, as we might have a command that apparently succeeded (no output) but eventually failed (returns code different from `0`).

There's more...

One important aspect of the return status of the commands is that it can be used to (conditionally) run the next command. Two important operators are used for this purpose: `&&` (AND) and `||` (OR).

In the two commands here, the second is run if—and only if—the first succeeds (the `&&` operator). `file.txt` is removed if it is copied to the project folder:

```
cp file.txt ~/projects && rm -f file.txt
```

Let's have a look at a second example:

```
cp file.txt ~/projects || echo 'copy failed!'
```

In the preceding example, the second command is run only if the first fails (the `||` operator). `copy failed!` is printed if the copy fails.

In this recipe, we just showed that commands can be combined on a shell script to create a more complex command, and by controlling the error code, we can control the flow of execution. Man pages are a great resource as they contain all the commands and error codes (for example, `man cp` and `man cat`).

Handling Linux code error

This recipe represents the second side of the coin in the topic of error handling: error handling at a source-code level. Linux *exposes* its kernel features through commands, as well as through a programming API. In this recipe, we'll see how to deal with error codes and `errno` through a C program, to open a file.

How to do it...

In this section, we'll see how to get the error from a system call in a C program. To do this, we'll create a program to open a non-existent file and show the details of the error returned by Linux:

1. Create a new file: `open_file.c`.
2. Edit the following code in the newly created file:

```c
#include <fcntl.h>
#include <stdio.h>
#include <stdlib.h>
#include <errno.h>
#include <string.h>

int main(int argc, char *argv[])
{
    int fileDesc = open("myFile.txt", O_RDONLY);
```

```
        if (fileDesc == -1)
        {
            fprintf(stderr, "Cannot open myFile.txt .. error: %d\n",
                fileDesc);
            fprintf(stderr, "errno code = %d\n", errno);
            fprintf(stderr, "errno meaningn = %s\n", strerror(errno));
            exit(1);
        }
    }
```

3. Save the file and exit (:x).
4. Compile the code: gcc open_file.c.
5. The preceding compilation (without parameters) will produce a binary file
   called a.out (which is the default name on the Linux and Unix operating
   systems).

How it works...

The program listed tries to open a file in reading mode. Errors are printed on standard
error, through the fprintf command. By running it, the output will be as follows:

```
root@229a73ca4c0e:/BOOK/chapter1# ./a.out
Cannot open myFile.txt .. error: -1
errno code = 2
errno meaningn = No such file or directory
root@229a73ca4c0e:/BOOK/chapter1#
```

There are a couple of considerations to highlight. The program is developed by strictly
following the man page of the open system call (man 2 open):

```
RETURN VALUES
       If successful, open() returns a non-negative integer, termed a
file descriptor. It
       returns -1 on failure, and sets errno to indicate the error
```

The developer (us, in this case) checked that the file descriptor was -1 (confirmed
by fprintf) to print errno too (with code 2). What does errno 2 mean? strerror is
useful exactly for this scope, to translate from errno (which is cryptic) to something the
programmer (or the user) would understand.

There's more...

In `Chapter 2`, *Revisiting C++*, we'll see how C++ helps programmers by providing higher-level mechanisms, and easy-to-write and more concise code. Even if we try to minimize the interaction with the kernel API directly, in favor of the use of the C++11-14-17 higher-level mechanism, there will be cases where we'll need to check the error status. In those cases, you are invited to pay attention to error management.

Revisiting C++ 2

This chapter acts as a refresher on C++ 11-20, which will be used throughout this book. We'll explain why C++ represents a great opportunity that shouldn't be missed when it comes to writing good quality code that's concise and more portable than ever.

This chapter does not contain *all* the new features introduced by C++ (11 through 20) – just the ones we will be using for the rest of this book. Specifically, you'll get a refresher (if you already know) or learn (if you are new) about the most essential new C++ skills needed to write modern code. You'll work, hands-on, with lambda expressions, atomics, and move semantics, just to mention a few.

This chapter will cover the following recipes:

- Understanding C++ primitive types
- Lambda expressions
- Automatic type deduction and `decltype`
- Learning how atomic works
- Learning how `nullptr` works
- Smart pointers – `unique_ptr` and `shared_ptr`
- Learning how semantics works
- Understanding concurrency
- Understanding the filesystem
- The C++ Core Guidelines
- Adding GSL to your makefile
- Understanding concepts
- Using span
- Learning how Ranges work
- Learning how modules work

Technical requirements

To let you try out the programs in this chapter immediately, we've set up a Docker image that has all the tools and libraries we'll need throughout this book. It's based on Ubuntu 19.04.

In order to set it up, follow these steps:

1. Download and install the Docker Engine from `www.docker.com`.
2. Pull the image from Docker Hub: `docker pull kasperondocker/system_programming_cookbook:latest`.
3. The image should now be available. Type in the following command to view the image: `docker images`.
4. Now, you should have the following image: `kasperondocker/system_programming_cookbook`.
5. Run the Docker image with an interactive shell with the help of the following command: `docker run -it --cap-add sys_ptrace kasperondocker/system_programming_cookbook:latest /bin/bash`.
6. The shell on the running container is now available. Use `root@39a5a8934370/#` `cd /BOOK/` to get all the programs that have been developed for the chapters in this book.

The `--cap-add sys_ptrace` argument is needed to allow GDB to set breakpoints in the Docker container which, by default, Docker does not allow.

 Disclaimer: The C++20 standard has been approved (that is, technically finalized) by WG21 in a meeting in Prague at the end of February. This means that the GCC compiler version that this book uses, 8.3.0, does not include (or has very, very limited support for) the new and cool C++20 features. For this reason, the Docker image does not include the C++20 recipe code. GCC keeps the development of the newest features in branches (you have to use appropriate flags for that, for example, `-std=c++2a`); therefore, you are encouraged to experiment with them by yourself. So, clone and explore the GCC contracts and module branches and have fun.

Understanding C++ primitive types

This recipe will show all the primitive data types defined by the C++ standard, as well as their size.

How to do it...

In this section, we'll have a closer look at what primitives the C++ standard defines and what other information is important. We'll also learn that although the standard does not define a size for each, it defines another important parameter:

1. First, open a new Terminal and type in the following program:

```cpp
#include <iostream>
#include <limits>

int main ()
 {
    // integral types section
    std::cout << "char " << int(std::numeric_limits<char>::min())
              << "-" << int(std::numeric_limits<char>::max())
              << " size (Byte) =" << sizeof (char) << std::endl;
    std::cout << "wchar_t " << std::numeric_limits<wchar_t>::min()
              << "-" <<   std::numeric_limits<wchar_t>::max()
              << " size (Byte) ="
              << sizeof (wchar_t) << std::endl;
    std::cout << "int " << std::numeric_limits<int>::min() << "-"
              << std::numeric_limits<int>::max() << " size
                 (Byte) ="
              << sizeof (int) << std::endl;
    std::cout << "bool " << std::numeric_limits<bool>::min() << "-"
              << std::numeric_limits<bool>::max() << "
                 size (Byte) ="
              << sizeof (bool) << std::endl;
    // floating point types
    std::cout << "float " << std::numeric_limits<float>::min() <<
                 "-"
              << std::numeric_limits<float>::max() << " size
                 (Byte) ="
              << sizeof (float) << std::endl;
    std::cout << "double " << std::numeric_limits<double>::min()
                 << "-"
              << std::numeric_limits<double>::max() << " size
                 (Byte) ="
              << sizeof (double) << std::endl;
```

```
        return 0;
    }
```

2. Next, build (compile and link) g++ primitives.cpp.
3. This will produce an executable file with the (default) name of a.out.

How it works...

The output of the preceding program will be something like this:

```
root@7205968ae436:/BOOK/chapter2/primitiveTypes# ./a.out
char -128-127 size (Byte) =1
wchar_t -2147483648-2147483647 size (Byte) =4
int -2147483648-2147483647 size (Byte) =4
bool 0-1 size (Byte) =1
float 1.17549e-38-3.40282e+38 size (Byte) =4
double 2.22507e-308-1.79769e+308 size (Byte) =8
root@7205968ae436:/BOOK/chapter2/primitiveTypes#
```

This represents the minimum and maximum values that a type can represent and the size in bytes for the current platform.

The C++ standard **does not** define the size of each type, but it does define the minimum **width**:

- char: Minimum width = 8
- short int: Minimum width = 16
- int: Minimum width = 16
- long int: Minimum width = 32
- long int int: Minimum width = 64

This point has huge implications as different platforms can have different sizes and a programmer should cope with this. To help us get some guidance regarding data types, there is the concept of a data model. A **data model** is a set of choices (a specific size for each type) made by each implementation (the psABI of the architecture that compilers and operating systems adhere to) to define all the primitive data types. The following table shows a subset of various types and data models that exist:

Data type	LP32	ILP32	LLP64	LP64
char	8	8	8	8

short int	16	16	16	16
int	16	32	32	32
long	32	32	32	64
pointer	32	32	64	64

The Linux kernel uses the LP64 data model for 64-bit architectures (x86_64).

We briefly touched on the psABI topic (short for **platform-specific Application Binary Interfaces (ABIs)**). Each architecture (for example, x86_64) has a psABI specification that the OS adheres to. The **GNU Compiler Collection (GCC)** has to know these details as it has to know the sizes of the primitive types it compiles. The `i386.h` GCC header file contains the size of the primitive data types for that architecture:

```
root@453eb8a8d60a:~# uname -a
 Linux 453eb8a8d60a 4.9.125-linuxkit #1 SMP Fri Sep 7 08:20:28 UTC 2018
 x86_64 x86_64 x86_64 GNU/Linux
```

The program output shows that the current OS (actually, the Ubuntu image we're running) uses the LP64 data model as expected and that the machine's architecture is x86_64.

There's more...

As we've seen, the C++ standard defines the following primitive data types:

- Integer: `int`
- Character: `char`
- Boolean: `bool`
- Floating point: `float`
- Double floating point: `double`
- Void: `void`
- Wide character: `wchar_t`
- Null pointer: `nullptr_t`

Data types can have other information so that their types can be defined:

- Modifiers: `signed`, `unsigned`, `long`, and `short`
- Qualifiers: `const` and `restrict`
- Storage type: `auto`, `static`, `extern`, and `mutable`

Obviously, not all these additional attributes can be applied to all the types; for example, `unsigned` cannot be applied to the `float` and `double` types (their respective IEEE standards would not allow that).

See also

Specifically for Linux, the Linux kernel documentation is generally a good place to start digging more into this: `https://www.kernel.org/doc/html/latest`. The GCC source code shows the sizes of the primitive data types for every supported architecture. Refer to the following link to find out more: `https://github.com/gcc-mirror/gcc`.

Lambda expressions

A **lambda expression** (or **lambda function**) is a convenient way of defining an anonymous, small, and one-time use function to be used in the place right where it is needed. Lambda is particularly useful with **Standard Template Library** (**STL**), as we'll see.

How to do it...

In this section, we'll write some code in order to get familiar with lambda expressions. Although the mechanics are important, pay attention to the code readability with lambda, especially in conjunction with STL. Follow these steps:

1. In this program, the lambda function gets an integer and prints it to standard output. Let's open a file named `lambda_01.cpp` and write the following code in it:

```
#include <iostream>
#include <vector>
#include <algorithm>
int main ()
{
    std::vector<int> v {1, 2, 3, 4, 5, 6};
    for_each (begin(v), end(v), [](int x) {std::cout << x
        << std::endl;});
    return 0;
}
```

2. In this second program, the lambda function captures a prefix by reference and prepends it to the integer in the standard output. Let's write the following code in a file called `lambda_02.cpp`:

```cpp
#include <iostream>
#include <vector>
#include <algorithm>
int main ()
{
    std::vector<int> v {1, 2, 3, 4, 5, 6};
    std::string prefix ("0");
    for_each (begin(v), end(v), [&prefix](int x) {std::cout
        << prefix << x << std::endl;});
    return 0;
}
```

3. Finally, we compile it with `g++ lambda_02.cpp`.

How it works...

In the first example, the lambda function just gets an integer as input and prints it. Note that the code is concise and readable. Lambda can capture the variables in scope by reference, `&`, or by value, `=`.

The output of the second program is as follows:

```
root@7205968ae436:/BOOK/chapter2/lambda# ./a.out
01
02
03
04
05
06
root@7205968ae436:/BOOK/chapter2/lambda#
```

In the second example, the lambda **captures** the variable prefix by reference, making it visible to the lambda. Here, we captured the `prefix` variable by reference, but we might have captured any of the following:

- All the variables by reference [`&`]
- All the variables by value [`=`]
- Specifying *what variables to capture* and *how to capture them* [`&var1, =var2`]

There are cases where we have to be explicit about the type to return, as in this case:

```
[](int x) -> std::vector<int>{
            if (x%2)
                return {1, 2};
            else
                return {3, 4};
});
```

The `-> std::vector<int>` operator, called **trailing return type**, tells the compiler that this lambda will return a vector of integers.

There's more...

Lambda can be decomposed into six parts:

1. Capture clause: `[]`
2. Parameter list: `()`
3. Mutable specification: `mutable`
4. Exception specification: `noexcept`
5. Trailing return type: `-> type`
6. Body: `{}`

Here, *1, 2,* and *6* are mandatory.

Although optional, mutable specification and exception specification are worth having a look at as they might be handy in some circumstances. The mutable specification allows a by-value parameter to be modified by the body of the lambda. A variable in the parameter list is typically captured *const-by-value*, so the mutable specification just removes this restriction. The second case is the exception specification, which we can use to specify the exceptions the lambda might throw.

See also

The books *Effective Modern C++* by Scott Meyers and *The C++ Programming Language* by Bjarne Stroustrup cover these topics in great detail.

Automatic type deduction and decltype

C++ offers two mechanisms for deducting types from an expression: `auto` and `decltype()`. `auto` is used to deduce a type from its initializer, while `decltype()` is used to deduce a type for more complex cases. This recipe will show examples of how to use both.

How to do it...

It might be handy (and it actually is) to avoid explicitly specifying the type of variable that will be used, especially when it is particularly long and used very locally:

1. Let's start with a typical example:

```
std::map<int, std::string> payslips;
// ...
for (std::map<int,
     std::string>::const_iterator iter = payslips.begin();
     iter !=payslips.end(); ++iter)
{
 // ...
}
```

2. Now, let's rewrite it with `auto`:

```
std::map<int, std::string> payslips;
// ...
for (auto iter = payslips.begin(); iter !=payslips.end(); ++iter)
{
    // ...
}
```

3. Let's look at another example:

```
auto speed = 123;          // speed is an int
auto height = calculate ();    // height will be of the
                          // type returned by calculate()
```

`decltype()` is another mechanism offered by C++ that can deduce the type of expression when the expression is more complex than the `auto` case.

4. Let's look at this using an example:

```
decltype(a) y = x + 1;  // deducing the type of a
decltype(str->x) y;     // deducing the type of str->x, where str
```

```
is
                                   // a struct and x
                                   // an int element of that struct
```

Could we use `auto` instead of `decltype()` in these two examples? We'll take a look in the next section.

How it works...

The first example with `auto` shows that the type is deduced, at compile time, from the right-hand parameter. `auto` is used in simple cases.

`decltype()` deduces the type of expression. In the example, it defines the `y` variable so that it's the same type as `a`. As you can imagine, this would not be possible with `auto`. Why? This is pretty simple: `decltype()` tells the compiler to *define a variable of a specific type*; in the first example, `y` is a variable with the same type as `a`. With `auto`, the type is deduced automatically.

We should use `auto` and `decltype()` anytime we don't have to explicitly specify the type of a variable; for example, when we need a `double` type (and not a `float`). It's worth mentioning that both `auto` and `decltype()` deduct types of expressions that are already known to the compiler, so **they are not runtime mechanisms**.

There's more...

There is a specific case that must be mentioned. When `auto` uses `{}` (uniform initializers) for type deduction, it can cause some headaches (or at least behaviors that we wouldn't expect). Let's look at an example:

```
auto fuelLevel {0, 1, 2, 3, 4, 5};
```

In this case, the type that's being deduced is `initializer_list<T>` and not an array of integers, as we could expect.

See also

The books *Effective Modern C++* by Scott Meyers and *The C++ Programming Language* by Bjarne Stroustrup cover these topics in great detail.

Learning how atomic works

Traditionally, C and C++ have a long tradition of portable code for system programming. The `atomic` feature that was introduced in the C++11 standard reinforces this by adding, natively, the guarantee that an operation is seen as atomic by other threads. Atomic is a template, such as `template <class T> struct atomic;` or `template <class T> struct atomic<T*>;`. C++20 has added `shared_ptr` and `weak_ptr` to T and T*. Any operation that's performed on the `atomic` variable is now protected from other threads.

How to do it...

`std::atomic` is an important aspect of modern C++ for dealing with concurrency. Let's write some code to master the concept:

1. The first snippet of code shows the basics of `atomic` operations. Let's write this now:

   ```cpp
   std::atomic<int> speed (0);          // Other threads have access to
   the speed variable
   auto currentSpeed = speed.load();    // default memory order:
   memory_order_seq_cst
   ```

2. In this second program, we can see that the `is_lock_free()` method returns `true` if the implementation is lock-free or if it has been implemented using a lock. Let's write this code:

   ```cpp
   #include <iostream>
   #include <utility>
   #include <atomic>
   struct MyArray { int z[50]; };
   struct MyStr { int a, b; };
   int main()
   {
       std::atomic<MyArray> myArray;
       std::atomic<MyStr> myStr;
       std::cout << std::boolalpha
                 << "std::atomic<myArray> is lock free? "
                 << std::atomic_is_lock_free(&myArray) << std::endl
                 << "std::atomic<myStr> is lock free? "
                 << std::atomic_is_lock_free(&myStr) << std::endl;
   }
   ```

3. Let's compile the program. When doing so, you may need to add the `atomic` library to g++ (due to a GCC bug) with `g++ atomic.cpp -latomic`.

How it works...

`std::atomic<int> speed (0);` defines a `speed` variable as an atomic integer. Although the variable will be atomic, this initialization **is not atomic**! Instead, the following code: `speed +=10;` atomically increases the speed of `10`. This means that there will not be race conditions. By definition, a race condition happens when among the threads accessing a variable, at least 1 is a writer.

The `std::cout << "current speed is: " << speed;` instruction reads the current value of the speed automatically. Pay attention to the fact that reading the value from speed is atomic but what happens next is not atomic (that is, printing it through `cout`). The rule is that read and write are atomic but the surrounding operations are not, as we've seen.

The output of the second program is as follows:

```
root@7205968ae436:/BOOK/chapter2/atomic# ./a.out
std::atomic<myArray> is lock free? false
std::atomic<myStr> is lock free? true
root@7205968ae436:/BOOK/chapter2/atomic#
```

The basic operations for atomic are load, store, swap, and **cas** (short for **compare and swap**), which are available on all types of atomics. Others are available, depending on the types (for example, `fetch_add`).

One question remains open, though. How come `myArray` uses locks and `myStr` is lock-free? The reason is simple: C++ provides a lock-free implementation for all the primitive types, and the variables inside `MyStr` are primitive types. A user will set `myStr.a` and `myStr.b`. `MyArray`, on the other hand, is not a fundamental type, so the underlying implementation will use locks.

The standard guarantee is that for each atomic operation, every thread will make progress. One important aspect to keep in mind is that the compiler makes code optimizations quite often. The use of atomics imposes restrictions on the compiler regarding how the code can be reordered. An example of a restriction is that no code that preceded the write of an `atomic` variable can be moved *after* the atomic write.

There's more...

In this recipe, we've used the default memory model called `memory_order_seq_cst`. Some other memory models that are available are:

- `memory_order_relaxed`: Only the current operation atomicity is guaranteed. That is, there are no guarantees on how memory accesses in different threads are ordered with respect to the atomic operation.
- `memory_order_consume`: The operation is ordered to happen once all accesses to memory in the releasing thread that carry a dependency on the releasing operation have happened.
- `memory_order_acquire`: The operation is ordered to happen once all accesses to memory in the releasing thread have happened.
- `memory_order_release`: The operation is ordered to happen before a consume or acquire operation.
- `memory_order_seq_cst`: The operation is sequentially consistent ordered.

See also

The books *Effective Modern C++* by Scott Meyers and *The C++ Programming Language* by Bjarne Stroustrup cover these topics in great detail. Furthermore, the *Atomic Weapons* talk from Herb Sutter, freely available on YouTube (`https://www.youtube.com/watch?v=A8eCGOqgvH4`), is a great introduction.

Learning how nullptr works

Before C++11, the `NULL` identifier was meant to be used for pointers. In this recipe, we'll see why this was a problem and how C++11 solved it.

How to do it...

To understand why `nullptr` is important, let's look at the problem with `NULL`:

1. Let's write the following code:

```
bool speedUp (int speed);
bool speedUp (char* speed);
int main()
```

```
    {
        bool ok = speedUp (NULL);
    }
```

2. Now, let's rewrite the preceding code using `nullptr`:

```
bool speedUp (int speed);
bool speedUp (char* speed);
int main()
{
    bool ok = speedUp (nullptr);
}
```

How it works...

The first program might not compile or (if it does) call the wrong method. We would expect it to call `bool speedUp (char* speed);` instead. The problem with NULL was exactly this: NULL was defined as 0, which is an integer type, and used by the **pre-processor** (which was replacing all the occurrences of NULL with 0). This is a huge difference as `nullptr` is now among the C++ primitives types and managed by the **compiler**.

For the second program, the `speedUp` (overloaded) method is called with the `char*` pointer to `nullptr`. There is no ambiguity here – we're calling the version with the `char*` type.

There's more...

`nullptr` represents *a pointer that does not point to any object*:

```
int* p = nullptr;
```

Due to this, there is no ambiguity, which means that readability improves. Another example that improves readability is as follows:

```
if (x == nullptr)
{
    // ...\
}
```

This makes the code more readable and clearly indicates that we're comparing a pointer.

See also

The books *Effective Modern C++* by Scott Meyers and *The C++ Programming Language* by Bjarne Stroustrup cover these topics in great detail.

Smart pointers – unique_ptr and shared_ptr

This recipe will show the basic usage of `unique_ptr` and `shared_ptr`. These smart pointers are the main helpers for programmers who don't want to deal with memory deallocation manually. Once you've learned how to use them properly, this will save headaches and nights of debugging sessions.

How to do it...

In this section, we'll look at the basic use of two smart pointers, `std::unique_ptr` and `std::shared_ptr`:

1. Let's develop a `unique_ptr` example by developing the following class:

```cpp
#include <iostream>
#include <memory>
class CruiseControl
{
public:
    CruiseControl()
    {
        std::cout << "CruiseControl object created" << std::endl;
    };
    ~CruiseControl()
    {
        std::cout << "CruiseControl object destroyed" << std::endl;
    }
    void increaseSpeedTo(int speed)
    {
        std::cout << "Speed at " << speed << std::endl;
    };
};
```

2. Now, let's develop a `main` class by calling the preceding class:

```cpp
int main ()
{
    std::cout << "unique_ptr test started" << std::endl;
    std::unique_ptr<CruiseControl> cruiseControl =
    std::make_unique<CruiseControl>();
    cruiseControl->increaseSpeedTo(12);
    std::cout << "unique_ptr test finished" << std::endl;
}
```

3. Let's compile `g++ unique_ptr_01.cpp`.

4. Another example with `unique_ptr` shows its behavior with arrays. Let's reuse the same class (`CruiseControl`):

```cpp
int main ()
{
    std::cout << "unique_ptr test started" << std::endl;
    std::unique_ptr<CruiseControl[]> cruiseControl =
        std::make_unique<CruiseControl[]>(3);
    cruiseControl[1].increaseSpeedTo(12);
    std::cout << "unique_ptr test finished" << std::endl;
}
```

5. Let's see `std::shared_ptr` in action with a small program:

```cpp
#include <iostream>
 #include <memory>
class CruiseControl
{
public:
    CruiseControl()
    {
        std::cout << "CruiseControl object created" << std::endl;
    },
    ~CruiseControl()
    {
        std::cout << "CruiseControl object destroyed" << std::endl;
    }
    void increaseSpeedTo(int speed)
    {
        std::cout << "Speed at " << speed << std::endl;
    };
};
```

`main` looks like this:

```cpp
int main ()
{
    std::cout << "shared_ptr test started" << std::endl;
    std::shared_ptr<CruiseControl> cruiseControlMaster(nullptr);
    {
        std::shared_ptr<CruiseControl> cruiseControlSlave =
            std::make_shared<CruiseControl>();
        cruiseControlMaster = cruiseControlSlave;
    }
    std::cout << "shared_ptr test finished" << std::endl;
}
```

The *How it works...* section will describe these three programs in detail.

How it works...

By running the first `unique_ptr` program, that is, `./a.out`, we get the following output:

```
root@7205968ae436:/BOOK/chapter2/smartPointer# ./a.out
unique_ptr test started
CruiseControl object created
Speed at 12
unique_ptr test finished
CruiseControl object destroyed
root@7205968ae436:/BOOK/chapter2/smartPointer#
```

`unique_ptr` is a **smart pointer** that embodies the concept of unique ownership.
Unique ownership, simply put, means that there is one and only one variable that can *own* a
pointer. The first consequence of this concept is that the copy operator is not allowed on
two unique pointer variables. Just `move` is allowed, where the ownership is transferred
from one variable to another. The executable that was run shows that the object is
deallocated at the end of the current scope (in this case, the `main`
function): `CruiseControl object destroyed`. The fact that the developer doesn't need
to bother remembering to call `delete` when needed, but still keep control over memory, is
one of the main advantages of C++ over garbage collector-based languages.

In the second `unique_ptr` example, with arrays, there are three objects of the `CruiseControl` type that have been allocated and then released. For this, the output is as follows:

```
root@7205968ae436:/BOOK/chapter2/smartPointer# ./a.out
unique_ptr test started
CruiseControl object created
CruiseControl object created
CruiseControl object created
Speed at 12
unique_ptr test finished
CruiseControl object destroyed
CruiseControl object destroyed
CruiseControl object destroyed
root@7205968ae436:/BOOK/chapter2/smartPointer#
```

The third example shows usage of `shared_ptr`. The output of the program is as follows:

```
root@7205968ae436:/BOOK/chapter2/smartPointer# ./a.out
shared_ptr test started
CruiseControl object created
shared_ptr test finished
CruiseControl object destroyed
root@7205968ae436:/BOOK/chapter2/smartPointer#
```

The `shared_ptr` smart pointer represents the concept that an object is being pointed at (that is, by the owner) by more than one variable. In this case, we're talking about shared ownership. It is clear that the rules are different from the `unique_ptr` case. An object **cannot be released** until at least one variable is using it. In this example, we defined a `cruiseControlMaster` variable pointing to `nullptr`. Then, we defined a block and in that block, we defined another variable: `cruiseControlSlave`. So far, so good! Then, still inside the block, we assigned the `cruiseControlSlave` pointer to `cruiseControlMaster`. At this point, the object allocated has two pointers: `cruiseControlMaster` and `cruiseControlSlave`. When this block is closed, the `cruiseControlSlave` destructor is called but the object is not freed as it is still used by another one: `cruiseControlMaster`! When the program finishes, we see the `shared_ptr test finished` log and immediately after the `cruiseControlMaster`, as it is the only one pointing to the `CruiseControl` object release, the object and then the constructor is called, as reported in the `CruiseControl object destroyed` log.

Clearly, the `shared_ptr` data type has a concept of **reference counting** to keep track of the number of pointers. These references are increased during the constructors (not always; the `move` constructor isn't) and the copy assignment operator and decreased in the destructors.

Can the reference counting variable be safely increased and decreased? The pointers to the same object might be in different threads, so manipulating this variable might be an issue. This is not an issue as the reference counting variable is atomically managed (that is, it is an atomic variable).

One last point about the size. `unique_ptr` is as big as a raw pointer, whereas `shared_ptr` is typically double the size of `unique_ptr` because of the reference counting variable.

There's more...

I strongly suggest always using `std::make_unique` and `std::make_shared`. Their usage removes code duplication and improves exception safety. Want more details? `shared_ptr.h` (https://github.com/gcc-mirror/gcc/blob/master/libstdc%2B%2B-v3/include/bits/shared_ptr.h) and `shared_ptr_base.h` (https://github.com/gcc-mirror/gcc/blob/master/libstdc%2B%2B-v3/include/bits/shared_ptr_base.h) contain the GCC `shared_ptr` implementation so that we can see how reference counting is manipulated.

See also

The books *Effective Modern C++* by Scott Meyers and *The C++ Programming Language* by Bjarne Stroustrup cover these topics in great detail.

Learning how move semantics works

We know copies are expensive, especially heavy objects. The move semantics that were introduced in C++11 help us avoid expensive copies. The foundational concept behind `std::move` and `std::forward` is the **rvalue reference**. This recipe will show you how to use `std::move`.

How to do it...

Let's develop three programs to learn about `std::move` and its universal reference:

1. Let's start by developing a simple program:

```cpp
#include <iostream>
#include <vector>
int main ()
{
    std::vector<int> a = {1, 2, 3, 4, 5};
    auto b = std::move(a);
    std::cout << "a: " << a.size() << std::endl;
    std::cout << "b: " << b.size() << std::endl;
}
```

2. Let's develop a second example:

```cpp
#include <iostream>
#include <vector>
void print (std::string &&s)
{
    std::cout << "print (std::string &&s)" << std::endl;
    std::string str (std::move(s));
    std::cout << "universal reference ==> str = " << str
              << std::endl;
    std::cout << "universal reference ==> s = " << s << std::endl;
}
void print (std::string &s)
{
    std::cout << "print (std::string &s)" << std::endl;
}
int main()
{
    std::string str ("This is a string");
    print (str);
    std::cout << "==> str = " << str << std::endl;
    return 0;
}
```

3. Let's look at an example with the universal reference:

```cpp
#include <iostream>
void print (std::string &&s)
{
    std::cout << "print (std::string &&s)" << std::endl;
    std::string str (std::move(s));
    std::cout << "universal reference ==> str = " << str
```

```
                << std::endl;
        std::cout << "universal reference ==> s = " << s << std::endl;
    }
    void print (std::string &s)
    {
        std::cout << "print (std::string &s)" << std::endl;
    }
    int main()
    {
        print ("this is a string");
        return 0;
    }
```

The next section will describe these three programs in detail.

How it works...

The output of the first program is as follows (g++ `move_01.cpp` and `./a.out`):

```
root@7205968ae436:/BOOK/chapter2/moveSemantics# ./a.out
a: 0
b: 5
root@7205968ae436:/BOOK/chapter2/moveSemantics#
```

In this program, `auto b = std::move(a);` does a couple of things:

1. It casts the vector, a, to the **rvalue reference**.
2. As it is an rvalue reference, the vector move constructor is called, which moves the content of the a vector to the b vector.
3. a doesn't have the original data anymore, b has.

The output of the second program is as follows (g++ `moveSemantics2.cpp` and `./a.out`):

```
root@7205968ae436:/BOOK/chapter2/moveSemantics# ./a.out
print (std::string &s)
==> str = this is a string
root@7205968ae436:/BOOK/chapter2/moveSemantics#
```

In this second example, the `str` string we pass to the `print` method is an **lvalue reference** (that is, we can take the address of that variable), so it is passed by reference.

The output of the third program is as follows (`g++ moveSemantics3.cpp` and `./a.out`):

```
root@7205968ae436:/BOOK/chapter2/moveSemantics# ./a.out
print (std::string &&s)
universal reference ==> str = this is a string
universal reference ==> s =
root@7205968ae436:/BOOK/chapter2/moveSemantics#
```

In the third example, the method that's being called is the one with the **universal reference** as a parameter: `print (std::string &&s)`. This is because we cannot take the address of `this is a string`, which means it is an rvalue reference.

It should be clear now that `std::move` doesn't actually move anything – it is a function template that **performs an unconditional cast** to an rvalue, as we saw in the first example. This allows us to move (and not copy) the data to the destination and invalidate the source. The benefits of `std::move` are huge, especially every time we see an rvalue reference parameter to a method (`T&&`) that would probably* be a copy in the previous versions of the language (C++98 and before).

*Probably: it depends on compiler optimizations.

There's more...

`std::forward` is somewhat similar (but with a different purpose). It is a conditional cast to an lvalue reference. You are invited to learn more about `std::forward`, rvalue, and lvalue by reading the books referenced in the next section.

See also

The books *Effective Modern C++* by Scott Meyers and *The C++ Programming Language* by Bjarne Stroustrup cover these topics in great detail.

Understanding concurrency

In the past, it was common for a C++ developer to write programs by using threading libraries or native threading mechanisms (for example `pthread`, a Windows thread). Since C++11, this has changed drastically and concurrency is another big feature that was added that goes in the direction of a self-consistent language. The two new features we'll look at in this recipe are `std::thread` and `std::async`.

How to do it...

In this section, we'll learn how to use `std::thread` with a basic scenario (create and join) and how to pass and receive parameters to it:

1. `std::thread`: By using the basic thread methods, `create` and `join`, write the following code:

```cpp
#include <iostream>
#include <thread>
void threadFunction1 ();
int main()
{
    std::thread t1 {threadFunction1};
    t1.join();
    return 0;
}
void threadFunction1 ()
{
    std::cout << "starting thread 1 ... " << std::endl;
    std::cout << "end thread 1 ... " << std::endl;
}
```

2. Compile it with `g++ concurrency_01.cpp -lpthread`.

The second example is similar to the previous one but in this case, we pass and get parameters:

1. `std::thread`: Create and join a thread, passing a parameter and getting a result. Write the following code:

```
#include <iostream>
#include <thread>
#include <vector>
#include <algorithm>
void threadFunction (std::vector<int> &speeds, int& res);
int main()
{
    std::vector<int> speeds = {1, 2, 3, 4, 5};
    int result = 0;
    std::thread t1 (threadFunction, std::ref(speeds),
                    std::ref(result));
    t1.join();
    std::cout << "Result = " << result << std::endl;
    return 0;
}
void threadFunction (std::vector<int> &speeds, int& res)
{
    std::cout << "starting thread 1 ... " << std::endl;
    for_each(begin(speeds), end(speeds), [](int speed)
    {
        std::cout << "speed is " << speed << std::endl;
    });
    res = 10;
    std::cout << "end thread 1 ... " << std::endl;
}
```

2. Compile it using `g++ concurrency_02.cpp -lpthread`.

The third example uses **async** to create a task, execute it, and get the result, as follows:

1. `std::async`: Here, we can see why async is called **task-based threading**. Write the following code:

```
root@b6e74d5cf049:/Chapter2# cat concurrency_03.cpp
#include <iostream>
#include <future>
int asyncFunction ();
int main()
{
    std::future<int> fut = std::async(asyncFunction);
    std::cout << "max = " << fut.get() << std::endl;
```

```
        return 0;
    }
    int asyncFunction()
    {
        std::cout << "starting asyncFunction ... " << std::endl;
        int max = 0;
        for (int i = 0; i < 100000; ++i)
        {
            max += i;
        }
        std::cout << " Finished asyncFunction ..." << std::endl;
        return max;
    }
```

2. Now, we need to compile the program. There is a catch here. Since we're using a threading mechanism, the compilers rely on the native implementations, which in our case turn out to be `pthread`. In order to compile and link without errors (we'd get an undefined reference), we need to include `-lpthread`:

g++ concurrency_03.cpp -lpthread

In the fourth example, `std::async` used in conjunction with `std::promise` and `std::future` is a good and easy way of making two tasks communicate with each other. Let's take a look:

1. `std::async`: This is another `std::async` example showing a basic communication mechanism. Let's code it:

```
    #include <iostream>
    #include <future>
    void asyncProducer(std::promise<int> &prom);
    void asyncConsumer(std::future<int> &fut);
    int main()
    {
        std::promise<int> prom;
        std::future<int> fut = prom.get_future();
        std::async(asyncProducer, std::ref(prom));
        std::async(asyncConsumer, std::ref(fut));
        std::cout << "Async Producer-Consumer ended!" << std::endl;
        return 0;
    }
    void asyncConsumer(std::future<int> &fut)
    {
        std::cout << "Got " << fut.get() << " from the producer ... "
            << std::endl;
    }
    void asyncProducer(std::promise<int> &prom)
```

```
        {
                std::cout << " sending 5 to the consumer ... " << std::endl;
                prom.set_value (5);
        }
```

2. And finally, compile it: `g++ concurrency_04.cpp -lpthread`

How it works...

Let's analyze the previous four programs:

1. `std::thread`: The following program shows basic thread usage for create and join:

```
root@7205968ae436:/BOOK/chapter2/concurrency# g++ concurrency.cpp -lpthread
root@7205968ae436:/BOOK/chapter2/concurrency# ./a.out
starting thread 1 ...
end thread 1 ...
root@7205968ae436:/BOOK/chapter2/concurrency#
```

There's nothing really complex in this first test. `std::thread` was initialized with a function through the uniform initialization and joined (waiting for the thread to be completed). The thread would accept a function object:

```
struct threadFunction
{
    int speed;
    void operator () ();
}
std::thread t (threadFunction);
```

2. `std::thread`: Create and join a thread, passing a parameter and getting a result:

```
root@7205968ae436:/BOOK/chapter2/concurrency# g++ concurrency_02.cpp -lpthread
root@7205968ae436:/BOOK/chapter2/concurrency# ./a.out
starting thread 1 ...
speed is 1
speed is 2
speed is 3
speed is 4
speed is 5
end thread 1 ...
Result = 10
root@7205968ae436:/BOOK/chapter2/concurrency#
```

This second test shows how to pass a parameter using `std::vector<int>&` `speeds` to the thread and get the return parameter, `int& ret`. This test shows how to pass parameters to a thread, and *is not* multithreaded code (that is, passing the same parameters to other threads will result in a race condition if *at least one* thread will be writing on them)!

3. `std::async`: Here, we can see why async is called **task-based threading**:

```
root@7205968ae436:/BOOK/chapter2/concurrency# g++ concurrency_03.cpp -lpthread
root@7205968ae436:/BOOK/chapter2/concurrency# ./a.out
max = starting asyncFunction ...
 Finished asyncFunction ...
704982704
root@7205968ae436:/BOOK/chapter2/concurrency#
```

Note that when we call `std::async(asyncFunction);`, we could use `auto fut = std::async(asyncFunction);` to deduce the type of the return from `std::async` at compile time.

4. `std::async`: This is another `std::async` example showing a basic communication mechanism:

```
root@7205968ae436:/BOOK/chapter2/concurrency# g++ concurrency_04.cpp -lpthread
.root@7205968ae436:/BOOK/chapter2/concurrency# ./a.out
 sending 5 to the consumer ...
Got 5 from the producer ...
Async Producer-Consumer ended!
root@7205968ae436:/BOOK/chapter2/concurrency#
```

The consumer, `void asyncConsumer(std::future<int> &fut)`, calls the `get()` method on the future to get the value set by the producer through the `set_value()` method on the promise. `fut.get()` waits for the value to be computed, if necessary (that is, it's a blocking call).

There's more...

The C++ concurrent library doesn't just include the features shown in this recipe, although these are the foundational ones. You are invited to explore the full set of concurrency tools that are available by going to *Chapter 5*, paragraph three of *The C++ Programming Language* by Bjarne Stroustrup.

See also

The books *Effective Modern C++* by Scott Meyers and *The C++ Programming Language* by Bjarne Stroustrup cover these topics in great detail.

Understanding the filesystem

C++17 marks another huge milestone in terms of new features. The `filesystem` library provides a simpler way of interacting with the filesystem. It was inspired by `Boost.Filesystem` (available since 2003). This recipe will show its basics features.

How to do it...

In this section, we'll show two examples of the `filesystem` library by using `directory_iterator` and `create_directories`. Although there is definitely more under this namespace, the goal of these two snippets is to highlight their simplicity:

1. `std::filesystem::directory_iterator`: Let's write the following code:

```
#include <iostream>
#include <filesystem>
int main()
{
    for(auto& p: std::filesystem::directory_iterator("/"))
    std::cout << p << std::endl;
}
```

2. Now, compile it with `g++ filesystem_01.cpp -std=c++17 -lstdc++fs`, where `-std=c++17` tells the compiler to use the C++17 standard and `-lstdc++fs` tells the compiler to use the `filesystem` library.

The second example is about creating a directory and a file:

1. `std::filesystem::create_directories`: Write the following code:

```
#include <iostream>
#include <filesystem>
#include <fstream>
int main()
{
    std::filesystem::create_directories("test/src/config");
    std::ofstream("test/src/file.txt") << "This is an example!"
```

```
                                              << std::endl;
    }
```

2. The compilation is as the same as the previous example:
    ```
    g++ filesystem_02.cpp -std=c++17 -lstdc++fs.
    ```

With just two lines of code, we've created a folder structure, a file, and have also written on it! It's as simple (and portable) as that.

How it works...

The `filesystem` library is located in the `<filesystem>` header under the `std::filesystem` namespace. These two tests, although pretty simple, were needed to show how powerful the `filesystem` library is. The output of the first program is as follows:

```
root@7205968ae436:/BOOK/chapter2/filesystem# g++ filesystem_01.cpp -std=c++17 -lstdc++fs
root@7205968ae436:/BOOK/chapter2/filesystem# ./a.out
"/etc"
"/media"
"/dev"
"/sbin"
"/mnt"
"/home"
"/root"
"/run"
"/lib"
"/tmp"
"/sys"
"/proc"
"/lib32"
"/opt"
"/boot"
"/usr"
"/srv"
"/bin"
"/libx32"
"/lib64"
"/var"
"/BOOK"
"/.dockerenv"
root@7205968ae436:/BOOK/chapter2/filesystem#
```

A complete list of `std::filesystem` methods can be found here: `https://en.cppreference.com/w/cpp/header/filesystem`.

`std::filesystem::create_directories` create a directory (recursively, if `test/src` does not exist) in the current folder, in this case. Of course, an absolute path is managed too and the current line would be perfectly valid, that is, `std::filesystem::create_directories("/usr/local/test/config");`.

The second line of the source code uses `ofstream` to create an output file stream named `test/src/file.txt` and appends << to the string: `This is an example!`.

There's more...

The `filesystem` library is heavily inspired by `Boost.Filesystem`, which has been available since 2003. If you want to experiment and debug a little, just add the `-g` option (add the debug symbols to the binary) to the compiler: `g++ -g fs.cpp -std=c++17 -lstdc++fs`.

See also

The books *Effective Modern C++* by Scott Meyers and *The C++ Programming Language* by Bjarne Stroustrup cover these topics in great detail.

The C++ Core Guidelines

The C++ Core Guidelines are a collaborative effort led by Bjarne Stroustrup, much like the C++ language itself. They are the result of many years of discussion and design across a number of organizations. Their design encourages general applicability and broad adoption but they can be freely copied and modified to meet your organization's needs. More precisely, these guidelines are referring to the C++14 standard.

Getting ready

Go over to GitHub and go to the C++ Core Guideline document (`http://isocpp.github.io/CppCoreGuidelines/CppCoreGuidelines`), as well as to the GitHub project page: `https://github.com/isocpp/CppCoreGuidelines`.

How to do it...

The C++ Core Guidelines are divided into sections that are easily browsable. The sections include class and class hierarchies, resource management, performance, and error handling. The C++ Core Guidelines are a collaborative effort led by Bjarne Stroustrup and Herb Sutter but, in total, they involve more than 200 contributors (to find out more about this, please visit https://github.com/isocpp/CppCoreGuidelines/graphs/contributors). The quality, suggestions, and best practices they've put in are incredible.

How it works...

The most common way to use the C++ Core Guidelines is to keep a browser tab open on the GitHub page and consult it continuously for your daily tasks.

There's more...

If you want to contribute to the issues that have already been provided, the GitHub page contains a lot of items, ready to be picked up. For more information, please visit https://github.com/isocpp/CppCoreGuidelines/issues.

See also

The *Adding GSL in your makefile* recipe of this chapter will be helpful.

Adding GSL in your makefile

"The GSL is the small set of types and aliases specified in these guidelines. At the time of writing, their specification herein is too sparse; we plan to add a WG21-style interface specification to ensure that different implementations agree, and to propose as a contribution for possible standardization, subject as usual to whatever the committee decides to accept/improve/alter/reject." – FAQ.50 of the C++ Core Guidelines.

Getting ready

Go to GitHub and go to the C++ Core Guideline document: http://isocpp.github.io/CppCoreGuidelines/CppCoreGuidelines.

How to do it...

In this section, we'll integrate the **Guideline Supporting Library** (gsl) to a program by modifying a makefile:

1. Download and copy a gsl implementation (for example, https://github.com/microsoft/GSL).
2. Copy the gsl folder into your project.
3. Add the include to the makefile: -I$HOME/dev/GSL/include.
4. In your source file, include #include <gsl/gsl>.

The gsl currently provides the following:

- GSL.view
- GSL.owner
- GSL.assert: Assertions
- GSL.util: Utilities
- GSL.concept: Concepts

How it works...

You might have noticed that to get the gsl working, you just need to specify the header file folder path in the makefile, that is, -I$HOME/dev/GSL/include. Another detail to note is that no library is specified in the makefile.

This is because the whole implementation is provided *inline* in the header files under the gsl folder.

There's more...

The Microsoft GSL (http://isocpp.github.io/CppCoreGuidelines/CppCoreGuidelines) is just one implementation maintained by Microsoft. You can find another implementation here: https://github.com/martinmoene/gsl-lite. Both implementations have been released under the MIT license type.

See also

The C++ Core Guidelines recipe of this chapter.

Understanding concepts

A **concept** is a compile-time predicate that's used in conjunction with templates. The C++20 standard definitely boosted generic programming by providing more compile-time opportunity for the developer to communicate its intention. We can visualize concepts such as requirements (or constraints) the user of the template must adhere to. Why do we need concepts? Do you have do define concepts by yourself? This recipe will answer these and many more questions.

How to do it...

In this section, we will develop a concrete template example using `concepts`:

1. We want to create our own version of the `std::sort` template function from the C++ standard library. Let's start by writing the following code in a `.cpp` file:

```
#include <algorithm>
#include <concepts>

namespace sp
{
    template<typename T>
        requires Sortable<T>
    void sort(T& container)
    {
        std::sort (begin(container), end(container));
    };
}
```

2. Now, let's use our new template class with the constraint that the type we pass, an `std::vector`, must be sortable; otherwise, the compiler will notify us:

```
int main()
{
    std::vector<int> myVec {2,1,4,3};
    sp::sort(vec);

    return 0;
}
```

We'll look at the details in the next section.

How it works...

I strongly believe `concepts` were the missing feature. Before them, a template didn't have a well-defined set of requirements, nor, in the case of a compilation error, a simple and brief description of it. These are the two pillars that drove the design of the `concepts` feature.

Step 1 includes the algorithms `include` for the `std::sort` method and the `concepts` header. To not confuse the compiler and ourselves, we encapsulated our new template in a namespace, `sp`. As you can see, there is a very minimal difference compared to the classical templates we used to use and the difference is with the `requires` keyword.

`requires` communicates to the compiler (and to the template user) that this template is only valid with a `T Sortable` type (`Sortable<T>`). OK; what is `Sortable`? This is a predicate that is only satisfied if it is evaluated to true. There are other ways to specify a constraint, as follows:

- With the trailing `requires`:

```
template<typename T>
void sort(T& container) requires Sortable<T>;
```

- As a `template` parameter:

```
template<Sortable T>
void sort(T& container)
```

I personally prefer the style in the *How to do it...* section as it is more idiomatic and, more importantly, allows us to keep all the `requires` together, like so:

```
template<typename T>
    requires Sortable<T> && Integral<T>
void sort(T& container)
{
    std::sort (begin(container), end(container));
};
```

In this example, we want to communicate that our `sp::sort` method is valid with type `T`, which is `Sortable` and `Integral`, for whatever reason.

Step 2 simply uses our new customized version of sort. To do this, we instantiated a vector (which is `Sortable`!) and passed in input to the `sp::sort` method.

There's more...

There might be cases where you need to create your own concept. The standard library contains plenty of them, so it is a remote probability that you'd need one. As we learned in the previous section, a concept is a predicate if and only if it is evaluated as true. The definition of a concept as a composite of two existing ones might look like this:

```
template <typename T>
concept bool SignedSwappable()
{
    return SignedIntegral<T>() && Swappable<T>();
}
```

Here, we can use the `sort` method:

```
template<typename T>
    requires SignedSwappable<T>
void sort(T& container)
{
    std::sort (begin(container), end(container));
};
```

Why is this cool? For a couple of reasons:

- It lets us immediately know what the template expects without getting lost in implementation details (that is, the requirements or constraints are explicit).
- At compile time, the compiler will evaluate whether the constraints have been met.

See also

- *A Tour of C++, Second Edition*, B. Stroustrup: *Chapter 7.2* and *Chapter 12.7* for a complete list of concepts defined in the standard library.
- `https://gcc.gnu.org/projects/cxx-status.html` for a list of C++20 features mapped with GCC versions and status.

Using span

We may come across cases where we need to write a method but we'd like to have the flexibility to accept a plain array or STL containers as input. `std::span` solves this problem. It gives the user a view into a contiguous sequence of elements. This recipe will teach you how to use it.

How to do it...

In this recipe, we'll write a method with one parameter (`std::span`) that can be used in different contexts. Then, we'll highlight the flexibility it offers:

1. Let's start by adding the includes we need. Then, we need to define the `print` method by passing the `container` variable of the `std::span` type:

```cpp
#include <iostream>
#include <vector>
#include <array>
#include <span>

void print(std::span<int> container)
{
    for(const auto &c : container)
        std::cout << c << "-";
}
```

2. In `main`, we want to print our arrays by calling the `print` method:

```cpp
int main()
{
    int elems[]{4, 2, 43, 12};
    print(elems);
    std::vector vElems{4, 2, 43, 12};
    print(vElems);
}
```

Let's see how this works.

How it works...

`std::span` describes an object that refers to a contiguous sequence of elements. The C++ standard defines an array as having a contiguous portion of memory. This definitely simplifies the `std::span` implementation, since a typical one includes a pointer to the first element of the sequence and the size.

Step 1 defines the `print` method of passing the `std::span`, which we can read as a sequence of integers. Any array type that has contiguous memory will be seen from the method as a sequence.

Step 2 uses the `print` method with two different arrays, one C-style and the second an `std::vector` part of the STL library. Since both arrays are defined in a contiguous portion of memory, `std::span` is able to seamlessly manage them.

There's more...

Our method considers `std::span` with the `int` type. You might need to make the method generic. In this case, you'd need to write something like this:

```
template <typename T>
void print(std::span<T> container)
{
    for(const auto &c : container)
        std::cout << c << "-";
}
```

As we learned in the *Understanding concepts* recipe, it is wise to specify some requirements in this template. Therefore, we might write to the following:

```
template <typename T>
    requires Integral<T>
void print(std::span<T> container)
{
    for(const auto &c : container)
        std::cout << c << "-";
}
```

The `requires Integral<T>` would make explicit the needs of an `Integral` type for the template.

See also

- The *Understanding concepts* recipe to review how to write concepts with templates and apply them to `std::span`.
- `https://gcc.gnu.org/projects/cxx-status.html` for a list of C++20 features mapped with GCC versions and their statuses.

Learning how Ranges work

The C++20 standard added Ranges, which are an abstraction of containers that allow the program to operate uniformly on containers' elements. Furthermore, Ranges represent a very modern and concise way of writing expressive code. We'll learn that this expressiveness is even greater with pipes and adaptors.

How to do it...

In this section, we'll write a program that will help us learn the main use case of Ranges in conjunction with pipes and adaptors. Given an array of temperatures, we want to filter out the negative ones and convert the positives (warm temperatures) into Fahrenheit:

1. On a new source file, type the following code. As you can see, two lambda functions and a `for` range loop does the job:

```cpp
#include <vector>
#include <iostream>
#include <ranges>

int main()
{
    auto temperatures{28, 25, -8, -3, 15, 21, -1};
    auto minus = [](int i){ return i <= 0; };
    auto toFahrenheit = [](int i) { return (i*(9/5)) + 32; };
    for (int t : temperatures | std::views::filter(minus)
                              |
std::views::transform(toFahrenheit))
        std::cout << t << ' ';  // 82.4 77 59 69.8
}
```

We'll analyze what's behind of Ranges in the next section. We'll also learn that Ranges are the first users of `concepts`.

How it works...

`std::ranges` represents a very modern way of describing a sequence of actions on a container in a readable format. This is one of the cases where the language improves readability.

Step 1 defines the `temperatures` vector, which contains some data. Then, we defined a lambda function that returns true if the input, `i`, is greater or equal to zero. The second lambda we defined converts `i` into Fahrenheit. Then, we looped over temperatures (`viewable_range`) and piped to the `filter` (called `adaptor`, in the scope of Ranges), which removed the negative temperatures based on the `minus` lambda function. The output is piped to another adaptor that converts every single item of the container so that the final loop can take place and print to the standard output.

C++20 provides another level on top of the one we used to iterate over the container's element, one that's more modern and idiomatic. By combining `viewable_range` with adaptors, the code is more concise, compact, and readable.

The C++20 standard library provides many more adaptors following the same logic, including `std::views::all`, `std::views::take`, and `std::views::split`.

There's more...

All of the adaptors are templates that use concepts to define the requirements that the specific adaptor needs. An example of this is as follows:

```
template<ranges::input_range V,
std::indirect_unary_predicate<ranges::iterator_t<V>> Pred >
    requires ranges::view<V> && std::is_object_v<Pred>
class filter_view : public ranges::view_interface<filter_view<V, Pred>>
```

This template is the `std::views::filter` we used in this recipe. This template takes two types: the first one is `V`, the input range (that is, the container), while the second one is `Pred` (which is the lambda function, in our case). We've specified two constraints for this template:

- `V` must be a view
- The predicate must be an object type: a function, lambda, and so on

See also

- The *Understanding concepts* recipe to review concepts.
- Go to `https://github.com/ericniebler/range-v3` to see the `range` implementation by the C++20 library proposal author (Eric Niebler).
- *Learning the Linux fundamentals – shell* recipe in `Chapter 1`, *Getting Started with System Programming*, to notice that the C++20 Ranges pipe is very similar to the concept of pipes we've seen on the shell.
- To read more about `std::is_object`, please visit the following link: `https://en.cppreference.com/w/cpp/types/is_object`.

Learning how modules work

Before C++20, there was only one way of structuring a program in parts: through the `#include` directive (which is resolved by the precompiler). The latest standard added another and more modern way of achieving the same result, called **module**. This recipe will show you how to write code using modules and the differences between `#include` and module.

How to do it...

In this section, we'll write a program composed of two modules. This program is an improvement of the one we developed in the *Learning how Range works* recipe. We'll encapsulate the temperature code in a module and use it in a client module. Let's get started:

1. Let's create a new `.cpp` source file called `temperature.cpp` and type in the following code:

```
export module temperature_engine;
import std.core
#include <ranges>

export
std::vector<int> toFahrenheitFromCelsius(std::vector<int>& celsius)
{
    std::vector<int> fahrenheit;
    auto toFahrenheit = [](int i) { return (i*(9/5)) + 32; };
    for (int t : celsius | std::views::transform(toFahrenheit))
        fahrenheit.push_back(t);
```

```
        return fahrenheit;
    }
```

2. Now, we have to use it. Create a new file (for example,
   `temperature_client.cpp`) and include the following code:

```
import temperature_engine;
import std.core;   // instead of iostream, containers
                   // (vector, etc) and algorithm
int main()
{
    auto celsius = {28, 25, -8, -3, 15, 21, -1};
    auto fahrenheit = toFahrenheitFromCelsius(celsius);
    std::for_each(begin(fahrenheit), end(fahrenheit),
        [&fahrenheit](int i)
    {
        std::cout << i << ";";
    });
}
```

The next section explains how modules work, what relationship they have with the
namespaces, and the advantages they have over the `#include` precompiler directive.

How it works...

A module is the C++20 solution to (possibly) the `#include` directive. Possibly is mandatory
here as the millions of lines of legacy code cannot be converted overnight to use modules.

Step 1 has the main goal of defining our `temperature_engine` module. The first
line, `export module temperature_engine;`, defines the module we want to export.
Next, we have `import std.core`. This is one of the biggest differences brought into
C++20: there is no need to use `#include` anymore. Specifically, `import std.core` is
equivalent to `#include <iostream>`. We also `#include` the range. In this case, we did it
the old way to show you that is possible to have code that mixes old and new solutions. This
is important as it'll allow us how to manage the transition to module better. Every time we
want to export something from our module, we just need to prefix it with the `export`
keyword, as we did with the `toFahrenheitFromCelsius` method. The method's
implementation is not affected, so its logic doesn't change.

Step 2 contains the code for the module client using `temperature_engine`. As we did in the previous step, we just need to use `import temperature_engine` and use the exported objects. We also used `import std.core` to replace `#include <iostream>`. Now, we can use the exported method as we normally would, calling `toFahrenheitFromCelsius` and passing the expected input parameters. The `toFahrenheitFromCelsius` method returns a vector of integers representing the converted temperatures in Fahrenheit, which means all we need to do is use the `for_each` template method to print the values by using `import std.core` where we normally would have used `#include <algorithm>`.

The main question at this point is: why should we use module instead of `#include`? `Module` does not just represent a syntactic difference – it's deeper than that:

- A module is compiled only once, while `#includes` are not. To make `#include` compile only once, we need to use the `#ifdef #define`, and `#endif` precompilers.
- Module can be imported in any order without affecting the meaning. This is not the same for `#include`.
- If a symbol is not exported from the module, the client code cannot use it and the compiler will notify with an error if the users do.
- Modules, unlike includes, are not transitive. Importing module A into module B, when module C uses module B, doesn't mean it automatically gains access to module A.

This has a great effect on maintainability, the structure of the code, and compilation time.

There's more...

One recurrent question is, aren't modules in conflict (or overlapping) with namespaces? This is a good point, and the answer is no. Namespaces and modules solve two different problems. A namespace is yet another mechanism that expresses the intention to group some declarations together. Other mechanisms that put group declaration together are functions and classes. What if two classes clash? We can encapsulate one of them into a namespace. You can see an example of this in the *Understanding concepts* recipe, where we created our own version of sort called `sp::sort`. A module, on the other hand, is a logical set of functionalities. The two concepts are **orthogonal**, which means I can have my namespace spread out over more modules. A concrete example is the `std::vector` and `std::list` containers, which are in two different modules but on the same `namespace`: `std`.

Another thing worth highlighting is that modules allow us to set a portion of the module as `private` to make it inaccessible to other **Translation Units** (**TUs**). This is useful if you want to export a symbol as an incomplete type, like so:

```
export module temperature_engine;
import std.core
#include <ranges>

export struct ConversionFactors;   //exported as incomplete type

export
void myMethod(ConversionFactors& factors)
{
    // ...
}

module: private;
struct ConversionFactors
{
    int toFahrenheit;
    int toCelsius;
};
```

See also

- Go to `https://gcc.gnu.org/projects/cxx-status.html` to check the module (and other C++20 features) support timeline.
- The *Lambda expressions* recipe for a refresher on lambdas.

3
Dealing with Processes and Threads

Processes and threads are the foundations of any computation. A program is rarely made of just one thread or process. In this chapter, you will learn the fundamental recipes for dealing with threads and processes. You will also learn how easy and convenient it is to deal with threads compared with the **Portable Operating System Interface (POSIX)**. Learning these skills is very important as part of the core skills of a system developer. C++ does not have the notion of *process* in its standard library, so the Linux native implementation will be used.

This chapter will cover the following recipes:

- Starting a new process
- Killing a process
- Creating a new thread
- Creating a daemon process

Technical requirements

In order to let you try the programs immediately, we've set up a Docker image that has all the tools and libraries we'll need throughout the book. This is based on Ubuntu 19.04.

In order to set it up, follow these steps:

1. Download and install Docker Engine from `www.docker.com`.
2. Pull the image from Docker Hub by running the following command: `docker pull kasperondocker/system_programming_cookbook:latest`.
3. The image should now be available. Type in the following command to view the image: `docker images`.

4. You should have at least this image now:
   `kasperondocker/system_programming_cookbook`.

5. Run the Docker image with an interactive shell, with the help of the following command: `docker run -it --cap-add sys_ptrace kasperondocker/system_programming_cookbook:latest /bin/bash`.

6. The shell on the running container is now available. Type in `root@39a5a8934370/# cd /BOOK/` to get all the programs developed, by chapters.

The `--cap-add sys_ptrace` argument is needed to allow the **GNU Project Debugger** (**GDB**) in the Docker container to set breakpoints, which, by default, Docker does not allow.

 Disclaimer: The C++20 standard has been approved (that is, technically finalized) by WG21 in a meeting in Prague at the end of February. This means that the GCC compiler version that this book uses, 8.3.0, does not include (or has very, very limited support for) the new and cool C++20 features. For this reason, the Docker image does not include the C++20 recipe code. GCC keeps the development of the newest features in branches (you have to use appropriate flags for that, for example, `-std=c++2a`); therefore, you are encouraged to experiment with them by yourself. So, clone and explore the GCC contracts and module branches and have fun.

Starting a new process

This recipe will show how to start a new process programmatically. The C++ standard does not include any support for processes, so the Linux native implementation will be used. Being able to manage processes in a program is an important skill, and this recipe will teach you the fundamental concepts of processes, the **process identifier** (**PID**), the parent PID, and the system calls needed.

How to do it...

This recipe will show how to start a child process and how to make the parent process wait for the child to finish by using Linux system calls. Two different techniques shall be shown: the first, where the parent just forks the child; and the second, where the child process uses the `execl` system call to run an application.

An alternative option to system calls is to use an external library (or framework), such as the **Boost** library.

1. First, type the program in a new file called `process_01.cpp`:

```cpp
#include <stddef.h>
#include <stdlib.h>
#include <unistd.h>
#include <sys/types.h>
#include <sys/wait.h>
#include <iostream>

int main(void)
{
    pid_t child;
    int status;
    std::cout << "I am the parent, my PID is " << getpid()
        << std::endl;
    std::cout << "My parent's PID is " << getppid() << std::endl;
    std::cout << "I am going to create a new process..."
        << std::endl;
    child = fork();
    if (child == -1)
    {
```

2. We have to consider the case that a child might not be forked, so we need to write this part:

```cpp
        // fork() returns -1 on failure
        std::cout << "fork() failed." << std::endl;
        return (-1);
    }
    else if (child == 0)
    {
```

3. This branch is a happy case, where the parent can fork its child correctly. The child, here, just prints its PID to the standard output:

```cpp
        std::cout << "I am the child, my PID is " << std::endl;
        std::cout << "My parent's PID is " << getppid() << std::endl;
    }
    else
    {
```

4. Now, we have to make the parent wait for the child process to finish:

```cpp
        wait(&status); // wait for the child process to finish...
        std::cout << "I am the parent, my PID is still "
```

```
                        << getpid() << std::endl;
        }
        return (0);
}
```

Now, let's develop the `fork-exec` version of the previous program.

1. First, type the program in a new file called `process_02.cpp`:

```cpp
#include <stddef.h>
#include <stdlib.h>
#include <stdio.h>
#include <unistd.h>
#include <sys/types.h>
#include <sys/wait.h>
#include <iostream>

int main(void)
{
    pxid_t child;
    int status;
    std::cout << "I am the parent, my PID is "
              << getpid() << std::endl;
    std::cout << "My parent's PID is "
              << getppid() << std::endl;
    std::cout << "I am going to create a new process..."
              << std::endl;
    child = fork();
    if (child == -1)
    {
        // fork() returns -1 on failure
        std::cout << "fork() failed." << std::endl;
        return 1;
    }
    else if (child == 0)
    {
```

2. The following code block shows the child section running `ls -l` with `execl`:

```cpp
if (execl("/usr/bin/ls", "ls", "-l", NULL) < 0)
{
    std::cout << "execl failed!" << std::endl;
    return 2;
}
std::cout << "I am the child, my PID is "
          << getpid() << std::endl;
std::cout << "My parent's PID is "
          << getppid() << std::endl;
```

```
        }
        else
        {
            wait(&status); // wait for the child process to finish...
        }
        return (0);
    }
```

The next section will describe the details of the two different approaches (`fork` versus `fork-exec`).

How it works...

Let's analyze the two preceding examples:

1. The `fork` system call: By compiling `g++ process_01.cpp` and running `./a.out`, the output would be as follows:

```
root@e36c5ccd6167:/BOOK/chapter3# ./a.out
I am the parent, my PID is 26
My parent's PID is 1
I am going to create a new process...
I am the child, my PID is 27
My parent's PID is 26
I am the parent, my PID is still 26
root@e36c5ccd6167:/BOOK/chapter3#
```

   The program, by calling `fork`, creates a copy of the calling process. This means that the two processes have the same code and, although they are two completely different processes, the code base will be the same. The user has to hook the child code in the `else if (child == 0)` section. The parent, eventually, will have to wait for the child to finish its task with the `wait(&status);` call. Another alternative is the `waitpid (123, &status, WNOHANG);` call, which waits for a specific PID (or waits for all the child processes if the first parameter is -1). `WNOHANG` makes `waitpid` immediately return, even if the status of a child is not immediately available.

What happens if the parent process does not wait for the child to finish? That is, what happens is there is no `wait(&status);` call? Technically, the parent will finish, and the child, still running, will become a **zombie**. This was a huge problem in the Linux kernel before version 2.6 as the zombie processes stayed in the system until they were *waited* for. The child's processes are now adopted by the `init` process (which has a PID of `1`), which, periodically, waits for children who can die.

2. The `fork-exec` system call:

```
root@e36c5ccd6167:/BOOK/chapter3# ./a.out
I am the parent, my PID is 53
My parent's PID is 1
I am going to create a new process...
total 28
-rwxr-xr-x 1 root root 17424 Jul  1 22:46 a.out
-rw-r--r-- 1 root root  1006 Jul  1 22:20 process_01.cpp
-rw-r--r-- 1 root root   946 Jul  1 22:46 process_02.cpp
root@e36c5ccd6167:/BOOK/chapter3#
```

The most common way of creating processes is the `fork/exec` combination. As we've seen, `fork` creates a completely new process with its own PID, but now, the `else if (child == 0)` section executes an external process, which has a different code base. This example just calls the `ls -l` command to list files and directories, but a developer can put any executable file here.

There's more...

Why a process should be used instead of a thread is an important aspect to consider. The answer depends, but in general, the following aspects should be considered.

- A thread runs in the same memory space of the process that launched it. This aspect has both pros and cons. The main implication is that if a thread crashes, the whole application crashes.
- Communication between threads is much faster than interprocess communications.
- A process can be spawned with lower privileges (through `setrlimit`) to limit the resources available to untrusted code.
- A program designed in processes is more segregated than one designed in threads.

There are many variations to the `fork/execl/wait` calls seen in this recipe. The `man pages` offer full comprehensive documentation to the whole family of calls. The following screenshot refers to `man execl`:

```
EXEC(3)                    BSD Library Functions Manual                    EXEC(3)

NAME
     execl, execle, execlp, execv, execvp, execvP -- execute a file

LIBRARY
     Standard C Library (libc, -lc)

SYNOPSIS
     #include <unistd.h>

     extern char **environ;

     int
     execl(const char *path, const char *arg0, ... /*, (char *)0 */);

     int
     execle(const char *path, const char *arg0, ... /*, (char *)0, char *const envp[] */);

     int
     execlp(const char *file, const char *arg0, ... /*, (char *)0 */);

     int
     execv(const char *path, char *const argv[]);

     int
     execvp(const char *file, char *const argv[]);

     int
     execvP(const char *file, const char *search_path, char *const argv[]);
```

See also

See `Chapter 1`, *Getting Started with System Programming,* for a refresher on `man pages` and Linux in general.

Killing a process

In the previous recipe, we've seen two ways to start a new process where the parent always waits for their children to finish the task. This is not always the case. Sometimes, a parent should be able to kill the child process. In this recipe, we will see an example of how to do that.

Getting ready

It's important to go through the *Starting a new process* recipe as a prerequisite.

How to do it...

In this section, we create a program where a parent process forks its child process, the child process will do an infinite loop, and the parent kills it:

1. Let's develop the child program that will be killed by the parent:

```cpp
#include <stddef.h>
#include <stdlib.h>
#include <stdio.h>
#include <unistd.h>
#include <sys/types.h>
#include <sys/wait.h>
#include <iostream>

int main(void)
{
    std::cout << "Running child ..." << std::endl;
    while (true)
        ;
}
```

2. Next, we have to develop the parent program (process_03.cpp in the /BOOK/Chapter03 folder):

```cpp
#include <stddef.h>
#include <stdlib.h>
#include <stdio.h>
#include <unistd.h>
#include <sys/types.h>
#include <sys/wait.h>
#include <iostream>
```

```
int main(void)
{
    pid_t child;
    int status;
    std::cout << "I am the parent, my PID is " << getpid()
                 << std::endl;
    child = fork();
    std::cout << "Forked a child process with PID = "
                 << child << std::endl;
    if (child == -1)
    {
        std::cout << "fork() failed." << std::endl;
        return 1;
    }
    else if (child == 0)
    {
```

3. Next, in the child section of the parent program, we start the child program developed in the previous step:

```
        std::cout << "About to run the child process with PID = "
                     << child << std::endl;
        if (execl("./child.out", "child.out", NULL) < 0)
        {
            std::cout << "error in executing child proceess "
                         << std::endl;
            return 2;
        }
    }
    else
    {
```

4. In the parent section (else section) of the parent program, we have to kill the child process and check that it is correctly killed:

```
        std::cout << "killing the child process with PID = "
                     << child << std::endl;
        int status = kill (child, 9);
        if (status == 0)
            std::cout << "child process killed ...." << std::endl;
        else
            std::cout << "there was a problem killing
                    the process with PID = "
                         << child << std::endl;
    }
    return (0);
}
```

We've seen both the parent and the child program, with the parent killing the child process. In the next section, we'll learn the mechanics of these programs.

How it works...

Before all this, we have to compile both the child and parent programs—g++ `process_03.cpp` and g++ -o child.out `process_04.cpp`.

When compiling `process_04.cpp`, we have to specify -o `child.out` as needed by the parent process (with the process name as a.out). By running it, the output produced is as follows:

```
root@90c65dec33d3:/BOOK/chapter3# ./a.out
I am the parent, my PID is 217
Forked a child process with PID = 218
killing the child process with PID = 218
child process killed ....
root@90c65dec33d3:/BOOK/chapter3#
```

The execution shows that the child process with `PID` = `218` is correctly killed by the parent process.

The code in this recipe is just a variation of the *Starting a new process* recipe. The difference is that now, the parent process, as part of its elaboration, kills the child process int `status = kill (child, 9);`. The `kill` system call accepts as the first parameter the PID of the process to kill, and, as the second parameter, the signal to send to the child process. The accepted signals are as follows:

- 1 = HUP (hangup)
- 2 = INT (interrupt)
- 3 = QUIT (quit)
- 6 = ABRT (abort)
- 9 = KILL (non-catchable, non-ignorable kill)
- 14 = ALRM (alarm clock)
- 15 = TERM (software termination signal)

 man 2 kill, the kill system call, sends a signal to a process. On success, return 0; otherwise, return −1. You need to include #include <sys/types.h> and #include <signal.h> to use it.

There's more...

In the *Understanding concurrency* recipe in `Chapter 2`, *Revisiting C++*, we offer two alternative solutions (and advocate them for the nature of this book) based on `std::thread` and `std::async`, if possible. The next recipe also offers a concrete example of `std::thread` use.

Creating a new thread

Processes are not the only way of structuring a software system; a lightweight alternative is to use threads. This recipe shows how to create and manage threads using the C++ standard library. We've seen that the main advantages of using the C++ standard library are its portability and the fact that it's not dependent on external libraries (for example, Boost).

How to do it...

The code we'll write will be the concurrent version of summing up a large vector of integers. The vector is split into two parts; each thread calculates the sum of its part, and the main thread shows the result.

1. Let's define a vector of 100,000 integers, and generate random numbers in the `main` method:

```cpp
#include <iostream>
#include <thread>
#include <vector>
#include <algorithm>

void threadFunction (std::vector<int> &speeds, int start, int
    end, int& res);

int main()
{
    std::vector<int> speeds (100000);
    std::generate(begin(speeds), end(speeds), [] ()
        { return rand() % 10 ; });
```

2. Next, start the first thread, passing the first 50,000 integers:

```cpp
int th1Result = 0;
std::thread t1 (threadFunction, std::ref(speeds), 0, 49999,
    std::ref(th1Result));
```

3. Then, start the second thread, passing the second 50,000 integers:

```
int th2Result = 0;
std::thread t2 (threadFunction, std::ref(speeds), 50000, 99999,
    std::ref(th2Result));
```

4. Wait for the results from the two threads:

```
t1.join();
t2.join();
std::cout << "Result = " << th1Result + th2Result
    << std::endl;
return 0;
}

void threadFunction (std::vector<int> &speeds, int start, int
    end, int& res)
{
    std::cout << "starting thread ... " << std::endl;
    for (int i = start; i <= end; ++i)
    res += speeds[i];
    std::cout << "end thread ... " << std::endl;
}
```

The next section explains the dynamics.

How it works...

By compiling the program with g++ thread_01.cpp -lpthread and executing it, the output is as follows:

In *step 1*, we defined the threadFunction method, which is the basic thread unit that will take care of summing up from start to end the elements in speeds, saving the result in the res output variable.

In *step 2* and *step 3*, we started two threads to do the calculation for the first 50,000 items for the t1 thread and the second 50,000 items for the t2 thread. These two threads ran concurrently, so we needed to wait for them to finish to do this. In *step 4*, we waited for the th1 and th2 results to be completed, summed up the two results—th1Results and th2Results— and printed them in the standard output (stdout).

There's more...

The *Starting a new process* recipe showed how to create a process, and in which circumstances a process suits the solution. One important aspect worth highlighting is that a thread runs in the **same address space** of the process that created it. Although threads are still a nice way of structuring a system software in a more independent (runnable) module, if a thread crashes (due to a segmentation fault, or if terminate is somehow called, among many others), the whole application crashes.

On the positive side, the ease of communication among threads, as we've seen in the preceding code, is extremely simple and efficient. Furthermore, threads share the **static** and the **heap** memory with each other, and with the process that created them.

The code in this recipe, although simple, has shown how a task (sum of a large array) can be executed concurrently. As a side note, a multithreaded application is worthless if the algorithm is not designed to be run concurrently—that is, if there are dependencies among threads.

It's important to note in this context that if the two threads were to run on two processors at the same time, we'd use the word **parallel**. We don't have this guarantee, in this case.

We've used std::thread from the C++ standard library, but the same example can be written using std::async. Chapter 2, *Revisiting C++*, shows an example of both. You are invited to rewrite this recipe's code using the second method.

See also

In the *Understanding concurrency* recipe in Chapter 2, *Revisiting C++*, there is an introduction to the concurrency topic with a recipe that includes both std::thread and std::async. You are also invited to read the section dedicated to threads in *Effective Modern C++* by Scott Meyers, and *The C++ Programming Language* by Bjarne Stroustrup.

Creating a daemon process

System programming is really about dealing closely with operating system resources, creating processes, threads, releasing resources, and much more. There are cases where we need a process to run *indefinitely;* that is, a process first offers some services or manages a resource, and then it keeps running all the time. A process that runs *indefinitely in the background* is called a **daemon**. This recipe will show how a daemon could be spawned programmatically.

How to do it...

As mentioned, a daemon is a process that runs indefinitely. A process, in order to be classified as a daemon, must have some well-defined properties that will be shown in this recipe with a program.

1. Type the following code to reset the initial access permission of the child process by calling the umask system call:

```
#include <unistd.h>
#include <sys/stat.h>
#include <iostream>

int main(void)
{
    pid_t child;
    int status;
    std::cout << "I am the parent, my PID is " << getpid()
        << std::endl;
    std::cout << "I am going to create a new daemon process..."
        << std::endl;
    // 1. clear file creation mask
    umask(0);
```

2. Type the code to fork for a child:

```
child = fork();
if (child == -1)
{
    std::cout << "fork() failed." << std::endl;
    return (-1);
}
else if (child == 0) // child (daemon) process
{
```

3. Type the `setsid` command on the child process:

```
setsid();
```

4. Change the working directory to the child process (which is a daemon now):

```
if (chdir("/") < 0)
        std::cout << "Couldn't change directly" << std::endl;
```

5. Run the daemon-specific task—in this case, just sleep for 10 seconds:

```
// Attach here the daemon specific long running
// tasks ... sleep for now.
sleep (10);
}
```

6. The parent process exits after `fork`:

```
return (0);
}
```

The next section will explain these six points in more detail.

How it works...

Compile the code with `g++ daemon_01.cpp` (in (`/BOOK/Chapter03`) folder of the Docker image) and run it. The output is as follows:

```
root@f0ebe118b21b:/BOOK/chapter3# ./a.out
I am the parent, my PID is 278
I am going to create a new daemon process...
root@f0ebe118b21b:/BOOK/chapter3# ps -efj
UID         PID  PPID  PGID   SID  C STIME TTY          TIME CMD
root          1     0     1     1  0 10:40 pts/0    00:00:00 /bin/bash
root        279     1   279   279  0 14:01 ?        00:00:00 ./a.out
root        280     1   280     1  0 14:01 pts/0    00:00:00 ps -efj
root@f0ebe118b21b:/BOOK/chapter3#
```

When we run a process on a shell, the Terminal waits for the children to finish before being ready for another command. We can run the command with the & symbol (for example, `ls -l &`), and the shell will prompt the Terminal for another command. Please note that the child process will still be in the same session as the parent process. For a process to be a daemon, the following rules should be applied (numbers 2 and 3 are mandatory; the others are optional):

1. **Call** `umask` **with parameter** 0 (`umask(0)`): When a parent creates a child process, the file mode creation mask is inherited (that is, the child process will inherit the initial access permission of the parent). We want to make sure we reset them.
2. **Have the parent exit after the fork**: In the preceding code, after the parent has created the child process, it returns.
3. **Call** `setsid`. This does three things:
    - The child process becomes the leader of a newly created session.
    - It becomes the leader of a new process group.
    - It gets disassociated from its controlling Terminal.
4. **Change working directory**: The parent process might run in a temporary (or mounted) folder that might not exist for long. It's a good practice to set the current folder to meet the long-term expectations of the daemon process.
5. **Logging**: Since the daemon service is not associated with any Terminal device anymore, it is a good practice to redirect the standard input, output, and error to `/dev/null`.

There's more...

A process, as seen so far, has a PID as its unique identifier. It also belongs to a group that has a **process group ID (PGID)**. A process group is a collection of one or more processes. All the processes in the same group can receive signals from the same Terminal. Each group has a leader, and the PGID has the same value as the leader's PID.

A session is a collection of one or more groups. This recipe showed that a new session can be created by calling the `setsid` method.

A session can have a (single) controlling Terminal. The `ps -efj` command shows all the processes running with the `PID`, `PPID`, and `PGID`, and the controlling Terminal (`TTY`) info for each process:

```
root@d776194f08f1:/BOOK/chapter3# ./a.out ; ps -axj
I am the parent, my PID is 18
I am going to create a new daemon process...
 PPID   PID  PGID   SID TTY       TPGID STAT   UID   TIME COMMAND
    0     1     1     1 pts/0        20 Ss       0   0:00 /bin/bash
    1    19    19    19 ?            -1 Ss       0   0:00 ./a.out
    1    20    20     1 pts/0        20 R+       0   0:00 ps -axj
root@d776194f08f1:/BOOK/chapter3#
```

The output shows that the `./a.out` daemon has `PID = 19` and it's a leader for the group (`PGID = 19`), and it is not attached to any controlling Terminal (`TTY= ?`).

See also

Chapter 13 of *Advanced Programming in the UNIX® Environment* by W.R. Stevens is dedicated to the daemon processes.

4
Deep Dive into Memory Management

Memory turns out to be one of the core concepts when dealing with systems development. Allocating, freeing, and learning how memory is managed, and knowing what C++ can offer to simplify and manage memory, are crucial. This chapter will help you grasp how memory works by learning how to use C++ smart pointers, aligned memory, memory-mapped I/O, and allocators.

This chapter will cover the following topics:

- Learning automatic versus dynamic memory
- Learning when to use `unique_ptr`, and the implications for size
- Learning when to use `shared_ptr`, and the implications for size
- Allocating aligned memory
- Checking whether the memory allocated is aligned
- Dealing with memory-mapped I/O
- Dealing with allocators hands-on

Technical requirements

In order to let you immediately try the programs, we've set up a Docker image that has all the tools and libraries we'll need throughout the book. This is based on Ubuntu 19.04.

In order to set it up, follow these steps:

1. Download and install Docker Engine from `www.docker.com`.
2. Pull the image from Docker Hub by running the following command: `docker pull kasperondocker/system_programming_cookbook:latest`.

3. The image should now be available. Type in the following command to view the image: `docker images`.

4. You should have at least this image now: `kasperondocker/system_programming_cookbook`.

5. Run the Docker image with an interactive shell, with the help of the following command: `docker run -it --cap-add sys_ptrace kasperondocker/system_programming_cookbook:latest /bin/bash`.

6. The shell on the running container is now available. Type in `root@39a5a8934370/# cd /BOOK/` to get all the programs developed, by chapter.

The `--cap-add sys_ptrace` argument is needed to allow the **GNU Project Debugger** (**GDB**) in the Docker container to set breakpoints, which, by default, Docker does not allow.

 Disclaimer: The C++20 standard has been approved (that is, technically finalized) by WG21 in a meeting in Prague at the end of February. This means that the GCC compiler version that this book uses, 8.3.0, does not include (or has very, very limited support for) the new and cool C++20 features. For this reason, the Docker image does not include the C++20 recipe code. GCC keeps the development of the newest features in branches (you have to use appropriate flags for that, for example, `-std=c++2a`); therefore, you are encouraged to experiment with them by yourself. So, clone and explore the GCC contracts and module branches and have fun.

Learning automatic versus dynamic memory

This recipe will focus on the two main strategies C++ offers to allocate memory: **automatic** and **dynamic** memory allocation. A variable is automatic when its scope lasts for the duration of the block in which it is defined, and its allocation and deallocation are automatic (that is, not up to the developer). The variable is allocated on the stack.

A variable is dynamic if allocated in the dynamic portion of the memory (free store, which is often referred to as the *heap*), and the allocation and deallocation are up to the developer. Greater flexibility offered by the dynamic memory allocation comes with a cost, in terms of more work for the developer to avoid memory leaks, dangling pointers, and so on.

How to do it...

This section will show two examples of automatic and dynamic variable allocation.

1. Let's create a utility class we're going to need:

```
class User
{
public:
    User(){
        std::cout << "User constructor" << std::endl;
    };
    ~User(){
        std::cout << "User Destructor" << std::endl;
    };

    void cheers()
    {
        std::cout << " hello!" << std::endl;};
    };
};
```

2. And now, let's create the `main` module to show automatic memory usage:

```
#include <iostream>

int main()
{
    std::cout << "Start ... " << std::endl;
    {
        User developer;
        developer.cheers();
    }
    std::cout << "End ... " << std::endl;
}
```

3. And now, we'll write the `main` module for dynamic memory usage:

```
#include <iostream>

int main()
{
    std::cout << "Start ... " << std::endl;
    {
        User* developer = new User();
        developer->cheers();
        delete developer;
    }
```

```
            std::cout << "End ... " << std::endl;
    }
```

These two programs, although with the same outcome, show two different ways of dealing with memory.

How it works...

In the first step, we defined a `User` class, which is used to show the difference between automatic and dynamic memory allocation. Its constructor and destructor will be used to show when the class is allocated and deallocated.

In *step 2*, we can see that the variable is just defined as `User developer;`. The C++ runtime will take care of allocating memory of the stack and freeing it, without additional work for the developer. This type of memory management is faster and easier, but comes with two major costs:

- The amount of memory is limited.
- The variable is only valid and visible in the inner `{ }` block, where it is allocated.

In *step 3*, the same object is allocated on the dynamic memory (that is, **heap**). The main difference is that the developer is now responsible for allocating and deallocating the quantity of memory needed. If the memory is not deallocated (by using `free`), there'll be a leak. The pros of managing the memory dynamically are as follows:

- Flexibility: The pointer, referencing to the allocated memory (the `developer` variable) can be used throughout the whole program.
- The quantity of memory available is way more than that for automatic memory management.

There's more...

With the newer C++ standard (from version 11 onward), `new` and `delete` can be safely avoided in favor of smart pointers (`shared_ptr` and `unique_ptr`). These two tools will take care of deallocating the memory when it is not used anymore. `Chapter 2`, *Revisiting C++*, provides a refresher on smart pointers.

See also

The next two recipes will show when to use `unique_ptr` and `shared_ptr`.

Learning when to use unique_ptr, and the implications for size

In the previous recipe, we've learned the two fundamental ways of managing memory in C++: automatic and dynamic. We've also learned that dynamic memory is available to the developer in a greater quantity compared to automatic memory (that is, available from the stack), and offers great flexibility. On the other hand dealing with dynamic memory can be an unpleasant experience:

- The pointer does not indicate whether it points to an array or to a single object.
- When freeing the allocated memory, you don't know if you have to use `delete` or `delete[]`, so you have to look at how the variable is defined.
- There is no explicit way to tell if the pointer is dangling.

These are just a few issues you might encounter when dealing with dynamic memory, and then, with `new` and `delete`. `unique_ptr` is a smart pointer, which means that it knows when the memory should be deallocated, removing the burden from the developer. In this recipe, you'll learn how to use `unique_ptr` and `make_unique` properly.

How to do it...

In this section, we'll develop a program to learn why `unique_ptr` is a convenient way of dealing with dynamic memory; and the second aspect is to learn whether `unique_ptr` is the same size as raw pointers:

1. We'll reuse the `User` class developed in the previous recipe.
2. Let's write the `main` program, allocating a `User` object with `make_unique` and using `unique_ptr`:

```
#include <iostream>

int main()
{
    std::cout << "Start ... " << std::endl;
    {
```

```
        auto developer = std::make_unique<User>();
        developer->cheers();
    }
    std::cout << "End ... " << std::endl;
}
```

3. Let's see the memory implications:

```
auto developer = std::make_unique<User>();
developer->cheers();

User* developer2 = new User();
std::cout << "developer size = " << sizeof (developer) <<
std::endl;
std::cout << "developer2 size = " << sizeof (developer2) <<
std::endl;
delete developer2;
```

What do you think will be the difference in size between `developer` and `developer2`?

How it works...

In *step 2*, we used `unique_ptr` to define a variable allocated using `std::make_unique`. Once the variable is allocated, there is no risk of memory leak as the destructor will automatically deallocate the memory for us. The output is as follows:

```
root@925b46908508:/BOOK/chapter4# ./a.out
Start ...
User Constructor
 hello!
User Destructor
End ...
root@925b46908508:/BOOK/chapter4#
```

In *step 3*, we wanted to check if `unique_ptr` added any memory compared to raw pointers. Well, the good news is that `unique_ptr` has the same size as the raw pointer version. The output of this step is as follows:

```
root@925b46908508:/BOOK/chapter4# ./a.out
Start ...
User Constructor
User Constructor
developer size = 8
developer2 size = 8
User Destructor
User Destructor
End ...
root@925b46908508:/BOOK/chapter4#
```

The `developer` and `developer2` variables are of the same size, and the developer can treat them the same way.

A rule of thumb is to use `unique_ptr` for variables that manage resources with **exclusive ownership only**, which represent most developers' use cases.

There's more...

By default, `unique_ptr` calls the default `delete` destructor for the object, but a custom `delete` destructor can be specified. If the pointer variable does not represent exclusive ownership but rather shared ownership converting it to `shared_ptr` is easy.

One important aspect to highlight is that `make_unique` is not part of the C++11 standard library, but part of the C++ 14 library. If you're using the C++11 standard library, its implementation is quite simple, though.

See also

`Chapter 2`, *Revisiting C++* has a dedicated recipe on smart pointers, with one recipe on shared and unique pointers. A suggested read is *Effective Modern C++* by Scott Meyers.

Learning when to use shared_ptr, and the implications for size

In the previous recipe, we've learned how to manage dynamic memory (allocated on the heap) in a very convenient way, by using `unique_ptr`. We've learned as well that `unique_ptr` must be used, just in case of exclusive ownership of the memory, or resources managed by the memory. But what if we have a resource that is co-owned by more entities? What if the memory we have to manage has to be released when all the owners have completed their job? Well, this is exactly the use case for `shared_ptr`. Just as with `unique_ptr`, for `shared_ptr` we don't have to allocate memory with `new`, but there is a template function (part of the C++ standard library), `make_shared`.

How to do it...

In this section, we'll develop a program to show how to use `shared_ptr`. You'll learn that the memory is only deallocated when none of the owners use the memory anymore:

1. We'll reuse the `User` class developed in the first recipe. Let's now write the `main` module:

```
int main()
{
    std::cout << "Start ... " << std::endl;
    auto shared1 = std::make_shared<User>();
    {
        auto shared2 = shared1;
        shared2->cheers(); std::cout << " from shared2"
            << std::endl;
        shared1->cheers(); std::cout << " from shared1"
            << std::endl;
    }
    std::cout << "End ... " << std::endl;
}
```

2. Now, let's see the memory used by `shared_ptr` by writing this program:

```
int main()
{
    std::cout << "Start ... " << std::endl;
    auto shared1 = std::make_shared<User>();
    {
        auto shared2 = shared1;
        User* newAllocation = new User();
```

```
auto uniqueAllocation = std::make_unique

std::cout << "shared2 size = " << sizeof (shared2)
    << std::endl;
std::cout << "newAllocation size = " <<
    sizeof (newAllocation) << std::endl;
std::cout << "uniqueAllocation size = " <<
    sizeof (uniqueAllocation) << std::endl;

delete newAllocation;
}
std::cout << "End ... " << std::endl;
}
```

At this point, we should know the size of `unique_ptr` compared to a raw pointer (as we learned in the *Learning when to use unique_ptr, and the implications for size* recipe). What is the size of the `shared_ptr` variable? Still the same? In the next section, we'll learn about this important aspect.

How it works...

In the preceding first program, we showed how to use `shared_ptr`. First, we allocated a block of memory, which contained an object of type `User` with `auto shared1 = std::make_shared<User>();`. So far, the `User` resource is owned by the `shared1` variable. Next, into the block, we assigned the `shared1` variable to `shared2` through `auto shared2 = shared1;`. This means that the memory containing the `User` object is now pointed by `shared1` and `shared2`. The same goal would have been achieved by using the constructor copy `auto shared2 (shared1);`. As `User` is now pointed by two variables, the deallocation of the used memory only happens when all the variables go out of scope. Indeed, the output proves that the memory is deallocated (`User`'s destructor is called) at the end of the main block, and not at the end of the inner block, as happened for `unique_ptr`:

```
root@9e43ae3f03da:/BOOK/chapter4# ./a.out
Start ...
User Constructor
 hello!
 from shared2
 hello!
 from shared1
End ...
User Destructor
root@9e43ae3f03da:/BOOK/chapter4#
```

The impact of `shared_ptr` on memory is not the same as `unique_ptr`. The reason is that the `shared_ptr` implementation needs one raw pointer to keep track of the memory (likewise with `unique_ptr`), and another raw pointer for the resource's reference counting.

This reference-counting variable must necessarily be an atomic one, as it can be incremented and decremented by different threads:

```
root@9e43ae3f03da:/BOOK/chapter4# ./a.out
Start ...
User Constructor
User Constructor
User Constructor
shared2 size = 16
newAllocation size = 8
uniqueAllocation size = 8
User Destructor
User Destructor
End ...
User Destructor
```

The memory size of a `shared_ptr` variable is, typically, twice the size of a raw pointer, as we see in the preceding output, on running the second program.

There's more...

One more interesting point not to overlook is that as `shared_ptr` contains an atomic variable, it is typically slower than normal variables.

See also

`Chapter 2`, *Revisiting C++*, has a dedicated recipe on smart pointers, with one recipe on shared and unique pointers. A suggested read is *Effective Modern C++* by Scott Meyers.

Allocating aligned memory

Writing system programs might require the use of data that is aligned in memory in order to access the hardware efficiently (and in some cases, to access it at all). For example, on a 32-bit architecture machine, we have the memory allocated aligned to a 4-byte boundary. In this recipe, you'll learn how to use the C++11 `std::aligned_storage` to allocate aligned memory. Of course, there are other, more traditional, mechanisms to allocate aligned memory, but the goal of this book is to use C++ standard library tools as much as possible.

How to do it...

In this section, we'll write a program that will use the allocated memory with `std::aligned_storage` and will show the use of `std::alignment_of`:

1. Let's start by writing a program to check what is the default alignment boundary for integers and doubles on the current machine:

```cpp
#include <type_traits>
#include <iostream>
int main()
{
    std::cout << "int alignment = " << std::alignment_of<int>
        ::value << std::endl;
    std::cout << "double alignment = " <<
        std::alignment_of<double>::value << std::endl;
    return (0);
}
```

2. Now, let's write a program to allocate memory aligned to a specific size. For this, let's use `std::aligned_storage`:

```cpp
#include <type_traits>
#include <iostream>
typedef std::aligned_storage<sizeof(int), 8>::type intAligned;
int main()
{
    intAligned i, j;
    new (&i) int();
    new (&j) int();

    int* iu = &reinterpret_cast<int&>(i);
    *iu = 12;
    int* ju = &reinterpret_cast<int&>(j);
    *ju = 13;
```

```
        std::cout << "alignment = " << std::alignment
          _of<intAligned>::value << std::endl;
        std::cout << "value = " << *iu << std::endl;
        std::cout << "value2 = " << reinterpret_cast<int&>(i)
            << std::endl;
        return (0);
    }
```

Allocating aligned memory can be tricky, and the C++ standard library (from version 11 onward) offers these two features (`std::alignment_of`, `std::aligned_storage`) to simplify it. The next section will describe the mechanics behind it.

How it works...

The first program, which is quite simple, shows the natural alignment in memory for two primitive types through `std::alignment_of`. By compiling (`g++ alignedStorage.cpp`) and running the program, we have the following output:

```
root@839836698e38:/BOOK/chapter4# ./a.out
int alignment = 4
double alignment = 8
root@839836698e38:/BOOK/chapter4#
```

This means that each integer will be aligned at 4 bytes of boundary and with floating-point types aligned to 8 bytes.

In the second program, we need an integer that is aligned to 8 bytes. By compiling it and running the executable, the output would be something like this:

```
root@839836698e38:/BOOK/chapter4# ./a.out
alignment = 8
value = 12
value2 = 12
root@839836698e38:/BOOK/chapter4#
```

You may have noticed that I've compiled with the −g option (to add debug symbols). We did this to show, with the memory dump in GDB, that the memory of the integer is correctly aligned at 8 bytes:

```
root@839836698e38:/BOOK/chapter4# gdb a.out
GNU gdb (Ubuntu 8.2.91.20190405-0ubuntu3) 8.2.91.20190405-git
Copyright (C) 2019 Free Software Foundation, Inc.
License GPLv3+: GNU GPL version 3 or later <http://gnu.org/licenses/gpl.html>
This is free software: you are free to change and redistribute it.
There is NO WARRANTY, to the extent permitted by law.
Type "show copying" and "show warranty" for details.
This GDB was configured as "x86_64-linux-gnu".
Type "show configuration" for configuration details.
For bug reporting instructions, please see:
<http://www.gnu.org/software/gdb/bugs/>.
Find the GDB manual and other documentation resources online at:
    <http://www.gnu.org/software/gdb/documentation/>.

For help, type "help".
Type "apropos word" to search for commands related to "word"...
Reading symbols from a.out...
(gdb) b 17
Breakpoint 1 at 0x11fe: file alignedStorage2.cpp, line 17.
(gdb) r
Starting program: /BOOK/chapter4/a.out
warning: Error disabling address space randomization: Operation not permitted

Breakpoint 1, main () at alignedStorage2.cpp:17
17              std::cout << "alignment = " << std::alignment_of<intAligned>::value << std::endl;
(gdb) x/20bd iu
0x7ffc57654468: 12       0       0       0       -103     85      0       0
0x7ffc57654470: 13       0       0       0       -4       127     0       0
0x7ffc57654478: 0        -86     94      51
(gdb)
```

From the debug session, we can see that through the x/20bd iu (x = *memory dump*) command, we dumped 20 bytes of the memory after the address of the iu variable. We can see something interesting here: both the iu and ju variables are aligned at 8 bytes. Each memory row displays 8 bytes (test it: 0x7ffc57654470 − 0x7ffc57654468 = 8).

There's more...

Playing with memory is always risky, and these new C++ features (and others available in the std namespace) help us to **play safe**. The recommendation is still the same: premature optimization must be used carefully; optimize (that is, use aligned memory) only when necessary. One last recommendation: using reinterpret_cast is discouraged, as it manipulates memory at a low level. You need to know what you're doing when using it.

See also

The latest version of *The C++ Programming Language, Fourth Edition* by Bjarne Stroustrup has a paragraph on *memory alignment* (6.2.9) and *aligned_storage* (35.4.1).

Checking whether the memory allocated is aligned

In the previous recipe, you have learned how to use C++11 to allocate aligned memory. The question now is: how do we know that memory is properly aligned? This recipe will teach you about this.

How to do it...

We'll be using the previous program, and by modifying it a little, we'll see how to check whether a pointer is aligned or not:

1. Let's modify the previous program, as follows:

```
#include <type_traits>
#include <iostream>

using intAligned8 = std::aligned_storage<sizeof(int), 8>::type;
using intAligned4 = std::aligned_storage<sizeof(int), 4>::type;

int main()
{
    intAligned8 i; new(&i) int();
    intAligned4 j; new (&j) int();

    int* iu = &reinterpret_cast<int&>(i);
    *iu = 12;
    int* ju = &reinterpret_cast<int&>(j);
    *ju = 13;

    if (reinterpret_cast<unsigned long>(iu) % 8 == 0)
        std::cout << "memory pointed by the <iu> variable
        aligned to 8 byte" << std::endl;
    else
        std::cout << "memory pointed by the <iu> variable NOT
        aligned to 8 bytes" << std::endl;
    if (reinterpret_cast<unsigned long>(ju) % 8 == 0)
```

```
            std::cout << "memory pointed by the <ju> variable aligned
    to
            8 bytes" << std::endl;
        else
            std::cout << "memory pointed by the <ju> variable NOT
            aligned to 8 bytes" << std::endl;

        return (0);
    }
```

We created on purpose two typedefs, one for the alignment to 8 bytes (intAligned8) and one for the alignment to 4 bytes (intAligned4).

How it works...

In the program, we defined two variables, i and j, of type intAligned8 and intAligned4 respectively. With the help of these two variables (with alignment to 8 and 4 bytes), we can see that they are properly aligned by checking that the result of the division by 8 is 0: ((unsigned long)iu % 8 == 0). This ensures that the iu pointer is aligned to 8 bytes. The same is done for the ju variable. By running the preceding program, we'll get this result:

```
root@839836698e38:/BOOK/chapter4# g++ isAligned.cpp
root@839836698e38:/BOOK/chapter4# ./a.out
memory pointed by the <iu> variable aligned to 8 byte
memory pointed by the <ju> variable NOT aligned to 8 bytes
root@839836698e38:/BOOK/chapter4#
```

As expected: iu is properly aligned to 8 bytes and ju is not.

There's more...

As you might have noticed, we used reinterpret_cast to allow the modulus (%) operator instead of the C-style cast ((unsigned long)iu % 8 == 0). If you are developing in C++, you're encouraged to use the named casts (static_cast, reinterpret_cast, const_cast, dynamic_cast) for two basic reasons:

- To allow the programmer to express the intent of the cast
- To make the cast safe

See also

More info on this topic can be found in *Advanced Programming in the UNIX® Environment* by W. Richard Stevens and Stephen A. Rago.

When a portion of memory is aligned, the compiler can make great optimization. A compiler doesn't have the possibility of knowing this, and therefore cannot make any optimizations. The last C++20 standard added the `std::assume_aligned` feature. This informs the compiler that the value of a pointer is a memory address aligned to a certain number of bytes. What can happen is that when we allocate some aligned memory, the pointer to that memory is then passed to other functions.

The `std::assume_aligned` feature informs the compiler to assume that the memory pointed by a pointer is already aligned, so it is safe to make optimizations:

```
void myFunc (int* p)
{
    int* pAligned = std::assume_aligned<64>(p);
    // using pAligned from now on.
}
```

The `std::assume_aligned<64>(p);` feature informs the compiler that p is already aligned to at least 64 bytes. You'll get undefined behavior if the memory is not aligned.

Dealing with memory-mapped I/O

Sometimes, we need to operate on memory in a way that is not conventional or, so to speak, not common. As we've seen, memory is allocated with `new` and released with `delete` (or, even better, with `make_unique` and `make_shared`). There might be cases in which we need to skip some layer—that is, using a Linux system call; for the sake of performance; or because of a custom behavior that we cannot map with the C++ standard library. This is the case with the `mmap` Linux system call (`man 2 mmap`). `mmap` is a POSIX-compliant system call that allows the programmer to map a file to a portion of memory. Among other things, `mmap` also allows memory to be allocated, and this recipe will teach you how to do it.

How to do it...

This section will show two mmap use cases: the first, how to map a file to a portion of memory; and the second, how to allocate memory using mmap. Let's first write a program that maps a file to memory.

1. In a shell, let's create a new source file called mmap_write.cpp. We need to open a file to map:

```
int fd = open(FILEPATH, O_RDWR | O_CREAT | O_TRUNC, (mode_t)0600);
if (fd == -1)
{
    std::cout << "Error opening file " << FILEPATH << std::endl;
    return 1;
}
```

2. Second, we have to create a space into the file that we'll use later (mmap does not do this):

```
int result = lseek(fd, FILESIZE-1, SEEK_SET);
if (result == -1)
{
    close(fd);
    std::cout << "Error calling lseek " << std::endl;
    return 2;
}

result = write(fd, "", 1);
if (result != 1)
{
    close(fd);
    std::cout << "Error writing into the file " << std::endl;
    return 3;
}
```

3. Then, we can map the file—represented by the fd file descriptor—to the map variable:

```
int* map = (int*) mmap(0, FILESIZE, PROT_READ | PROT_WRITE,
    MAP_SHARED, fd, 0);
if (map == MAP_FAILED)
{
    close(fd);
    std::cout << "Error mapping the file " << std::endl;
    return 4;
}
```

4. And finally, we need to write some value into it:

```
for (int i = 1; i <=NUM_OF_ITEMS_IN_FILE; ++i)
    map[i] = 2 * i;
```

5. Let's not forget to close the resources used:

```
if (munmap(map, FILESIZE) == -1)
    std::cout << "Error un-mapping" << std::endl;

close(fd);
```

6. The steps seen so far are related to writing a file with mmap. For the sake of completeness, in this step, we develop the program to read a file called mmap_read.cpp, which is very similar to the one we've seen. Here, we'll just see the important part (the Docker image contains the complete version of both the reader and the writer):

```
int* map = (int*) mmap(0, FILESIZE, PROT_READ, MAP_SHARED, fd, 0);
if (map == MAP_FAILED)
{
    close(fd);
    std::cout << "Error mapping the file " << std::endl;
    return 4;
}

for (int i = 1; i <= NUM_OF_ITEMS_IN_FILE; ++i)
    std::cout << "i = " << map[i] << std::endl;
```

Let's now learn how to use mmap to allocate memory.

1. Let's now allocate memory with mmap:

```
#include <sys/mman.h>
#include <iostream>
#include <cstring>

constexpr auto SIZE = 1024;

int main(int argc, char *argv[])
{
    auto* mapPtr = (char*) mmap(0, SIZE,
                            PROT_READ | PROT_WRITE,
                            MAP_PRIVATE | MAP_ANONYMOUS,
                            -1, 0);
    if (mapPtr == MAP_FAILED)
    {
```

```
        std::cout << "Error mapping memory " << std::endl;
        return 1;
    }
    std::cout << "memory allocated available from: " << mapPtr
      << std::endl;

    strcpy (mapPtr, "this is a string!");
    std::cout << "mapPtr val = " << mapPtr << std::endl;

    if (munmap(mapPtr, SIZE) == -1)
        std::cout << "Error un-mapping" << std::endl;

    return 0;
}
```

Although simple, these two programs show you how to allocate memory and manage a file with `mmap`. In the next section, we'll see how it works.

How it works...

In the first program, we've learned the most common use of `mmap`: to map a file to a portion of memory. As almost any resource can be mapped to a file in Linux, it means that we can map almost anything to memory with `mmap`. It indeed accepts a file descriptor. By compiling and running the `mmap_write.cpp` program first, we are able to write a file in memory with a list of integers. The file generated will be called `mmapped.txt`. The interesting part is to run the `mmap_read.cpp` reader program. Let's compile and run it:

```
root@839836698e38:/BOOK/chapter4# ./a.out
i = 2
i = 4
i = 6
i = 8
i = 10
i = 12
i = 14
i = 16
i = 18
i = 20
```

As we can see, it correctly prints out all the integers from the file.

Strictly speaking, mmap does not allocate memory in the heap memory, nor on the stack. It is a separate memory area, still in the virtual space of the process. munmap does the inverse: it releases the mapped memory, and flushes data to file (this behavior can be controlled with the msync system call).

The second program shows the second use case of mmap: Allocating memory in an alternative way to new and malloc. We can see a few differences in the call to mmap:

- MAP_PRIVATE: The modifications are private. Any modification made to the memory is not reflected back to the file or to other mappings. The file is mapped as copy-on-write.
- MAP_ANONYMOUS: It indicates that a portion of the memory of size SIZE will be allocated and not associated with any specific file.
- The fifth parameter we passed -1 as we want to allocate memory (that is, no file descriptor).

We allocated 1 KB of memory and used a string. The output is as follows:

```
root@839836698e38:/BOOK/chapter4# g++ mmap_allocate.cpp
root@839836698e38:/BOOK/chapter4# ./a.out
memory allocated availabe from:
mapPtr val =  this is a string!
root@839836698e38:/BOOK/chapter4#
```

Likewise, when we deallocate memory with free or delete, we need to release the mapped memory with munmap.

There's more...

There are a few advantages worth mentioning about mmap:

1. Reading from and writing to a memory-mapped file avoids the copy needed by the read() and write() from the actual file if mmap is used with MAP_SHARED or MAP_SHARED_VALIDATE flags. Indeed, when we write a chunk of data to a file, a buffer is moved from the user space to the kernel space, and the same is true when reading a chunk of data.
2. Reading and writing a memory-mapped file turns out to be a simple memory access. A memory-mapped file is only read and written in memory; at the munmap call, the memory is flushed back in the file. This behavior can be controlled by the MS_SYNC, MS_ASYNC, and MS_INVALIDATE flag parameters of the msync system call.

3. Very conveniently, when multiple processes map the same file in memory, the data is shared among all the processes (`MAP_SHARED`).

See also

Check `man 2 mmap` for more information. Further information can be found in *Linux System Programming, Second Edition* by Robert Love.

Dealing with allocators hands-on

C++ **Standard Template Library** (**STL**) containers are a simple, as well as effective, way of managing resources. One huge benefit of containers is that they can manage (almost) any type of data. When dealing with system programming, though, we may need to provide an alternative way of managing memory for our container. Allocators are exactly this: they provide a custom implementation to a container.

How to do it...

In this recipe, you'll learn to implement your own custom allocator (based on `mmap`, in this case) to provide to a standard library container (`std::vector`):

1. Let's create an empty allocator template first:

```
template<typename T>
class mmap_allocator
{
public:
    using value_type = T;
    template<typename U> struct rebind {
        using alloc = mmap_allocator<U>;
    };

    mmap_allocator(){};
    template <typename U>
    mmap_allocator(const mmap_allocator<U> &alloc) noexcept {};

    T* allocate(std::size_t n){};

    void deallocate(T* p, std::size_t n) {}
};
```

2. As you can see, there are copy constructor, `allocate`, and `deallocate` methods to implement. Let's implement them one by one (there is no need to implement the default constructor, in this case):

```cpp
mmap_allocator(const mmap_allocator<U> &alloc) noexcept {
    (void) alloc; };
```

3. Next, implement the `allocate` method:

```cpp
std::cout << "allocating ... n = " << n << std::endl;
auto* mapPtr = static_cast<T*> (mmap(0, sizeof(T) * n,
                                PROT_READ | PROT_WRITE,
                                MAP_PRIVATE | MAP_ANONYMOUS,
                                -1, 0));
if (mapPtr != MAP_FAILED)
    return static_cast<T*>(mapPtr);
throw std::bad_alloc();
```

4. And finally, implement the `deallocate` method:

```cpp
std::cout << "deallocating ... n = " << n << std::endl;
(void) n;
munmap(p, sizeof(T) * n);
```

5. The `main` method looks like this:

```cpp
int main ()
{
    std::vector<int, mmap_allocator<int>> mmap_vector = {1, 2,
        3, 4, 5};

    for (auto i : mmap_vector)
        std::cout << i << std::endl;

    return 0;
}
```

The use of `std::vector`, as you can see, is seamless from the user's point of view. The only difference is to specify which allocator we want to use. This container will allocate and deallocate memory, using solely `mmap` and `munmap` and not the default implementation, based on `new` and `delete`.

How it works...

The central part of this program is the two methods: `allocate`, which returns a pointer representing the memory allocated, and `deallocate`, which takes a pointer to the memory to be released.

In the first step, we've sketched the interface we're going to use to allocate and deallocate the memory. It's a template class, as we want it to be valid for any type. The two methods we have to implement, as discussed previously, are `allocate` and `deallocate`.

In the second step, we've developed the copy constructor, which will be called when we want to construct an object, passing in the input of an object of the same type. We're just returning a `typedef` that will communicate which allocator to use for the new object.

In the third step, we've implemented the constructor, which basically allocates the space of object n of type `T` with `mmap`. We've seen the use of `mmap` already in the previous recipe, so you're invited to read that recipe again.

In the fourth step, we've implemented the `deallocate` method, which in this case is calling the `munmap` method, which deletes the mappings for the specified address range.

Finally, the `main` method shows how to use our custom allocator with `std::vector` (it could have been any container—for example, list). In the definition of the variable, `mmap_vector`, we pass two parameters: the first one, `int`, to inform the compiler that it'll be a vector of integers, and the second one, `mmap_allocator<int>`, to instruct the use of our custom allocator, `mmap_allocator`, instead of the default one.

There's more...

In system programming, there is the concept of a **pool** of (pre-allocated) memory that the system reserves upfront and that must be used throughout the life of a resource. The `map_allocator` class seen in this recipe can be easily modified to pre-allocate a portion of memory in the constructor, and acquire and release it from the pool without affecting the system memory.

See also

The books *Effective Modern C++* by Scott Meyers and *The C++ Programming Language* by Bjarne Stroustrup cover these topics in great detail. Refer to the *Dealing with memory-mapped I/O* recipe for more details on `mmap`.

5
Using Mutexes, Semaphores, and Condition Variables

This chapter will focus on the most common mechanisms you can use to synchronize access to a shared resource. The synchronization mechanisms we will look at prevent a critical section (the program segment responsible for a resource) from being executed concurrently from two or more processes or threads. In this chapter, you'll learn how to use both POSIX and C++ standard library synchronization building blocks such as mutexes, `std::condition_variable`, `std::promise`, and `std::future`.

This chapter will cover the following recipes:

- Using POSIX mutexes
- Using POSIX semaphores
- POSIX semaphores advanced usage
- Synchronization building blocks
- Learning inter-thread communication with simple events
- Learning inter-thread communication with condition variables

Technical requirements

So that you can try out all the programs in this chapter immediately, we've set up a Docker image that contains all the tools and libraries we'll need throughout this book. It is based on Ubuntu 19.04.

In order to set it up, follow these steps:

1. Download and install the Docker Engine from `www.docker.com`.
2. Pull the image from Docker Hub: `docker pull kasperondocker/system_programming_cookbook:latest`.
3. The image should now be available. Type in the `docker images` command to view the image.
4. You should have the following image: `kasperondocker/system_programming_cookbook`.
5. Run the Docker image with an interactive shell using the `docker run -it -- cap-add sys_ptrace kasperondocker/system_programming_cookbook:latest /bin/bash` command.
6. The shell on the running container is now available. Use `root@39a5a8934370/# cd /BOOK/` to get all the programs that will be developed in this book.

The `--cap-add sys_ptrace` argument is needed to allow GDB to set breakpoints. Docker doesn't allow this by default.

Using POSIX mutexes

This recipe will teach you how to use POSIX mutexes to synchronize access to a resource from multiple threads. We'll do this by developing a program that contains a method (the critical section) that will perform a task that cannot run concurrently. We'll use the `pthread_mutex_lock, pthread_mutex_unlock`, and `pthread_mutex_init` POSIX methods to synchronize the threads' access to it.

How to do it...

In this recipe, we'll create a multi-threaded program just to increment an integer to `200000`. To do this, we'll develop the critical section that's responsible for incrementing the counter, which must be protected. Then, we'll develop the main section, which will create the two threads and manage the coordination between them. Let's proceed:

1. Open a new file called `posixMutex.cpp` and develop its structure and critical section method:

```cpp
#include <pthread.h>
#include <iostream>
```

```
struct ThreadInfo
{
    pthread_mutex_t lock;
    int counter;
};

void* increment(void *arg)
{
    ThreadInfo* info = static_cast<ThreadInfo*>(arg);
    pthread_mutex_lock(&info->lock);

    std::cout << "Thread Started ... " << std::endl;
    for (int i = 0; i < 100000; ++i)
        info->counter++;
    std::cout << "Thread Finished ... " << std::endl;

    pthread_mutex_unlock(&info->lock);
    return nullptr;
}
```

2. Now, in the `main` section, add the `init` method for the lock that's needed for synchronization between threads:

```
int main()
{
    ThreadInfo thInfo;
    thInfo.counter = 0;
    if (pthread_mutex_init(&thInfo.lock, nullptr) != 0)
    {
        std::cout << "pthread_mutex_init failed!" << std::endl;
        return 1;
    }
```

3. Now that we have the method that will execute the `increment` (that is, the critical section to protect) and the lock that will manage the synchronization between threads, let's create the threads:

```
    pthread_t t1;
    if (pthread_create(&t1, nullptr, &increment, &thInfo) != 0)
    {
        std::cout << "pthread_create for t1 failed! " << std::endl;
        return 2;
    }

    pthread_t t2;
    if (pthread_create(&t2, nullptr, &increment, &thInfo) != 0)
    {
        std::cout << "pthread_create for t2 failed! " << std::endl;
```

```
        return 3;
    }
```

4. Now, we have to wait for the threads to complete the tasks:

```
pthread_join(t1, nullptr);
pthread_join(t2, nullptr);
std::cout << "Threads elaboration finished. Counter = "
          << thInfo.counter << std::endl;
pthread_mutex_destroy(&thInfo.lock);
return 0;
```

This program (available in the Docker image under the /BOOK/Chapter05/ folder) showed us how to use the POSIX mutex interfaces to synchronize the use of a shared resource – a counter, in this case – between threads. We will explain this process in detail in the next section.

How it works...

In the first step, we created the struct that was needed to pass the parameters to the threads: struct ThreadInfo. In this struct, we put the lock that's needed to protect the resource counter and the counter itself. Then, we developed the increment feature. increment, logically, needs to lock the pthread_mutex_lock(&info->lock); resource, increment the counter (or any other action needed by the critical section), and unlock the pthread_mutex_unlock(&info->lock); resource to let the other threads do the same.

In the second step, we started developing the main method. The first thing we did is initialize the lock mutex with pthread_mutex_init. Here, we need to pass a pointer to the locally allocated resource.

In the third step, we created two threads, th1 and th2. These are responsible for running the increment method concurrently. The two threads are created with the pthread_create POSIX API by passing the address of thInfo that was allocated in *step 2*. If the thread is created successfully, it starts the elaboration immediately.

In the fourth and last step, we waited for both th1 and th2 to finish printing the value of the counter to the standard output, which we expect to be 200000. By compiling g++ posixMutex.cpp -lpthread and running the ./a.out program, we get the following output:

```
root@839836698e38:/BOOK/chapter5# g++ posixMutex.cpp -lpthread
root@839836698e38:/BOOK/chapter5# ./a.out
Thread Started ...
Thread Finished ...
Thread Started ...
Thread Finished ...
Threads elaboration finished. Counter = 200000
root@839836698e38:/BOOK/chapter5#
```

As we can see, the two threads never overlap the execution. Thus, the counter resource in the critical section is managed properly and the output is what we expected.

There's more...

In this recipe, we used `pthread_create` for the sake of completeness. The exact same goal could have been achieved by using `std::thread` and `std::async` from the C++ standard library.

 The `pthread_mutex_lock()` function locks the mutex. If the mutex is already locked, the calling thread will be blocked until the mutex becomes available. The `pthread_mutex_unlock` function unlocks the mutex if the current thread holds the lock on a mutex; otherwise, it results in undefined behavior.

See also

You are invited to modify this program and use `pthread_mutex_lock` and `pthread_mutex_unlock` in conjunction with `std::thread` or `std::async` from the C++ standard library. See Chapter 2, *Revisiting C++*, to refresh yourself on this topic.

Using POSIX semaphores

POSIX mutexes are clearly not the only mechanism you can use to synchronize access to a shared resource. This recipe will show you how to use another POSIX tool to achieve the same result. Semaphores are different from mutexes, and this recipe will teach you their basic usage, while the next will show you more advanced ones. A semaphore is a notification mechanism between threads and/or processes. As a rule of the thumb, try to use a mutex as a synchronization mechanism and semaphores as a notification mechanism. In this recipe, we'll develop a program that's similar to the one we built in the *Using POSIX mutexes* recipe, but this time, we'll protect the critical section with semaphores.

How to do it...

In this recipe, we'll create a multi-threaded program to increment an integer until it reaches 200000. Again, the code section that takes care of the increments must be protected and we'll use POSIX semaphores. The main method will create the two threads and ensure that the resources are destroyed correctly. Let's get started:

1. Let's open a new file called posixSemaphore.cpp and develop the structure and the critical section method:

```cpp
#include <pthread.h>
#include <semaphore.h>
#include <iostream>

struct ThreadInfo
{
    sem_t sem;
    int counter;
};

void* increment(void *arg)
{
    ThreadInfo* info = static_cast<ThreadInfo*>(arg);
    sem_wait(&info->sem);

    std::cout << "Thread Started ... " << std::endl;
    for (int i = 0; i < 100000; ++i)
        info->counter++;
    std::cout << "Thread Finished ... " << std::endl;
    sem_post(&info->sem);
    return nullptr;
}
```

2. Now, in the `main` section, add the `init` method for the lock that's needed for the synchronization between threads:

```cpp
int main()
{
    ThreadInfo thInfo;
    thInfo.counter = 0;
    if (sem_init(&thInfo.sem, 0, 1) != 0)
    {
        std::cout << "sem_init failed!" << std::endl;
        return 1;
    }
```

3. Now that the `init` section is complete, let's write the code that will start the two threads:

```cpp
pthread_t t1;
if (pthread_create(&t1, nullptr, &increment, &thInfo) != 0)
{
    std::cout << "pthread_create for t1 failed! " << std::endl;
    return 2;
}

pthread_t t2;
if (pthread_create(&t2, nullptr, &increment, &thInfo) != 0)
{
    std::cout << "pthread_create for t2 failed! " << std::endl;
    return 3;
}
```

4. Finally, here's the closing part:

```cpp
pthread_join(t1, nullptr);
pthread_join(t2, nullptr);

std::cout << "posixSemaphore:: Threads elaboration
    finished. Counter = "
            << thInfo.counter << std::endl;
sem_destroy(&thInfo.sem);
return 0;
}
```

The same program we used for POSIX mutexes now runs with POSIX semaphores. As you can see, the program's design doesn't change – what really changes is the APIs we used to protect the critical section.

How it works...

The first section contains the structure that's used to communicate with the `increment` method and the definition of the method itself. The main difference, compared to the mutex version of the program, is that we now include the `#include <semaphore.h>` headers so that we can use the POSIX semaphores APIs. Then, in the structure, we use the `sem_t` type, which is the actual semaphore that is going to protect the critical section. The `increment` method has two barriers to protect the actual logic: `sem_wait(&info->sem);` and `sem_post(&info->sem);`. All these two methods do is atomically decrement and increment the `sem` counter, respectively. `sem_wait(&info->sem);` acquires the lock by decrementing the counter by 1. If the value of the counter is greater than 0, then the lock is acquired and the thread can enter the critical region. `sem_post(&info->sem);` just increments the counter by one while exiting the critical region.

In the second step, we initialize the semaphore by calling the `sem_init` API. Here, we passed three parameters:

- The semaphore to initialize.
- The `pshared` argument. This indicates whether the semaphore is to be shared between the threads of a process or between processes. `0` indicates the first option.
- The last parameter indicates the initial value of the semaphore. By passing `1` to `sem_init`, we are asking the semaphore to protect one resource. The semaphore, through `sem_wait` and `sem_post`, will internally increase and decrease that counter automatically, letting each thread enter the critical section one at a time.

In the third step, we created the two threads that use the `increment` method.

In the last step, we waited for the two threads to finish the elaboration with `pthread_join` and, most relevant in this section, we destroyed the semaphore structure with `sem_destroy` by passing the semaphore structure we've used so far.

Let's compile and execute the program: `g++ posixSemaphore.cpp -lpthread`. Even in this case, we need to link the program with the `libpthread.a` by passing the `-lpthread` option to g++ as we use `pthreads`. The output of doing this is as follows:

```
root@839836698e38:/BOOK/chapter5# g++ posixSemaphore.cpp -lpthread
root@839836698e38:/BOOK/chapter5# ./a.out
Thread Started ...
Thread Finished ...
Thread Started ...
Thread Finished ...
posixSemaphore:: Threads elaboration finished. Counter = 200000
root@839836698e38:/BOOK/chapter5#
```

As expected, the output shows the counter at 200000. It also shows that the two threads are not overlapping.

There's more...

We used `sem_t` as a binary semaphore by passing the value 1 to the `sem_init` method. Semaphores can be used as *counting semaphores*, which means passing a value greater than 1 to the `init` method. In this case, it means that the critical section will be accessed concurrently by *N* threads.

 For more information on the GNU/Linux man pages, type `man sem_init` in a shell.

See also

You can find out more about *counting semaphores* in the next recipe, where we'll learn about the difference between mutexes and semaphores.

You are invited to modify this program and use `pthread_mutex_lock` and `pthread_mutex_unlock` in conjunction with `std::thread` or `std::async` from the C++ standard library.

POSIX semaphores advanced usage

The *Using POSIX semaphores* recipe showed us how to use POSIX semaphores to protect a critical region. In this recipe, you'll learn how to use it as a counting semaphore and notification mechanism. We'll do this by developing a classical publish-subscriber program where there is one publisher thread and one consumer thread. The challenge here is that we want to limit the maximum number of items in the queue to a defined value.

How to do it...

In this recipe, we'll write a program representing a typical use case for a counting semaphore – a producer-consumer problem in which we want to limit the number of items in the queue to a certain number. Let's get started:

1. Let's open a new file called `producerConsumer.cpp` and code the structure we'll need in the two threads:

```
#include <pthread.h>
#include <semaphore.h>
#include <iostream>
#include <vector>

constexpr auto MAX_ITEM_IN_QUEUE = 5;

struct QueueInfo
{
    sem_t mutex;
    sem_t full;
    sem_t empty;
    std::vector<int> queue;
};
```

2. Now, let's write the code for `producer`:

```
void* producer(void *arg)
{
    QueueInfo* info = (QueueInfo*)arg;
    std::cout << "Thread Producer Started ... " << std::endl;
    for (int i = 0; i < 1000; i++)
    {
        sem_wait(&info->full);

        sem_wait(&info->mutex);
        info->queue.push_back(i);
        std::cout << "Thread Producer Started ... size = "
```

```
            << info->queue.size() << std::endl;
        sem_post(&info->mutex);

        sem_post(&info->empty);
    }
    std::cout << "Thread Producer Finished ... " << std::endl;
    return nullptr;
}
```

3. We do the same for `consumer`:

```
void* consumer(void *arg)
{
    QueueInfo* info = (QueueInfo*)arg;
    std::cout << "Thread Consumer Started ... " << std::endl;
    for (int i = 0; i < 1000; i++)
    {
        sem_wait(&info->empty);

        sem_wait(&info->mutex);
        if (!info->queue.empty())
        {
            int b = info->queue.back();
            info->queue.pop_back();
        }
        sem_post(&info->mutex);

        sem_post(&info->full);
    }
    std::cout << "Thread Consumer Finished ... " << std::endl;
    return nullptr;
}
```

4. Now, we need to code the `main` method in order to initialize the resources (for example, semaphores):

```
int main()
{
    QueueInfo thInfo;
    if (sem_init(&thInfo.mutex, 0, 1) != 0 ||
        sem_init(&thInfo.full, 0, MAX_ITEM_IN_QUEUE) != 0 ||
        sem_init(&thInfo.empty, 0, 0) != 0)
    {
        std::cout << "sem_init failed!" << std::endl;
        return 1;
    }

    pthread_t producerPthread;
```

```
if (pthread_create(&producerPthread, nullptr, &producer,
    &thInfo) != 0)
{
    std::cout << "pthread_create for producer failed! "
        << std::endl;
    return 2;
}
pthread_t consumerPthread;
if (pthread_create(&consumerPthread, nullptr, &consumer,
    &thInfo) != 0)
{
    std::cout << "pthread_create for consumer failed! "
        << std::endl;
    return 3;
}
```

5. Finally, we need to code the section that will release the resources:

```
pthread_join(producerPthread, nullptr);
pthread_join(consumerPthread, nullptr);

sem_destroy(&thInfo.mutex);
sem_destroy(&thInfo.full);
sem_destroy(&thInfo.empty);
return 0;
}
```

This program, which is the typical implementation of a consumer-producer problem based on semaphores, shows how to limit the use of a resource to *N* (in our case, MAX_ITEM_IN_QUEUE). This concept can be applied to other problems, including how to limit the number of connections to a database, and so on. What would happen if, instead of one producer, we started two producer threads?

How it works...

In the first step of the program, we defined struct that's needed to let the two threads communicate. It contains the following:

- A full semaphore (counting semaphore): This semaphore is set to MAX_ITEM_IN_QUEUE. This limits the number of the item on the queue.
- An empty semaphore (counting semaphore): This semaphore notifies the process when the queue is empty.

- A `mutex` semaphore (binary semaphore): This is a mutex that's implemented with semaphores and is needed to provide mutual exclusion on the queue's access.
- Queue: Implemented with `std::vector`.

In the second step, we implemented the `producer` method. The core part of the method is the `for` loop implementation. The producer goal is to push items into the queue with no more than `MAX_ITEM_IN_QUEUE` items at the same time so that the producer tries to enter the critical region by decrementing the `full` semaphore (which we initialized to `MAX_ITEM_IN_QUEUE` in `sem_init`), then push the item into the queue and increment the empty semaphore (this gives the consumer permission to go on and read from the queue). Why do we need to notify that the consumer can read an item? In other words, why do we need to call `sem_post(&info->empty);` in the producer? If we didn't, the consumer thread would read items continuously and would keep incrementing the `full` semaphore to values greater than `MAX_ITEM_IN_QUEUE` with the effect of more than `MAX_ITEM_IN_QUEUE` item in the queue.

In the third step, we implemented the `consumer` method. This is specular to `producer`. What the consumer does is wait for the notification to read an item from the queue with `sem_wait(&info->empty);`, reads from the queue, and then increments the `full` semaphore. This last step can be read like so: I've just consumed one item from the queue.

The fourth step is where we started the two threads and initialized the three semaphores.

The fifth step is the closing section.

If we start more producers, the code would still work as the `full` and `empty` semaphores would ensure the behavior we described previously and the `mutex` on the queue ensures that just one item at a time writes/read on it.

Both POSIX mutexes and semaphores can be used among threads and processes. To make a semaphore working among processes, we just need to pass a value different from 0 in the second parameter of `sem_init`. For mutexes, we need to pass the `PTHREAD_PROCESS_SHARED` flag when calling `pthread_mutexattr_setpshared`. By building and running the program we'd have output like the following:

```
root@839836698e38:/BOOK/chapter5# g++ producerConsumer.cpp -pthread
root@839836698e38:/BOOK/chapter5# ./a.out
Thread Consumer Started ...
Thread Producer Started ...
Thread Producer Started ... size = 1
Thread Producer Started ... size = 2
Thread Producer Started ... size = 3
Thread Producer Started ... size = 4
Thread Producer Started ... size = 5
Thread Consumer Started ... size = 4
Thread Consumer Started ... size = 3
Thread Consumer Started ... size = 2
Thread Consumer Started ... size = 1
Thread Consumer Started ... size = 0
Thread Producer Started ... size = 1
Thread Producer Started ... size = 2
Thread Producer Started ... size = 3
Thread Producer Started ... size = 4
```

Let's see something more about this recipe in the next section.

There's more...

It's worth highlighting that a semaphore can be initialized (the third parameter of the `sem_init` method) to three possible values:

- To 1: In this case, we're using the semaphore as a mutex.
- To N: In this case, we're using the semaphore as a *counting semaphore*.
- To 0: We're using the semaphore like a notification mechanism (see the `empty` semaphore example previously).

In general, semaphores must be seen as a notification mechanism between threads or processes.

When should we use POSIX semaphores and POSIX mutexes? Try to use a mutex as a synchronization mechanism and semaphores as a notification mechanism. Furthermore, consider that POSIX mutexes are generally faster than POSIX semaphores in Linux kernels.

One last thing: remember that both POSIX mutexes and semaphores make the tasks go to sleep, as opposed to spinlocks, which don't. Indeed, when a mutex or semaphore is locked, the Linux scheduler puts the task in the waiting queue.

See also

Please have look at the following list for further information:

- The *Using POSIX mutexes* recipe in this chapter to learn how to program POSIX mutexes
- The *Using POSIX semaphores* recipe in this chapter to learn how to program POSIX mutexes
- *Linux Kernel Development*, by Robert Love

Synchronization building blocks

From this recipe and the next two, we'll be back in the C++ world. In this recipe, we'll learn about the C++ synchronization building blocks. Specifically, we'll look at using `std::lock_guard` and `std::unique_lock` in combination with **Resource Acquisition Is Initialization (RAII)**, an object-oriented programming idiom that makes the code more robust and readable. `std::lock_guard` and `std::unique_lock` wrap the C++ concept of mutexes around two classes with the RAII concept. `std::lock_guard` is the simplest and smallest guard, while `std::unique_lock` adds some functionality on top of it.

How to do it...

In this recipe, we'll develop two programs in order to learn how to use `std::unique_lock` and `std::lock_guard`. Let's get started:

1. From a shell, create a new file called `lock_guard.cpp`. Then, write the code for the `ThreadInfo` structure and the `increment` (thread) method:

```
#include <iostream>
#include <mutex>
#include <thread>
```

```
struct ThreadInfo
{
    std::mutex mutex;
    int counter;
};

void increment(ThreadInfo &info)
{
    std::lock_guard<std::mutex> lock(info.mutex);
    std::cout << "Thread Started ... " << std::endl;

    for (int i = 0; i < 100000; ++i)
        info.counter++;

    std::cout << "Thread Finished ... " << std::endl;
}
```

2. Now, write the code for the `main` method, as follows:

```
int main()
{
    ThreadInfo thInfo;

    std::thread t1 (increment, std::ref(thInfo));
    std::thread t2 (increment, std::ref(thInfo));

    t1.join();
    t2.join();

    std::cout << "Threads elaboration finished. Counter = "
              << thInfo.counter << std::endl;
    return 0;
}
```

3. Let's write the same program for `std::unique_lock`. From a shell, create a new file called `unique_lock.cpp` and write the code for the `ThreadInfo` structure and the `increment` (thread) method:

```
#include <iostream>
#include <mutex>
#include <thread>
struct ThreadInfo
{
    std::mutex mutex;
    int counter;
};

void increment(ThreadInfo &info)
```

```
{
    std::unique_lock<std::mutex> lock(info.mutex);
    std::cout << "Thread Started ... " << std::endl;
    // This is a test so in a real scenario this is not be needed.
    // it is to show that the developer here has the possibility to
    // unlock the mutex manually.
    // if (info.counter < 0)
    // {
    //     lock.unlock();
    //     return;
    // }
    for (int i = 0; i < 100000; ++i)
        info.counter++;
    std::cout << "unique_lock:: Thread Finished ... " << std::endl;
}
```

4. Regarding the `main` method, there are no differences here to what we saw in the *Using POSIX mutexes* recipe:

```
int main()
{
    ThreadInfo thInfo;

    std::thread t1 (increment, std::ref(thInfo));
    std::thread t2 (increment, std::ref(thInfo));

    t1.join();
    t2.join();

    std::cout << "Unique_lock:: Threads elaboration finished.
        Counter = "
            << thInfo.counter << std::endl;
    return 0;
}
```

These two programs are the C++ versions of the one we wrote in the *Using POSIX mutexes* recipe. Note the conciseness of the code.

How it works...

Step 1 of the `lock_guard.cpp` program defines the `ThreadInfo` struct and the `increment` method that's needed. The first thing we can see is the use of `std::mutex` as a protection mechanism for the critical section. The `increment` method is now simplified with fewer headaches for the developer. Note that we have the `std::lock_guard<std::mutex> lock(info.mutex);` variable definition. As we can see in the method, there is no `unlock()` call at the end – why is this? Let's see how `std::lock_guard` works: its constructor locks the mutex. Since `std::lock_guard` is a class, when the object goes out of scope (at the end of the method, in this case), the destructor is called. The unlock of the `std::mutex` object is called in the `std::lock_guard` destructor. This means that whatever happens to the `increment` method, the constructor is called so there's no risk of a deadlock and the developer doesn't have to take care of the `unlock()`. What we described here is the RAII C++ technique, which binds the life cycle of the `info.mutex` object with the lifetime of the `lock` variable.

Step 2 contains the main code that's used to manage the two threads. In this case, C++ has a much cleaner and simpler interface. A thread is created with `std::thread t1 (increment, std::ref(thInfo));`. Here, `std::thread` accepts two parameters: the first is the method that the thread will call, while the second is the `ThreadInfo` that's passed to the increment method.

The `unique_lock.cpp` program is the version of the `lock_guard` we've described so far. The main difference is that `std::unique_lock` gives the developer more freedom. In this case, we've modified the `increment` method to simulate the needs of the mutex unlock for the `if (info.counter < 0)` case. With the use of `std::unique_lock`, we are able to `unlock()` the mutex and return from the method. We wouldn't be able to do the same on the `std::lock_guard` class. Of course, the `lock_guard` would unlock at the end of the scope no matter what, but what we want to highlight here is that with `std::unique_lock`, the developer has the freedom to unlock the mutex manually, at any time.

By compiling `lock_guard.cpp`: `g++ lock_guard.cpp -lpthread` and running the generated executable, we get the following output:

```
root@839836698e38:/BOOK/chapter5# g++ lock_guard.cpp -lpthread
root@839836698e38:/BOOK/chapter5# ./a.out
Thread Started ...
Thread Finished ...
Thread Started ...
Thread Finished ...
lock_guard:: Threads elaboration finished. Counter = 200000
root@839836698e38:/BOOK/chapter5#
```

The same happens for `unique_lock.cpp`: g++ `unique_lock.cpp -lpthread`, the output is as follows:

```
root@839836698e38:/BOOK/chapter5# g++ unique_lock.cpp -lpthread
root@839836698e38:/BOOK/chapter5# ./a.out
Thread Started ...
Thread Finished ...
Thread Started ...
Thread Finished ...
Unique_lock:: Threads elaboration finished. Counter = 200000
root@839836698e38:/BOOK/chapter5#
```

As expected, both outputs are exactly the same, with the advantage that the code that uses `lock_guard` looks cleaner and definitely more safe from the developer's point of view.

There's more...

As we've seen in this recipe, `std::lock_guard` and `std::unique_lock` are template classes that we used with the `std::mutex object. lock_guard. unique_lock` can be defined with other mutex objects, such as `std::timed_mutex`, which allows us to get a lock for a specific amount of time:

```
#include <chrono>
using std::chrono::milliseconds;

std::timed_mutex timedMutex;
std::unique_lock<std::timed_mutex> lock {timedMutex, std::defer_lock};
lock.try_lock_for(milliseconds{5});
```

The `lock` object will try to acquire the lock for 5 milliseconds. We have to be careful when adding `std::defer_lock`, which will not lock the mutex automatically on construction. This will only happen when `try_lock_for` succeeds.

See also

Here is a list of references you may refer to:

- *Linux Kernel Development*, by Robert Love
- The *Using POSIX mutexes* recipe in this chapter
- The *Using POSIX semaphores* recipe in this chapter
- `Chapter 2`, *Revisiting C++*, for a refresher on C++

Learning inter-thread communication with simple events

So far, we know how to use both POSIX and C++ standard library mechanisms to synchronize a critical section. There are use cases where we don't need to explicitly use locks; instead, we can use more simple communication mechanisms. `std::promise` and `std::future` can be used to allow two threads to communicate without the hassle of the synchronization.

How to do it...

In this recipe, we will write a program that splits a problem into two parts: thread 1 will run a highly intensive computation and will send the result to thread 2, which is the consumer of the results. We'll do this by using `std::promise` and `std::future`. Let's get started:

1. Open a new file called `promiseFuture.cpp` and type the following code into it:

```
#include <iostream>
#include <future>

struct Item
{
    int age;
    std::string nameCode;
```

```
        std::string surnameCode;
    };

    void asyncProducer(std::promise<Item> &prom);
    void asyncConsumer(std::future<Item> &fut);
```

2. Write the `main` method:

```
    int main()
    {
        std::promise<Item> prom;
        std::future<Item> fut = prom.get_future();

        std::async(asyncProducer, std::ref(prom));
        std::async(asyncConsumer, std::ref(fut));

        return 0;
    }
```

3. The consumer is responsible for getting the result through `std::future` and using it:

```
    void asyncConsumer(std::future<Item> &fut)
    {
        std::cout << "Consumer ... got the result " << std::endl;
        Item item = fut.get();
        std::cout << "Age = " << item.age << " Name = "
            << item.nameCode
                << " Surname = " << item.surnameCode << std::endl;
    }
```

4. The producer performs an elaboration to get the item and sends it to the waiting consumer:

```
    void asyncProducer(std::promise<Item> &prom)
    {
        std::cout << "Producer ... computing " << std::endl;

        Item item;
        item.age = 35;
        item.nameCode = "Jack";
        item.surnameCode = "Sparrow";

        prom.set_value(item);
    }
```

This program shows the typical use case for `std::promise` and `std::future`, where a mutex or semaphore is not needed for a one-shot form of communication.

How it works...

In *step 1*, we defined the `struct Item` to use between the producer and the consumer and declared the two method's prototypes.

In *step 2*, we defined two tasks using `std::async` by passing the defined promise and future.

In *step 3*, the `asyncConsumer` method waits for the result of the elaboration with the `fut.get()` method, which is a blocking call.

In *step 4*, we implemented the `asyncProducer` method. This method is simple – it just returns a canned answer. In a real scenario, the producer performs a highly intensive elaboration.

This simple program showed us how to simply decouple a problem from the producer of the information (promise) and the consumer of the information without taking care of the synchronization between threads. This solution of using `std::promise` and `std::future` only works for a one-shot type of communication (that is, we cannot have loops in the two threads sending and getting items).

There's more...

`std::promise` and `std::future` are just concurrency tools offered by the C++ standard library. The C++ standard library also provides `std::shared_future` in addition to `std::future`. In this recipe, we had one information producer and one information consumer, but what if we have more consumers? `std::shared_future` allows multiple threads to wait for the same information (coming from `std::promise`).

See also

The books *Effective Modern C++* by Scott Meyers and *The C++ Programming Language* by Bjarne Stroustrup cover these topics in great detail.

 You're also invited to read more about concurrency through the C++ Core Guideline in the *CP: Concurrency and parallelism* (`https://github.com/isocpp/CppCoreGuidelines/blob/master/CppCoreGuidelines.md#cp-concurrency-and-parallelism`) section.

Learning inter-thread communication with condition variables

In this recipe, you'll learn about another C++ tool that's available in the standard library that allows multiple threads to communicate. We'll be using `std::condition_variable` and `std::mutex` to develop a producer-consumer program.

How to do it...

The program in this recipe will use `std::mutex` to protect the queue from concurrent access and `std::condition_variable` to notify the consumer that an item has been pushed to the queue. Let's get started:

1. Open a new file called `conditionVariable.cpp` and type the following code into it:

```cpp
#include <iostream>
#include <queue>
#include <condition_variable>
#include <thread>

struct Item
{
    int age;
    std::string name;
    std::string surname;
};

std::queue<Item> queue;
std::condition_variable cond;
std::mutex mut;

void producer();
void consumer();
```

2. Now, let's write the `main` method, which creates the threads for the consumer and the producer:

```cpp
int main()
{
    std::thread t1 (producer);
    std::thread t2 (consumer);
```

```
        t1.join();
        t2.join();
        return 0;
}
```

3. Let's define the `consumer` method:

```
void consumer()
{
    std::cout << "Consumer ... " << std::endl;
    while(true)
    {
        std::unique_lock<std::mutex> lck{mut};
        std::cout << "Consumer ... loop ... START" << std::endl;
        cond.wait(lck);
        // cond.wait(lck, []{ return !queue.empty();});
        auto item = queue.front();
        queue.pop();
        std::cout << "Age = " << item.age << " Name = "
                  << item.name << " Surname = " << item.surname
                    << std::endl;
        std::cout << "Queue Size = " << queue.size() << std::endl;
        std::cout << "Consumer ... loop ... END" << std::endl;
        lck.unlock();
    }
}
```

4. Finally, let's define the `producer` method:

```
void producer()
{
    while(true)
    {
        Item item;
        item.age = 35;
        item.name = "Jack";
        item.surname = "Sparrow";
        std::lock_guard<std::mutex> lock {mut};
        std::cout << "Producer ... loop ... START" << std::endl;
        queue.push(item);
        cond.notify_one();
        std::cout << "Producer ... loop ... END" << std::endl;
    }
}
```

Although the program we've developed solves the typical producer-consumer problem we saw in the previous recipe, the code is more idiomatic, easy to read, and less error-prone.

How it works...

In the first step, we defined `struct Item` that we need to pass from the producer to the consumer. The interesting point in this step is the definition of the `std::queue` variable; it uses a mutex that synchronizes access to the queue and `std::condition_variable` to communicate an event to the consumer from the producer.

In the second step, we defined the producer and consumer threads and called the `join()` method.

In the third step, the consumer method does essentially four things: acquires the lock to read the item from the queue, waits for a notification from the producer with the condition variable, `cond`, pops an item from the queue, and then releases the lock. Interestingly, the condition variable uses `std::unique_lock` and not `std::lock_guard` for one simple reason: as soon as the `wait()` method on the condition variable is called, the lock is (internally) released so that the producer isn't blocked. When the producer calls the `notify_one` method, the `cond` variable on the consumer gets woken up and locks the mutex again. This allows it to safely pop an item from the queue and release the lock again at the end with `lck.unlock()`. Immediately after `cond.wait()` (the commented out code), there is an alternative way of calling `wait()` by passing a second parameter, a predicate, which will wait further if the second parameter returns false. In our case, the consumer will not wait if the queue isn't empty.

The last step is quite simple: we create an item, lock it with `lock_guard` on a mutex, and push it onto the queue. Note that by using `std::lock_guard`, we don't need to call unlock; the destructor of the `lock` variable will take care of that. The last thing we need to do before ending the current loop is notify the consumer with the `notify_one` method.

The `g++ conditionVariable.cpp -lpthread` compilation and the execution of the `./a.out` program will produce the following output:

```
Age = 35 Name = Jack Surname = Sparrow
Queue Size = 761
Consumer ... loop ... END
Consumer ... loop ... START
Producer ... loop ... START
Producer ... loop ... END
Producer ... loop ... START
Producer ... loop ... END
Age = 35 Name = Jack Surname = Sparrow
Queue Size = 762
Consumer ... loop ... END
Consumer ... loop ... START
Producer ... loop ... START
Producer ... loop ... END
Producer ... loop ... START
Producer ... loop ... END
Producer ... loop ... START
Producer ... loop ... END
Age = 35 Name = Jack Surname = Sparrow
Queue Size = 764
Consumer ... loop ... END
Consumer ... loop ... START
Producer ... loop ... START
Producer ... loop ... END
Producer ... loop ... START
Producer ... loop ... END
```

Note that since the producer is way faster than the consumer due to the `condition_variable`, which is asynchronous, there is a latency to pay. As you may have noticed, the producer and the consumer run infinitely, so you have to stop the process manually (*Ctrl + C*).

There's more...

In this recipe, we used the `notify_one` method on the `condition_variable` in the producer. An alternative method is to use `notify_all`, which notifies all the waiting threads.

Another important aspect to highlight is that condition variables are best used when the producer wants to notify one of the waiting thread about an event occurred in the computation so that the consumer can take action. For example, let's say that the producer notifies the consumer that a special item has been pushed or that the producer notifies a queue manager that the queue is full so that another consumer has to be spawned.

See also

- The *Creating a new thread* recipe in `Chapter 2`, *Revisiting C++*, to find out more or refresh yourself on threading in C++.
- *C++ Programming Language*, by Bjarne Stroustrup, covers these topics in great detail.

6
Pipes, First-In First-Out (FIFO), Message Queues, and Shared Memory

Communication between processes is an important part of software systems, and choosing the appropriate communication technique is not a simple task. One important distinction that developers should keep in mind when making a choice is whether processes are going to run on the same machine or not. This chapter focuses on the first category, where you'll learn how to develop **interprocess communication** (**IPC**) solutions based on pipes, **First-In First-Out** (**FIFO**), message queues, and shared memory. It'll start with an overview of the four types of IPC in the first recipe, their characteristics, and the differences between the types. Then, a recipe for each type will provide hands-on information needed to apply them to your daily work. This chapter does not contain any C++-specific solutions, in order to let you familiarize yourself with the Linux native mechanisms.

This chapter will cover the following topics:

- Learning the different types of IPC
- Learning how to use the oldest form of IPC—pipes
- Learning how to use FIFO
- Learning how to use message queues
- Learning how to use shared memory

Technical requirements

In order to let you try the programs immediately, we've set up a Docker image that has all the tools and libraries we'll need throughout the book. This is based on Ubuntu 19.04.

In order to set it up, follow these steps:

1. Download and install Docker Engine from `www.docker.com`.
2. Pull the image from Docker Hub by running the following command: `docker pull kasperondocker/system_programming_cookbook:latest`.
3. The image should now be available. Type in the following command to view the image: `docker images`.
4. You should have at least this image now: `kasperondocker/system_programming_cookbook`.
5. Run the Docker image with an interactive shell, with the help of the following command: `docker run -it --cap-add sys_ptrace kasperondocker/system_programming_cookbook:latest /bin/bash`.
6. The shell on the running container is now available. Type in `root@39a5a8934370/# cd /BOOK/` to get all the programs developed, by chapters.

The `--cap-add sys_ptrace` argument is needed to allow the **GNU Project Debugger (GDB)** in the Docker container to set breakpoints, which, by default, Docker does not allow.

 Disclaimer: The C++20 standard has been approved (that is, technically finalized) by WG21 in a meeting in Prague at the end of February. This means that the GCC compiler version that this book uses, 8.3.0, does not include (or has very, very limited support for) the new and cool C++20 features. For this reason, the Docker image does not include the C++20 recipe code. GCC keeps the development of the newest features in branches (you have to use appropriate flags for that, for example, `-std=c++2a`); therefore, you are encouraged to experiment with them by yourself. So, clone and explore the GCC contracts and module branches and have fun.

Learning the different types of IPC

This recipe's goal is to provide guidance among the different IPC solutions typically used with processes running on the same machine. It'll provide an overview of the main characteristics seen from the developer's point of view (your point of view!), explaining how they are different from each other.

How to do it...

The following table shows the four types of IPC always available on a Linux machine, where the columns represent what we believe are the distinctive factors that a developer should consider when making design choices:

	Processes' relation required?	Synchronization required?	Communication type	Scope	Kernel involved?
Pipe	Yes	Generally no	Half-duplex	Same machine	Yes
FIFO	No	Generally no	Half-duplex	Typically same machine	Yes
Message queue	No	Generally no	Half-duplex	Same machine	Yes
Shared memory	No	Yes	Half-duplex	Same machine	Yes

The columns of the table have the following descriptions:

- **Processes' relation required?**: This indicates whether a relation between processes (for example, parent-child) is required or not to implement the specific IPC.

- **Synchronization required?**: This indicates whether you have to take into consideration any form of synchronization between processes (for example, mutex, semaphores, and so on; see Chapter 5, *Using Mutexes, Semaphores, and Condition Variables*) or not.

- **Communication type**: A communication between two or more entities can be half-duplex (the closest analogy is the walkie-talkie, where just one individual can talk at any given time) or full-duplex (the telephone, for example, whereby two people can talk simultaneously). This can have a profound impact on the solution designed.

- **Scope**: This indicates if the solution can be applied to a broader scope, in terms of IPC among processes on different machines.
- **Kernel involved?**: This warns you about the kernel involvement in the communication process. The *How it works...* section will explain why this is important.

In the next section, we'll analyze row by row the single characteristics highlighted in the table.

How it works...

The first IPC mechanism in the list is a **pipe**. A pipe requires a relation between two processes (parent-child, for example) for it to work. This relation is needed in order to make the pipe **visible** by both the processes (as opposed to FIFO). It is like a variable that must be visible by a method in order to be usable. In the pipe recipe, we'll see how this works technically.

The communication type is half-duplex: the data flows from process *A* to process *B*, and for this reason, there is no need for synchronization. In order to achieve a full-duplex communication type between two processes, two pipes must be used. For the same reason that two processes must have a relationship in order to be able to use a pipe, a pipe cannot be used as a communication mechanism between processes on two different machines. The Linux kernel is involved in the communication as the data is copied to the kernel, which is then further copied to the receiver process.

The second IPC mechanism in the table is the **FIFO** (or **named pipe**). It is a named pipe as it requires a pathname to be created, and indeed, it is a special kind of a file. This makes the FIFO usable by any processes even without a relationship between them. All they need is the path of the FIFO (likewise, a filename) that all the process will use. Synchronization is not required in this case either. We have to be careful, though, as there are cases where synchronization is required, as the man page specifies.

POSIX.1 says that writes (http://man7.org/linux/man-pages/man2/write.2.html) of less than pipe_BUF bytes must be atomic (that is, the output data is written to the pipe as a contiguous sequence). Writes of more than pipe_BUF bytes may be nonatomic (that is, the kernel may interleave the data with data written by other processes). POSIX.1 requires pipe_BUF to be at least 512 bytes. (On Linux, pipe_BUF is 4,096 bytes.) The precise semantics depends on whether the file descriptor is nonblocking (O_NONBLOCK); whether there are multiple writers to the pipe; and on *n*, the number of bytes to be written.

The general rule is that, if you have any doubts about how much data exchange should happen between the processes, always provide a synchronization mechanism (for example, mutex, semaphores, and many others). A FIFO (likewise, a pipe) provides a half-duplex communication mechanism unless two FIFOs are provided for each process (one reader and one writer for each process); in that case, it would make it a full-duplex communication. FIFOs are typically used for IPC between processes on the same machine but, as it is based on files, if the file is visible by other machines, a FIFO could potentially be used for IPC between processes on different machines. Even in this case, the kernel is involved in the IPC, with data copied from kernel space to the user space of the processes.

A **message queue** is a linked list of messages stored in the kernel. This definition already contains a piece of information; this is a communication mechanism provided by the kernel, and again, it means that the data is copied back and forth from/to the kernel. Message queues do not require any relation between processes; they have to share a key to be able to access the same queue. The Linux kernel guarantees the atomicity of the operations on the queue if the message is smaller than or equal to `pipe_BUF`. In that case, a synchronization mechanism is required. A message queue cannot be used outside the scope of a machine.

The last IPC mechanism in the table is **shared memory**. This is the fastest form of IPC. This comes with a cost, in the sense that the processes using shared memory should use a form of synchronization (for example, mutexes or semaphores), as the `man page` suggests (`man shm_overview`).

 Any time there is a critical section to protect, processes must synchronize the access using a mechanism we've seen in `Chapter 5`, *Using Mutexes, Semaphores, and Condition Variables*.

Processes must be running on the same machine to use the same shared memory, and it is identified with a key, likewise for message queues. As the shared memory resides in the kernel space, data is copied from the kernel space to the processes that read and delete it.

There's more...

These four forms of IPC are the ones originally developed on the Unix System V and then reimplemented in the more modern POSIX standard, which Linux supports. There are cases where the processes are not on the same machine, and in those cases, we need to use other mechanisms such as sockets, which we'll see in the next chapter. Of course, a socket has wider applicability as it puts in communication processes, regardless of the position on the network.

This generality, so to speak, comes at a cost: they are slower than the mechanisms described in this recipe. So, as developers, this is a factor that must be taken into consideration when making a design choice.

See also

- `Chapter 5`, *Using Mutexes, Semaphores, and Condition Variables*: About the synchronization mechanisms you can use.
- `Chapter 7`, *Network Programming*: To complement this chapter with the notion of sockets (connection-oriented and connectionless).

Learning how to use the oldest form of IPC – pipes

In the previous recipe, you learned how to choose an IPC based on some key factors. It's now time to get hands-on with the four communication types, and this recipe focuses on pipes. In this recipe, you'll learn how to use pipes to make two processes communicating full-duplex by using two pipes. We'll not use any form of synchronization as generally, it is not required. In the *How it works...* section, we'll see why and when is it not required.

How to do it...

In this section, we'll develop a program that will create two processes, with the unique goal of sending a message to each other. With a pipe, as we've seen, the data flows in one direction. To make a bidirectional communication, and to simulate the general case, we will make use of two pipes:

1. We instantiate the two messages to send, and their size, which we'll need later:

```
#include <stdio.h>
#include <unistd.h>
#include <string.h>
#include <sys/types.h>
#include <sys/wait.h>

char* msg1 = "Message sent from Child to Parent";
char* msg2 = "Message sent from Parent to Child";
#define MSGSIZE 34
```

```
#define IN      0
#define OUT 1
```

2. Next, we move on to the initialization section. We need to instantiate the space for the message received, both the `childToParent` and `parentToChild` pipes, and the **process identifier** (**PID**) that we use to track the child:

```
int main()
{
    char inbufToParent[MSGSIZE];
    char inbufToChild[MSGSIZE];
    int childToParent[2], parentToChild[2], pid, nbytes;

    inbufToParent[0] = 0;
    inbufToChild[0] = 0;
    if (pipe(childToParent) < 0)
        return 1;

    if (pipe(parentToChild) < 0)
        return 1;
```

3. Now, let's see the child section. This section has two parts: the first, where the child sends the `msg1` message to the parent; and the second, where the child receives the `msg2` message from the parent:

```
if ((pid = fork()) > 0)
{
    printf("Created child with PID = %d\n", pid);
    close(childToParent[IN]);
    write(childToParent[OUT], msg1, strlen(msg1));
    close(childToParent[OUT]);

    close (parentToChild[OUT]);

    read(parentToChild[IN], inbufToChild, strlen(msg2));
    printf("%s\n", inbufToChild);
    close (parentToChild[IN]);
    wait(NULL);

}
```

4. And finally, let's see the parent code. It has two sections: one to receive the message from the child, and the second to reply to it:

```
else
{
    close (childToParent[OUT]);
    read(childToParent[IN], inbufToParent, strlen(msg1));
```

```
                        printf("%s\n", inbufToParent);
                        close (childToParent[IN]);

                        close (parentToChild[IN]);
                        write(parentToChild[OUT], msg2, strlen(msg2));
                        close (parentToChild[OUT]);
                }
        return 0;
```

We've implemented programmatically what we learned in Chapter 1, *Getting Started with System Programming,* for the shell (see the *Learning the Linux fundamentals – shell* recipe). These steps are detailed in the next section.

How it works...

In the first step, we just defined msg1 and msg2 to be used by the two processes and defined MSGSIZE for the message length needed to read them.

The second step essentially defines the two pipes, childToParent and parentToChild, as an array of two integers each. They are used by the pipe system call to create two communication buffers, which the processes can access through the childToParent[0] and childToParent[1] file descriptors. The message is written to childToParent[1] and read from childToParent[0] with the FIFO policy. In order to avoid a situation where buffers are not initialized, this step sets the pointer of inbuf1 and inbuf2 to 0.

The third step deals with the child's code. It writes to childToParent[1], then reads from parentToChild[0]. Writes to childToParentp[1] by the child process can be read on childToParent[0] by the parent process. The read and write system call causes the process to step in kernel mode and save the input data temporarily in kernel space until the second process reads it. One rule to follow is that the unused end of the pipes has to be closed. In our case, we write to childToParent[1]; so, we close the read end of the pipe, childToParent[0], and once read, we close the write end as this is not used.

The fourth step, pretty similar to the third, has the symmetric code to the child code. It reads on the childToParent[0] pipe and writes on parentToChild[1], following the same rule of closing the end of the pipe not used.

From the code analyzed, the reason why pipes are not usable by processes that are not ancestors should now be clear: childToParent and parentToChild file descriptors must be visible to parents and children at runtime.

If we compile the code with `gcc pipe.c` in the Docker container's `/BOOK/Chapter06/` folder and run it, the output would be as follows:

This shows that the parent and the child send and receive the two messages correctly.

There's more...

For the vast majority of use cases, pipes are intended to be used with small amounts of data, but there might be scenarios where a larger amount is needed. The standard POSIX, to which we adhere in this chapter, says that a `write` of less than `pipe_BUF` bytes must be atomic. It furthermore dictates that `pipe_BUF` must be at least 512 bytes (on Linux, it is 4 KB); otherwise, you have to take care of the synchronization at the user level by using mechanisms such as semaphores and mutexes.

See also

- `Chapter 1`, *Getting Started with System Programming*, shows the pipe concept from the shell point of view.
- `Chapter 5`, *Using Mutexes, Semaphores, and Condition Variables* has the tools necessary to add the synchronization, in case the data to send and receive is larger than `pipe_BUF`.

Learning how to use FIFO

The pipes we've seen in the previous recipe are temporary, in the sense that when no process has them open, they cease to exist. **FIFOs** (also called **named pipes**) are different; they are special pipes that exist as a special file on the filesystem. In principle, any process, assuming it has the right permissions, can access a FIFO. This last one is the FIFO-distinctive characteristic. Using files allows us to program a more general communication mechanism to put processes in communication, even without an ancestor relationship; or, in other words, we can use FIFO to get any two files to communicate. In this recipe, you'll learn how to program FIFO.

How to do it...

In this section, we'll develop a very primitive chat program based on FIFOs, resulting in two different programs that at runtime will allow two users to chat:

1. Let's create a file called `fifo_chat_user1.c` and add the includes that we need later, and the MAX_LENGTH define to determine the max length of messages the two users can exchange:

```
#include <stdio.h>
#include <string.h>
#include <fcntl.h>
#include <sys/stat.h>
#include <unistd.h>

#define MAX_LENGTH 128
```

2. Next, start with `main`. Here, we need to define the `fd` file descriptor to open the file; the path in which we intend to store the file; the two strings we'll use to store the `msgReceived` and `msgToSend` messages; and, finally, the `mkfifo` system call to create the FIFO in the defined path:

```
int main()
{
    char* fifoChat = "/tmp/chat";
    mkfifo(fifoChat, 0600);

    char msgReceived[MAX_LENGTH], msgToSend[MAX_LENGTH];
```

3. We now need an infinite loop to `write` and `read` continuously. We do this by creating two sections: in the `write` section, we open the `fifoChat` file in write mode, get the message from the user with `fgets`, and write `msgToSend` to the file, represented by the `fd` file descriptor. In the reader's section, we open the file in reading mode and read the content of the file with the `read` method, print the output, and close `fd`:

```
while (1)
{
    int fdUser1 = open(fifoChat, O_WRONLY);
    printf("User1: ");
    fgets(msgToSend, MAX_LENGTH, stdin);
    write(fdUser1, msgToSend, strlen(msgToSend)+1);
    close(fdUser1);

    int fdUser2 = open(fifoChat, O_RDONLY);
```

```
                read(fdUser2, msgReceived, sizeof(msgReceived));
                printf("User2: %s\n", msgReceived);
                close(fdUser2);
        }
        return 0;
}
```

4. The second program is very similar. The only difference is the `while` loop, which is the other way around. Here, we have the `read` section, and then, the `write` section. You can copy the `fifo_chat_user1.c` file into `fifo_chat_user2.c` and modify it, like the following:

```
while (1)
{
        int fdUser2 = open(myfifo, O_RDONLY);
        read(fdUser2, msgReceived, sizeof(msgReceived));
        printf("User1: %s\n", msgReceived);
        close(fdUser2);

        int fdUser1 = open(myfifo, O_WRONLY);
        printf("User2: ");
        fgets(msgToSend, MAX_LENGTH, stdin);
        write(fdUser1, msgToSend, strlen(msgToSend)+1);
        close(fdUser1);
}
```

Although this is not the most interactive chat you'll find around, it's definitely useful to experiment with FIFO. In the next section, we'll analyze the steps seen in this section.

How it works...

Let's first compile and run the two programs. In this case, we want to give a different name to the executables, so as to distinguish them:

```
gcc fifo_chat_user1.c -o chatUser1
```

```
gcc fifo_chat_user2.c -o chatUser2
```

This creates two executables: `chatUser1` and `chatUser2`. Let's run them in two separate Terminals, and let's chat:

```
root@d73a2ef8d899:/BOOK/chapter6# ./chat1            root@d73a2ef8d899:/BOOK/chapter6# ./chat2
User1: hey, how are you ?                            User2: hey, how are you ?
User2: great! you ?
                                                     User1: great! you ?
User1: fine ... I'm working! cannot wait to play footbal tonight :)  User2: fine ... I'm working! cannot wait to play footbal tonight :)
User2: yea ... definitely ... mee to
                                                     User1: yea ... definitely ... mee to
User1: ^C                                            ^C
root@d73a2ef8d899:/BOOK/chapter6#                    root@d73a2ef8d899:/BOOK/chapter6#
```

In *step 1*, we essentially defined `MAX_LENGTH` to the `128` bytes and added the defines we need.

In *step 2*, we created the `mkfifo` FIFO at the path specified by `fifoChat`, which points to the `/tmp/chat` file, with permissions 6 (read and write for the user), 0 (no read, no write, no execution for the group the user belongs to), and 0 (no read, no write, no execution for others). These settings can be checked once `mkfifo` is called:

```
root@d73a2ef8d899:/BOOK/chapter6# ls -latr /tmp/chat
prw------- 1 root root 0 Oct 1 23:40 /tmp/chat
```

In *step 3*, we opened the FIFO with the `open` method. It's worth mentioning that `open` is the same method used to open regular files, and on the descriptor returned, we can call `read` and `write`, as we would do on normal files. In this step, we made an infinite loop to allow the user to chat as long as they want. The `read` and `write` sections, as you can see, are swapped in *step 4* to allow the second user to read if the first is writing, and vice versa.

A FIFO is managed internally by the kernel with the FIFO policy. Every time we `write` or `read` data from/to the FIFO, the data is passed from/to the kernel. You should keep this aspect in mind. The message passes from the `chat1` executable, then, in the kernel space, and back in the user space again when the `chat2` program calls the `read` method.

There's more...

It should be clear so far that a FIFO is a special pipe. This means the same limitation we have for pipes applies to FIFO too. For example, there is no need for synchronization unless the amount of data sent exceeds the `pipe_BUF` limit, which the standard POSIX defines as 512 bytes, and Linux sets to 4 KB.

Another aspect to highlight is that a named pipe (FIFO) can be used in *N* to *M* communication types (that is, multiple readers and multiple writers). The kernel guarantees the atomicity of the operations (`read` and `write` calls) if the preceding conditions are met.

See also

- `Chapter 3`, *Dealing with Processes and Threads*
- `Chapter 5`, *Using Mutexes, Semaphores, and Condition Variables*

Learning how to use message queues

Another mechanism directly supported by POSIX-compliant operating systems (and then, the Linux kernel) is a message queue. A message queue, in its essence, is a linked list of messages stored in the kernel, where each queue is identified by an ID. In this recipe, we'll rewrite the chat program using a message queue, highlighting the key pros and cons.

How to do it...

In this section, we'll rewrite the chat program from the *Learning how to use FIFO* recipe. This will allow you to see, hands-on, similarities and differences between FIFO and a message queue:

1. Create a new file called `mq_chat_user_1.c`, and add the following includes and defines:

   ```
   #include <stdio.h>
   #include <string.h>
   #include <mqueue.h>

   #define MAX_MESSAGES 10
   #define MAX_MSG_SIZE 256
   ```

2. In the `main` method, let's now define the two message queue descriptors (`user1Desc` and `user2Desc`) needed to store the result from the `mq_open` method later. We have to define and initialize the `mq_attr` struct to store the configuration of the message queues we'll create:

   ```
   int main()
   {
   ```

```
mqd_t user1Desc, user2Desc;
char message[MAX_MSG_SIZE];
char message2[MAX_MSG_SIZE];

struct mq_attr attr;
attr.mq_flags = 0;
attr.mq_maxmsg = MAX_MESSAGES;
attr.mq_msgsize = MAX_MSG_SIZE;
attr.mq_curmsgs = 0;
```

3. We can open the two /user1 and /user2 message queues:

```
if ((user1Desc = mq_open ("/user1", O_WRONLY | O_CREAT,
    "0660", &attr)) == -1)
{
    perror ("User1: mq_open error");
    return (1);
}
if ((user2Desc = mq_open ("/user2", O_RDONLY | O_CREAT,
    "0660", &attr)) == -1)
{
    perror ("User2: mq_open error");
    return (1);
}
```

4. The central part of the program is the loop to send and receive the messages from the two users. To do this, we have to:

   1. Send a message to the user 2 with the mq_send method, using the user1Desc message queue descriptor.

   2. Receive an eventual message that the user 2 sent us with mq_receive, using the user2Desc message queue descriptor:

```
while (1)
{
    printf("USER 1: ");
    fgets(message, MAX_MSG_SIZE, stdin);
    if (mq_send (user1Desc, message, strlen (message)
        + 1, 0) == -1)
    {
        perror ("Not able to send message to User 2");
        continue;
    }
    if (mq_receive (user2Desc, message2, MAX_MSG_SIZE,
        NULL) == -1)
    {
        perror ("tried to receive a message from User 2
            but I've failed!");
```

```
                    continue;
              }
              printf("USER 2: %s\n", message2);
        }
        return 0;
  }
```

5. We need another program that would reply to user 1. This program is very similar; the only difference is that it sends messages on `user2Desc` (which is open in write mode this time) and reads from `user1Desc` (which is open in read mode).

Let's run the program now. We need to compile the `mq_chat_user_1.c` and `mq_chat_user_2.c` programs by typing the following two commands in the shell:

```
gcc mq_chat_user_1.c -o user1 -g -lrt
gcc mq_chat_user_2.c -o user2 -g -lrt
```

We're compiling and linking the programs, and generating `user1` and `user2` executables. We've added `-lrt` (which is the POSIX.1b Realtime Extensions library) as we need to include the POSIX message queue implementation. Remember that with `-l`, you're asking the compiler to consider a specific library for the linker phase. In the next section, we'll see the output, and analyze all the steps seen previously.

How it works...

By running the `./user1` and `./user2` executables, we'd have the following output:

Let's have a look at the following steps:

1. **Step 1**: We need `#include <stdio.h>` for the user input/output, `#include <string.h>` to get the length of string through `strlen`, and `#include <mqueue.h>` to have access to the message queue interfaces. In this step, we've defined the max number of messages in the queue (`10`) and the max size of a message in the queue (`256` bytes).

2. **Step 2**: In the `main` method of the program, we've defined the two message queue descriptors (`user1Desc` and `user2Desc`) to keep a reference to message queues; the two message arrays (`message` and `message2`) to store the messages to send and receive between the two users; and finally, we've defined and initialized the `struct mq_attr` structure, used to initialize the message queues we'll use in the next step.

3. **Step 3**: In this step, we've opened the two message queues. These are `/user1` and `/user2`, and they are located in `/dev/mqueue`:

   ```
   root@1f5b72ed6e7f:/BOOK/chapter6# ll /dev/mqueue/user*
   ------x--- 1 root root 80 Oct 7 13:11 /dev/mqueue/user1*
   ------x--- 1 root root 80 Oct 7 13:11 /dev/mqueue/user2*
   ```

   `mq_chat_user_1.c` opens the `/user1` message queue in write-only mode and creates it if it's not present. It also opens `/user2` in read-only mode and creates it if it's not present. It should be clear that if the current process doesn't have access rights to the message queue (which we open with `660`), `mq_open` will fail.

4. **Step 4**: This step contains the main logic of our program. It has an infinite loop, which sends a message from user 1 to user 2 and receives from user 2 to user 1. The method used to send messages is `mq_send`. It needs the message queue descriptor, the message to send, its length (+1, as we need to include the terminator), and the message priority (which we didn't use in this case). `mq_send` (see `man mq_send` for more info) blocks if there is no space in the queue until enough becomes available.

   After the send, we call the `mq_receive` method (see `man mq_receive` for more info) to get an eventual message from the user 2. It needs the message queue descriptor, an array that will contain the message, the max size we can receive, and the priority. Keep in mind that `mq_receive` blocks if there are no messages in the queue.

For more info, see the `man mq_receive` page.

As send and receive are core concepts, let's analyze them a little deeper with a schema:

```
                          (1)                  (2)
    User 1 Process [Write] ··········→ User1Desc ··········→ [Read] User 2 Process
                          (3)                  (4)
    User 2 Process [Write] ··········→ User2Desc ··········→ [Read] User 1 Process
```

(1) In this case, the user 1 process calls `mq_send`. The Linux kernel makes a copy of the message to send from the user space to the kernel space. The same happens in case **(3)**.

(2) When the user 2 process calls `mq_receive` on the same message queue (`user1Desc`), the Linux kernel makes a copy of the message from the kernel space to the user space, copying the data in the `message2` buffer. The same happens in case **(4)**.

There's more...

There might be cases where you may need to get the messages from the queue based on priority, which we didn't use in this case. Can you modify this recipe's program to include the priority? What do you have to modify?

You may have noticed that we used the `perror` method in this recipe. The `perror` method prints in the standard output the last error (`errno`), which occurs in a descriptive format. The advantage for the developer is that you don't have to explicitly get the `errno` value and translate it to a string; it is done automatically for you.

The same concept of atomicity that we described for pipes and FIFOs is valid for message queues. The delivery of a message is guaranteed to be atomic if the message is smaller than `pipe_BUF`. Otherwise, a synchronization mechanism must be provided by the developer.

See also

Recipes in `Chapter 3`, *Dealing with Processes and Threads* (about threading) and `Chapter 5`, *Using Mutexes, Semaphores, and Condition Variables* (about synchronization). As usual, `man pages` offer a great source of information, and a suggested starting point is `man mq_overview`.

Learning how to use shared memory

In all the IPC mechanisms we've seen so far, the kernel plays an active part in the communication between processes, as we've learned. The information indeed flows through from the Linux kernel to the processes, and vice versa. In this recipe, we'll learn the fastest form of interprocess communication that does not require the kernel as the mediator between processes. As usual, although the System V APIs are widely available, we'll be using the newest, simpler, and better-designed POSIX APIs. We'll rewrite our chat application using the shared memory, digging into it in greater detail.

How to do it...

In this section, we'll focus on developing a simple chat application by using the POSIX shared memory APIs. As the kernel does not take part in the communication process (directly), we need to provide a synchronization mechanism to protect the critical section—the shared memory—from the reads and the writes of the two processes:

1. Let's start by adding the include and defines we need. We'll have two shared memory spaces (STORAGE_ID1 and STORAGE_ID2) to have bidirectional communication between the processes:

   ```c
   #include <stdio.h>
   #include <sys/mman.h>
   #include <fcntl.h>
   #include <unistd.h>
   #include <string.h>

   #define STORAGE_ID1 "/SHM_USER1"
   #define STORAGE_ID2 "/SHM_USER2"
   #define STORAGE_SIZE 32
   ```

2. In the main method, we need two arrays to store the sent and received messages. Furthermore, we need to open two shared memory spaces with the following flags: read and write mode, create if not existing, and flags indicating read and write permission for the owner of the file (S_IRUSR and S_IWUSR, respectively):

   ```c
   int main(int argc, char *argv[])
   {
       char message1[STORAGE_SIZE];
       char message2[STORAGE_SIZE];
       int fd1 = shm_open(STORAGE_ID1, O_RDWR | O_CREAT, S_IRUSR |
           S_IWUSR);
       int fd2 = shm_open(STORAGE_ID2, O_RDWR | O_CREAT, S_IRUSR |
   ```

```
        S_IWUSR);
    if ((fd1 == -1) || (fd2 == -1))
    {
        perror("open");
        return 10;
    }
```

3. As shared memory is based on `mmap` (we essentially map a file to a portion of memory), we need to expand the file pointed by the file descriptor 1 (`fd1`) to the size `STORAGE_SIZE` that we need. Then, we need to map the two file descriptors to a portion of memory in shared mode (`MAP_SHARED`) and, of course, check for errors:

```
    // extend shared memory object as by default it's initialized
    //  with size 0
    int res1 = ftruncate(fd1, STORAGE_SIZE);
    if (res1 == -1)
    {
        perror("ftruncate");
        return 20;
    }

    // map shared memory to process address space
    void *addr1 = mmap(NULL, STORAGE_SIZE, PROT_WRITE, MAP_SHARED,
        fd1, 0);
    void *addr2 = mmap(NULL, STORAGE_SIZE, PROT_WRITE, MAP_SHARED,
        fd2, 0);
    if ((addr1 == MAP_FAILED) || (addr2 == MAP_FAILED))
    {
        perror("mmap");
        return 30;
    }
```

4. In the `main` loop, as with the previous two recipes, we `read` and `write` in the two shared memory instances:

```
while (1)
{
    printf("USER 1: ");
    fgets(message1, STORAGE_SIZE, stdin);
    int len = strlen(message1) + 1;
    memcpy(addr1, message1, len);
    printf("USER 2 (enter to get the message):"); getchar();
    memcpy(message2, addr2, STORAGE_SIZE);
    printf("%s\n", message2);
}
```

```
    return 0;
}
```

5. The second program mirrors this one. You can find both of them in
    the `/BOOK/Chapter06` folder: `shm_chat_user1.c` (the one we described)
    and `shm_chat_user2.c`.

Let's compile and link the two `shm_chat_user1.c` and `shm_chat_user2.c` programs by
typing the following two commands on the shell:

```
gcc shm_chat_user1.c -o user1 -g -lrt
gcc shm_chat_user2.c -o user2 -g -lrt
```

The outputs will be two binary files: `user1` and `user2`. We've added `-lrt` in this case too
as we need to include the POSIX shared memory implementation (without it, the linking
phase will throw an `undefined reference to 'shm_open'` error). In the next section,
we'll analyze all the steps seen in this section.

How it works...

Running the `./user1` and `./user2` programs would give the following interactions:

```
root@1f5b72ed6e7f:/BOOK/chapter6# ./user1     root@1f5b72ed6e7f:/BOOK/chapter6# ./user2
USER 1: Hi 2                                   USER 2: Hi 1
USER 2 (enter to get the message):             USER 1 (enter to get the message):
Hi 1                                           Hi 2

USER 1: I've built it ... it workd :)          USER 2: how are you?
USER 2 (enter to get the message):             USER 1 (enter to get the message):
how are you?                                    I've built it ... it workd :)

USER 1: █                                      USER 2: ▯
```

Let's perform the steps, as follows:

- **Step 1**: The first step just includes a few headers we need: `stdio.h` for the
  standard input/output (for example, `perror`, `printf`, and so on); `mman.h` for
  the shared memory APIs; `mmap` and `fcntl.h` for the `shm_open` flags (for
  example, `O_CREAT`, `O_RDWR`, and many others); `unistd.h` for the `ftruncate`
  method; and `string.h` for `strlen` and `memcpy` methods.

We defined `STORAGE_ID1` and `STORAGE_ID2` to identify the two shared memory objects, which will be available in the `/dev/shm` folder:

```
root@1f5b72ed6e7f:/BOOK/chapter6# ll /dev/shm/SHM_USER*
-rw------- 1 root root 32 Oct  7 23:26 /dev/shm/SHM_USER1
-rw------- 1 root root  0 Oct  7 23:26 /dev/shm/SHM_USER2
```

- **Step 2**: In this step, we allocated the space on the stack for the two messages (`message1` and `message2`) that we'll use to send and receive messages between processes. We then created and opened two new shared memory objects and checked for any errors.
- **Step 3**: Once the two shared memory objects are available, we need to extend the two files (through the two file descriptors `fd1` and `fd2`, one for each program) and—very important—mapping `fd1` and `fd2` to a virtual address space of the current process.
- **Step 4**: This step is the central part of the program. Here, there are a couple of interesting things to note. First, we can see that there is none of the movement of data between user space and kernel space that there was with FIFOs, pipes, and message queues. We just do memory copies between local buffers (allocated on the stack) and the memory we mapped, and vice versa. The second factor is that as we just deal with memory copy, the performance will be better than other IPC mechanisms.

The mechanic of this step is pretty simple: we ask the user to type a message and store it in the `message1` buffer, and then copy the buffer to the memory-mapped address with `addr1`. The read section (where we read the message from the second user) is simple too: we copy the message from the memory to the local buffer, `message2`.

There's more...

As you can see, there was no synchronization between the two processes in this recipe. That was to let you focus on one aspect only: communication with shared memory. The reader is again invited to improve this code to make it more interactive by using threads, and more secure by using a synchronization mechanism.

Since kernel 2.6.19, Linux supports the use of **access control lists** (**ACLs**) to control the permissions of objects in the virtual filesystem. For more info, see `man acl`.

See also

Recipes about threading and synchronization:

- `Chapter 3`, *Dealing with Processes and Threads*
- `Chapter 5`, *Using Mutexes, Semaphores, and Condition Variables*

Network Programming

7

In Chapter 6, *Pipes, First-In First-Out (FIFO), Message Queues, and Shared Memory*, we learned different IPC techniques to allow processes running on the same machine to communicate with each other. In this chapter, (which compliments what was covered in Chapter 6, *Pipes, First-In First-Out (FIFO), Message Queues, and Shared Memory*, you'll learn how two processes running on two different computers can achieve the same result. The topics presented here are the foundation of how the internet today works. You'll learn, hands-on, the difference between connection-oriented and connectionless-oriented communication, the characteristics that define an endpoint, and finally two recipes that will teach you how to use TCP/IP and UDP/IP.

This chapter will cover the following topics:

- Learning the basics of connection-oriented communication
- Learning the basics of connectionless-oriented communication
- Learning what a communication endpoint is
- Learning to use TCP/IP to communicate with processes on another machine
- Learning to use UDP/IP to communicate with processes on another machine
- Dealing with endianness

Technical requirements

In order to let you start using the programs immediately, we've set up a Docker image that has all the tools and libraries that we'll need throughout the book. It is based on Ubuntu 19.04.

In order to set it up, follow these steps:

1. Download and install Docker Engine from `www.docker.com`.
2. Pull the image from Docker Hub using `docker pull kasperondocker/system_programming_cookbook:latest`.
3. The image should now be available. Type in `docker images` to view the image.
4. You should have at least `kasperondocker/system_programming_cookbook` now.
5. Run the Docker image with an interactive shell by using `docker run -it -- cap-add sys_ptrace kasperondocker/system_programming_cookbook:latest /bin/bash`.
6. The shell on the running container is now available. Use `root@39a5a8934370/# cd /BOOK/` to get all the programs, listed by chapter.

The `--cap-add sys_ptrace` argument is needed to allow **GNU Project Debugger** (**GDB**) in the Docker container to set breakpoints, which by default Docker does not allow. To launch a second shell on the same container, run the `docker exec -it container-name bash` command. You can get the container name from the `docker ps` command.

Disclaimer: The C++20 standard has been approved (that is, technically finalized) by WG21 in a meeting in Prague at the end of February. This means that the GCC compiler version that this book uses, 8.3.0, does not include (or has very, very limited support for) the new and cool C++20 features. For this reason, the Docker image does not include the C++20 recipe code. GCC keeps the development of the newest features in branches (you have to use appropriate flags for that, for example, -std=c++2a); therefore, you are encouraged to experiment with them by yourself. So, clone and explore the GCC contracts and module branches and have fun.

Learning the basics of connection-oriented communication

If you sit at your desk and you browse the internet, it is likely that you're using a connection-oriented type of communication. When you request a page via HTTP or HTTPS, under the hood, a connection between your machine and the server you're trying to contact is established before the actual communication takes place. The *de facto* standard for internet communications is the **Transport Control Protocol** (**TCP**). In this chapter, you will learn what it is and why it is important, and you will also learn (on the command line) what a connection is.

How to do it...

In this section, we'll explore use of the command line to understand what happens when we make a connection with a remote machine. Specifically, we'll learn the internal aspects of a TCP/IP connection. Let's go through the following steps:

1. With the Docker image running, open a shell, type the following command, and press *Enter*:

   ```
   tcpdump -x tcp port 80
   ```

2. Open another shell, type the following command, and press *Enter*:

   ```
   telnet amazon.com 80
   ```

3. In the first shell, you'll see an output similar to the following:

```
root@5c77a7f1ed73:/BOOK/chapter7# tcpdump -x tcp port 80
tcpdump: verbose output suppressed, use -v or -vv for full protocol decode
listening on eth0, link-type EN10MB (Ethernet), capture size 262144 bytes
23:21:21.620119 IP 5c77a7f1ed73.59634 > s3-console-us-standard.console.aws.amazon.com.http: Flags [S], seq 2129791745, win 29200, options [mss 146
0,sackOK,TS val 610320 ecr 0,nop,wscale 7], length 0
        0x0000:  4510 003c 5b11 4000 4006 7324 ac11 0002
        0x0010:  cdfb f267 e8f2 0050 7ef2 0b01 0000 0000
        0x0020:  a002 7210 6ca5 0000 0204 05b4 0402 080a
        0x0030:  0009 5010 0000 0000 0103 0307
23:21:21.666326 IP s3-console-us-standard.console.aws.amazon.com.http > 5c77a7f1ed73.59634: Flags [S.], seq 452865147, ack 2129791746, win 65535,
options [mss 1460,wscale 2,eol], length 0
        0x0000:  4500 0030 7bcf 0000 2506 ad82 cdfb f267
        0x0010:  ac11 0002 0050 e8f2 1afe 2c7b 7ef2 0b02
        0x0020:  7012 ffff 5be8 0000 0204 05b4 0303 0200
23:21:21.666362 IP 5c77a7f1ed73.59634 > s3-console-us-standard.console.aws.amazon.com.http: Flags [.], ack 1, win 229, length 0
        0x0000:  4510 0028 5b12 4000 4006 7337 ac11 0002
        0x0010:  cdfb f267 e8f2 0050 7ef2 0b02 1afe 2c7c
        0x0020:  5010 00e5 6c91 0000
```

All of this might seem cryptic, but it's actually simple. The next section will explain to you, in great detail, how it works.

How it works...

A connection-oriented communication is based on the assumption that a connection between two entities is made. In this section, we'll explore what exactly a connection is.

The first step uses tcpdump (man tcpdump), which is a command-line tool that dumps all the traffic on a network. In our case, it writes all the TCP traffic from port 80 on the standard output showing the data in a hexadecimal representation. Once *Enter* is pressed, tcpdump will switch to listening mode.

The second step uses telnet to establish a connection with a remote service running on port 80 at amazon.com. Once *Enter* is pressed, after a few moments, the connection will be established.

In the third step, we see the output of the connection between the local machine through the telnet (or man telnet, to give it its full name) service and a remote machine at amazon.com (translated to the IP). The first thing to keep in mind is that a connection in TCP is a three-step process called a **three-way handshake**. The client sends *SYN*, the server replies *SYN+ACK*, and the client replies *ACK*. The following diagram represents the TCP header specification:

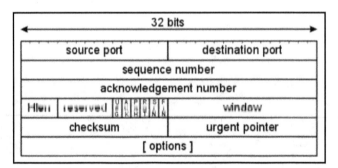

What data do the client and the server exchange in the *SYN | SYN+ACK | ACK* phase in order to successfully establish a connection? Let's go through it, step by step:

1. The client sends *SYN* to the server (amazon.com):

```
23:29:42.802531 IP 5c77a7f1ed73.59636 > s3-console-us-standard.console.aws.amazon.com.http: Flags [S], seq 2614145300, win 29200, options [mss 146
0,sackOK,TS val 660438 ecr 0,nop,wscale 7], length 0
        0x0000:  4510 003c a2c2 4000 4006 2b73 ac11 0002
        0x0010:  cdfb f267 e8f4 0050 9bd0 b114 0000 0000
        0x0020:  a002 7210 6ca5 0000 0204 05b4 0402 080a
        0x0030:  000a 13d6 0000 0000 0103 0307
```

Let's start from `0xe8f4` and `0x050` (the Ethernet header is before this, which is beyond the scope of this chapter). As we can see from the preceding TCP header, the first two bytes represent the source port (`0xe8f4` = `59636`) and the second two bytes represent the destination port (`0x0050` = `80`). In the next four bytes, the client sets a random number called the sequence number: `0x9bd0 | 0xb114`. The acknowledgment number is not set in this case. In order to mark this packet as *SYN*, the client has to set the *SYN* bit to `1` and indeed the value of the next two bytes is `0xa002`, which in binary is `1010 0000 0000 0010`. We can see that the second to last bit is set to 1 (compare this with the TCP header, as seen in the preceding screenshot).

2. The server sends *SYN+ACK* to the client:

```
23:29:42.846514 IP s3-console-us-standard.console.aws.amazon.com.http > 5c77a7f1ed73.59636: Flags [S.], seq 452877854, ack 2614145301, win 65535,
options [mss 1460,wscale 2,eol], length 0
        0x0000:  4500 0030 b116 0000 2506 783b cdfb f267
        0x0010:  ac11 0002 0050 e8f4 1afe 5e1e 9bd0 b115
        0x0020:  7012 ffff 6751 0000 0204 05b4 0303 0200
```

The server, which has received the *SYN* from the client, has to respond with *SYN+ACK*. Leaving out the first 16 bytes, the Ethernet header, we can see the following content: 2 bytes represent the source port (`0x0050` = `80`) and the second 2 bytes represent the destination port (`0xe8f4` = `59636`). Then we start to see a few interesting things: the server puts a random number in the sequence number, which in this case is `0x1afe = | 0x5e1e`, and in the acknowledgment number, the sequence number received from the client + 1 = `0x9bd0 | 0xb115`. As we learned, the server must set the flag to *SYN+ACK* and, according to the TCP header, the specification is correctly implemented by setting the two bytes to `0x7012` = `0111 0000 0001 0010`. The highlighted parts are *ACK* and *SYN* respectively. The TCP packet is then sent back to the client.

3. The client sends *ACK* to the server (`amazon.com`):

```
23:29:42.846557 IP 5c77a7f1ed73.59636 > s3-console-us-standard.console.aws.amazon.com.http: Flags [.], ack 1, win 229, length 0
        0x0000:  4510 0028 a2c3 4000 4006 2b86 ac11 0002
        0x0010:  cdfb f267 e8f4 0050 9bd0 b115 1afe 5e1f
        0x0020:  5010 00e5 6c91 0000
```

The last step of the three-way handshake algorithm is the reception of the ACK packet sent by the client to the server. The message consists of two bytes representing the source port (0xe8f4 = 59636) and the destination port (0x050 = 80); the sequence number this time contains the value the server originally received from the client, 0x9bd0 | 0xb115; and the acknowledgement number contains the random value received from the server + 1: 0x1afe = | 0x5e1**f**. Finally, the *ACK* is sent by setting the value 0x5010 = 0101 0000 000**1** 0000 (the part of the value that is highlighted is the *ACK*; compare it to the previous TCP header picture).

There's more...

The protocol you have learned so far is described in the RFC 793 (https://tools.ietf.org/html/rfc793). If the internet works, it is because all the network vendors, device driver implementations, and many programs implement this RFC (and other related standards) perfectly. The TCP RFC defines much more than what we've learned in this recipe, which was strictly focused on the connectivity. It defines the flow control (through the concept of a window) and reliability (through the concept of a sequence number and the *ACK* in it).

See also

- The *Learning to use TCP/IP to communicate with processes on another machine* recipe shows programmatically how two processes on two machines can communicate. The connection part is hidden in a system call, as we'll see.
- Chapter 3, *Dealing with Processes and Threads*, for a refresher on processes and threads.

Learning the basics of connectionless-oriented communication

In the *Learning the basics of connection-oriented communication* recipe, we learned that a connection-oriented communication with flow control is reliable. To make two processes in communication, we must establish a connection first. This obviously comes at a cost in terms of performance, which we cannot always pay—for example, when you watch an online movie, the available bandwidth might not be enough to support all the features that TCP takes with it.

In this case, it is likely that the underlying communication mechanism is connectionless. The *de facto* standard protocol for connectionless communication is the **User Data Protocol** (**UDP**), which is on the same logical level as TCP. In this recipe, we'll learn what UDP looks like on the command line.

How to do it...

In this section, we'll use `tcpdump` and `netcast` (`nc`) to analyze a connectionless link over UDP:

1. With the Docker image running, open a shell, type the following command, and press *Enter*:

   tcpdump `-i lo udp port 45998 -X`

2. Let's open another shell, type the following command, and press *Enter*:

   echo -n "welcome" | nc -w 1 -u localhost 45998

3. On the first shell, you'll see an output similar to the following:

```
root@c3f1474e0170:/BOOK# tcpdump -i lo udp port 45998 -X
tcpdump: verbose output suppressed, use -v or -vv for full protocol decode
listening on lo, link-type EN10MB (Ethernet), capture size 262144 bytes
03:20:40.006512 IP localhost.56101 > localhost.45998: UDP, length 7
        0x0000:  4500 0023 914a 4000 4011 ab7d 7f00 0001  E..#.J@.@..}....
        0x0010:  7f00 0001 db25 b3ae 000f fe22 7765 6c63  .....%....."welc
        0x0020:  6f6d 65                                   ome
```

This seems cryptic too, but it's actually simple. The next section will explain the steps in great detail.

How it works...

In a UDP connection, there is no concept of connection. In this case, a packet is sent to a receiver. There is no flow control and the link is not reliable. The UDP header is indeed very simple, as you can see from the following diagram:

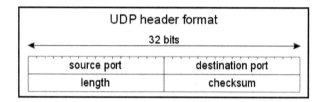

Step 1 uses `tcpdump` to listen on port `45998` using the UDP protocol on the `loopback` interface (`-i lo`) by printing the data of each packet in `hex` and `ASCII`.

Step 2 uses the `netcast` command `nc` (`man nc`) to send a UDP packet (`-u`) containing the string `welcome` to the localhost.

Step 3 shows the details of the UDP protocol. We can see that the source port (randomly picked by the sender) is `0xdb255` = `56101` and the destination port is correctly set to `0xb3ae` = `459998`. Next, we set the length to `0x000f` = `15` and the checksum to `0xfe22` = `65058`. The length is `15` bytes, as `7` bytes is the length of the data received and `8` bytes is the length of the UDP header (source port + destination port + length + checksum).

No retransmission, no control flow, no connection. A connectionless link is really just a message the sender sends to the receiver knowing that it might not receive it.

There's more...

We've talked about connections and we've seen the concepts of the source port and destination port in the UDP header. The address of the sender and receiver is stored somewhere else, in the **IP** (short for **Internet Protocol**) layer, logically right below the UDP layer. The IP layer has the information of the sender and receiver addresses (the IP addresses), which are used to route the UDP packet from the client to the server and vice versa.

The UDP is elaborately defined in RFC 768, at `https://www.ietf.org/rfc/rfc768.txt`.

See also

- `Chapter 1`, *Getting Started with System Programming*, for a review of the pipe of commands
- The *Learning the basics of a connectionless-oriented communication* recipe for a comparison with the TCP protocol

Learning what a communication endpoint is

When two entities communicate with each other they essentially exchange information. In order to make this happen, each entity must be clear as to where to send the information. From the programmer's point of view, each entity involved in the communication must have a clear endpoint. This recipe will teach you what an endpoint is and will show, on the command line, how to identify them.

How to do it...

In this section, we'll be using the `netstat` command-line utility to inspect and learn what an endpoint is:

1. With the Docker image running, open a shell, type the following command, and press *Enter*:

```
b07d3ef41346:/# telnet amazon.com 443
```

2. Open a second shell and type this command:

```
b07d3ef41346:/# netstat -ntp
```

The next section will explain these two steps.

How it works...

In *step 1*, we used the `telnet` utility to connect to the local machine, with the `amazon.com` remote host on port `443` (HTTP). The output of this command is the following:

```
root@839836698e38:/BOOK/chapter7# telnet amazon.com 443
Trying 205.251.242.103...
Connected to amazon.com.
Escape character is '^]'.
```

It is waiting for commands, which we won't send, as what we really care about is the connection.

In *step 2*, we want to know the details of the connection that we established between our local machine (`localhost`) and the remote host (`amazon.com` port `443`). For this, we executed the command in *step 2*. The output is as follows:

```
root@839836698e38:/BOOK/chapter7# netstat -ntp
Active Internet connections (w/o servers)
Proto Recv-Q Send-Q Local Address          Foreign Address         State       PID/Program name
tcp        0      0 172.17.0.3:53386        205.251.242.103:443     ESTABLISHED 558/telnet
root@839836698e38:/BOOK/chapter7#
```

What information can we retrieve from the output in this command line? Well, we can retrieve a few very useful pieces of information. Let's go through what we can learn from the preceding screenshot, reading the code from left to right:

- `tcp` represents the type of connection. It is a connection-oriented connection, which means that the local and remote hosts went through the three-way handshake that we saw in the *Learning the basics of connection-oriented communication* recipe.
- `Recv-Q` is a queue containing the data to be processed by the current process on localhost.
- `Send-Q` is a queue containing the data to be sent by the current process on localhost to a remote process.
- `Local Address` is a combination of the IP address and port number, which really represent the first endpoint of our communication, the local endpoint. Such an endpoint is often called, from a programming perspective, `Socket`, which is an integer representing, in its essence, `IP` and `PORT`. In this case, the endpoint is `172.17.0.2:40850`.

- Foreign Address, like the Local Address, is a combination of IP and PORT, and represents the remote endpoint, in this case, 176.32.98.166:443. Note that 443 is a well-known port and represents the https service.
- State represents the state of the connection between the two endpoints, ESTABLISHED in this case.
- PID/Program Name, or in our case, 65/telnet, represents the local process using both the endpoints to communicate with the remote host.

When programmers talk about socket, they are talking about IP and PORT for each endpoint of the communication. As we've seen, Linux makes it easy to analyze both the endpoints of the communication and the process they are attached to.

One important aspect to highlight is that a PORT represents a service. In our example, the local process telnet was connected with the remote host using IP 176.32.98.166 at port 80, where we know an HTTP daemon is running. But how do we know the port number for a specific service? There is a list of well-known ports (https://www.iana.org/assignments/service-names-port-numbers/service-names-port-numbers.xhtml) maintained by the **IANA** (short for the **Internet Assigned Numbers Authority**), which assigns PORTS to services. For example, the HTTPS service is expected to run at PORT 443, the sftp (short for **Secure File Transfer Protocol**) runs at PORT 22, and so on.

There's more...

The port info is a 16 bits unsigned integer value (that is, unsigned int), is maintained by the IANA (https://www.iana.org/) and is split into these ranges:

- 0-1023: Well-known ports. Ports that are well known, for example, HTTP, SFTP, and HTTPS.
- 1024-49151: Registered ports. Ports that organizations can ask to register for their purpose.
- 49152-65535: Dynamic, private, or ephemeral ports. Free to be used.

See also

- The *Learning the basics of connectionless-oriented communication* recipe to learn how communication without a connection works
- The *Learning the basics of connection-oriented communication* recipe to learn how communication with a connection works

- The *Learning to use TCP/IP to communicate with processes on another machine* recipe to learn how to develop a connection-oriented program
- The *Learning to use UDP/IP to communicate with processes on another machine* recipe to learn how to develop a connectionless-oriented program

Learning to use TCP/IP to communicate with processes on another machine

This recipe will show you how to connect two programs by using a connection-oriented mechanism. This recipe will use TCP/IP, which is the *de facto* standard on the internet. So far, we've learned that TCP/IP is a reliable form of communication, and its connection is made in three phases. It is time now to write a program to learn how to make two programs communicate with each other. Although the language used will be C++, the communication part will be written using the Linux system calls, as it is not supported by the C++ standard library.

How to do it...

We'll develop two programs, a client and a server. The server will start and `listen` on a specific port that is ready to accept an incoming connection. The client will start and connect to the server identified by an IP and a port number:

1. With the Docker image running, open a shell and create a new file, `clientTCP.cpp`. Let's add some headers and constants that we'll need later:

```
#include <stdio.h>
#include <stdlib.h>
#include <unistd.h>
#include <string.h>
#include <sys/types.h>
#include <sys/socket.h>
#include <netinet/in.h>
#include <netdb.h>
#include <iostream>

constexpr unsigned int SERVER_PORT = 50544;
constexpr unsigned int MAX_BUFFER = 128;
```

2. Let's start writing the `main` method now. We start by initializing `socket` and getting the information that is related to the server:

```cpp
int main(int argc, char *argv[])
{
    int sockfd = socket(AF_INET, SOCK_STREAM, 0);
    if (sockfd < 0)
    {
        std::cerr << "socket error" << std::endl;
        return 1;
    }
    struct hostent* server = gethostbyname(argv[1]);
    if (server == nullptr)
    {
        std::cerr << "gethostbyname, no such host" << std::endl;
        return 2;
    }
```

3. Next, we want to `connect` to the server, but we need the correct information, namely the `serv_addr`:

```cpp
    struct sockaddr_in serv_addr;
    bzero((char *) &serv_addr, sizeof(serv_addr));
    serv_addr.sin_family = AF_INET;
    bcopy((char *)server->h_addr,
          (char *)&serv_addr.sin_addr.s_addr,
          server->h_length);
    serv_addr.sin_port = htons(SERVER_PORT);
    if (connect(sockfd, (struct sockaddr *) &serv_addr, sizeof
        (serv_addr)) < 0)
    {
        std::cerr << "connect error" << std::endl;
        return 3;
    }
```

4. The server will reply with a connection `ack`, so we call the `read` method:

```cpp
    std::string readBuffer (MAX_BUFFER, 0);
    if (read(sockfd, &readBuffer[0], MAX_BUFFER-1) < 0)
    {
        std::cerr << "read from socket failed" << std::endl;
        return 5;
    }
    std::cout << readBuffer << std::endl;
```

5. We can now send the data to the server by just calling the `write` system call:

```
std::string writeBuffer (MAX_BUFFER, 0);
std::cout << "What message for the server? : ";
getline(std::cin, writeBuffer);
if (write(sockfd, writeBuffer.c_str(), strlen(write
    Buffer.c_str())) < 0)
{
    std::cerr << "write to socket" << std::endl;
    return 4;
}
```

6. Finally, let's go through the cleaning part, where we have to close the socket:

```
close(sockfd);
return 0;
}
```

7. Let's now develop the server program. In a second shell, we create the `serverTCP.cpp` file:

```
#include <stdio.h>
#include <stdlib.h>
#include <string.h>
#include <unistd.h>
#include <sys/types.h>
#include <sys/socket.h>
#include <netinet/in.h>
#include <iostream>
#include <arpa/inet.h>

constexpr unsigned int SERVER_PORT = 50544;
constexpr unsigned int MAX_BUFFER = 128;
constexpr unsigned int MSG_REPLY_LENGTH = 18;
```

8. On a second shell, first of all, we need a `socket` descriptor that will identify our connection:

```
int main(int argc, char *argv[])
{
    int sockfd =  socket(AF_INET, SOCK_STREAM, 0);
    if (sockfd < 0)
    {
        std::cerr << "open socket error" << std::endl;
```

```
        return 1;
    }

    int optval = 1;
    setsockopt(sockfd, SOL_SOCKET, SO_REUSEADDR, (const
      void *)&optval , sizeof(int));
```

9. We have to bind the `socket` to a port and `serv_addr` on the local machine:

```
    struct sockaddr_in serv_addr, cli_addr;
    bzero((char *) &serv_addr, sizeof(serv_addr));
    serv_addr.sin_family = AF_INET;
    serv_addr.sin_addr.s_addr = INADDR_ANY;
    serv_addr.sin_port = htons(SERVER_PORT);
    if (bind(sockfd, (struct sockaddr *) &serv_addr, sizeof
       (serv_addr)) < 0)
    {
        std::cerr << "bind error" << std::endl;
        return 2;
    }
```

10. Next, we have to wait for and accept any incoming connection:

```
    listen(sockfd, 5);
    socklen_t clilen = sizeof(cli_addr);
    int newsockfd = accept(sockfd, (struct sockaddr *) &cli_addr,
        &clilen);
    if (newsockfd < 0)
    {
        std::cerr << "accept error" << std::endl;
        return 3;
    }
```

11. As soon as we get a connection, we log who connected to the standard output (using their IP and port) and send a confirmation *ACK*:

```
    std::cout << "server: got connection from = "
            << inet_ntoa(cli_addr.sin_addr)
            << " and port = " << ntohs(cli_addr.sin_port)
              << std::endl;
    write(incomingSock, "You are connected!", MSG_REPLY_LENGTH);
```

12. We made the connection (a three-way handshake, remember?), so now we can read any data coming from the client:

```
std::string buffer (MAX_BUFFER, 0);
if (read(incomingSock, &buffer[0], MAX_BUFFER-1) < 0)
{
    std::cerr << "read from socket error" << std::endl;
    return 4;
}
std::cout << "Got the message:" << buffer << std::endl;
```

13. Finally, we close both the sockets:

```
close(incomingSock);
close(sockfd);
return 0;
}
```

We've written quite a lot of code, so it is time to explain how all of this works.

How it works...

Both the client and the server have a very common algorithm, which we have to describe in order for you to understand and generalize this concept. The client's algorithm is as follows:

```
socket() -> connect() -> send() -> receive()
```

Here, `connect()` and `receive()` are blocking calls (that is, the calling program will wait for their completion). The `connect` phrase specifically initiates the three-way handshake that we described in detail in the *Learning the basics of connection-oriented communication recipe*

The server's algorithm is as follows:

```
socket() -> bind() -> listen() -> accept() -> receive() -> send()
```

Here, `accept` and `receive` are blocking the call. Let's now analyze in detail both the client's and server's code.

The client code analysis is as follows:

1. The first step just contains the necessary includes that are needed to correctly use the four APIs that we listed in the preceding client's algorithm section. Just note that the constants, in pure C++ style, are not defined using the `#define` macro, but by using `constexpr`. The difference is that the latter is managed by the compiler, whereas the former is managed by the preprocessor. As a rule of thumb, you should always try to rely on the compiler.

2. The `socket()` system call creates a socket descriptor that we named `sockfd`, which will be used to send and receive information to/from the server. The two parameters indicate that the socket will be a TCP (`SOCK_STREAM`)/IP (`PF_INET`) socket type. Once we have a valid socket descriptor, and before calling the `connect` method, we need to know the server's details; for this, we use the `gethostbyname()` method, which, given a string like `localhost`, will return a pointer to `struct hostent *` with information about the host.

3. We're now ready to call the `connect()` method, which will take care of the three-way-handshake process. By looking at its prototype (`man connect`), we can see that as well as the socket, it needs a `const struct sockaddr *address` struct, so we need to copy the respective information into it and pass it to the `connect()`; that's why we use the `utility` method `bcopy()` (`bzero()` is just a helper method to reset the `sockaddr` struct before using it).

4. We are now ready to send and receive data. Once the connection is established, the server will send an acknowledgment message (`You are connected!`). Have you noticed that we're using the `read()` method to receive information from the server through a socket? This is the beauty and simplicity of programming in a Linux environment. One method can support multiple interfaces—indeed, we're able to work with the same method to read files, receive data with sockets, and do many other things.

5. We can send a message to the server. The method used is, as you may have guessed, `write()`. We pass `socket` to it, which identifies the connection, the message we want the server to receive, and the length of the message so that Linux will know when to stop reading from the buffer.

6. As usual, we need to close, clean, and free any resource used. In this case, we have to close the socket by just using the `close()` method, passing the socket descriptor.

The server code analysis is as follows:

1. We use a similar code to the one we used for the client, but include some headers and three defined constants, which we will use and explain later.

2. We have to define a socket descriptor by calling the `socket()` API. Note that there is no difference between the client and the server. We just need a socket that is able to manage a TCP/IP type of a connection.

3. We have to bind the socket descriptor created in the previous step to the network interface and port it on the local machine. We do this with the `bind()` method, which assigns an address (`const struct sockaddr *address` passed as the second parameter) to the socket descriptor passed as the first parameter. The call to the `setsockopt()` method is just to avoid the bind error, `Address already in use`.

4. We start listening for any incoming connection by calling the `listen()` API. The `listen()` system call is pretty simple: it gets the `socket` descriptor on which we are listening and the maximum number of connections to keep in the queue of pending connections, which in our case we set to 5. Then we call `accept()` on the socket descriptor. The `accept` method is a blocking call: it means that it'll block until a new incoming connection is available, and then it'll return an integer representing the socket descriptor. The `cli_addr` structure is filled in with the connection's information, which we use to log who connected (`IP` and `port`).

5. This step is just a logical continuation of step 10. Once the server accepts a connection, we log on the standard output who connected (in terms of their `IP` and `port`). We do this by querying the information that was filled in the `cli_addr` struct by the `accept` method.

6. In this step, we receive information from the connected client through the `read()` system call. We pass in the input, the socket descriptor of the incoming connection, the `buffer` where the data will be saved, and the maximum length of the data that we want to read (`MAX_BUFFER-1`).

7. We then clean up and free any eventual resource that is used and/or allocated. In this case, we have to close the two sockets' descriptors that were used (`sockfd` for the server and `incomingSock` for the incoming connection).

By building and running both the server and the client (in this order), we get the following output:

- The server build and output are as follows:

```
root@839836698e38:/BOOK/chapter7# g++ serverTCP.cpp -o server
root@839836698e38:/BOOK/chapter7# ./server
server: got connection from = 127.0.0.1 and port = 36702
Got the message:hi
root@839836698e38:/BOOK/chapter7#
```

- The client build and output are as follows:

```
root@839836698e38:/BOOK/chapter7# g++ clientTCP.cpp -o client
root@839836698e38:/BOOK/chapter7# ./client localhost
You are connected!
What message for the server? : hi
root@839836698e38:/BOOK/chapter7#
```

This proves what we learned in this recipe.

There's more...

How can we improve the server application to manage multiple concurrent incoming connections? The server's algorithm that we implemented is sequential; after `listen()`, we just wait on `accept()` until the end, where we close the connections. You should go through the following steps as an exercise:

1. Run an infinite loop over `accept()` so that a server is always up and ready to serve clients.
2. Spin off a new thread for each accepted connection. You can do this by using `std::thread` or `std::async`.

Another important practice is to pay attention to the data that the client and server exchange with each other. Usually, they agree to use a protocol that they both know. It might be a web server, which in that case will involve the exchange of HTML, files, resources, and so on between the client and the server. If it is a supervision and control system, it might be a protocol defined by a specific standard.

See also

- Chapter 3, *Dealing with Processes and Threads,* to refresh your memory as to how processes and threads work to improve the server solution described here
- The *Learning the basics of connection-oriented communication* recipe to learn how the TCP connection works
- The *Learning what a communication endpoint* recipe to learn what an endpoint is and how it is related to a socket

Learning to use UDP/IP to communicate with processes on another machine

When a process communicates with another, reliability is not always the main criterion to use when deciding the communication mechanism. Sometimes, what we need is fast communication without the burden or the connection, flow control, and all the other controls that the TCP protocol implemented to make it reliable. This is the case for video streaming, **Voice over Internet Protocol** (**VoIP**) calls, and many others. In this recipe, we'll learn how to program UDP code that makes two (or more) processes communicate with each other.

How to do it...

We'll develop two programs, a client and a server. The server will start, bind the socket to a local address, and then will just receive data from the clients:

1. With the Docker image running, open a shell, create a new file, serverUDP.cpp, and add some headers and constants that we'll need later:

```
#include <stdio.h>
#include <stdlib.h>
#include <string.h>
#include <unistd.h>
#include <sys/types.h>
#include <sys/socket.h>
#include <netinet/in.h>
#include <iostream>
#include <arpa/inet.h>
```

```
constexpr unsigned int SERVER_PORT = 50544;
constexpr unsigned int MAX_BUFFER = 128;
```

2. In the `main` function, we have to instantiate the socket of the `DATAGRAM` type and set the option to reuse the address each time the server is rerun:

```
int main(int argc, char *argv[])
{
    int sockfd =  socket(AF_INET, SOCK_DGRAM, 0);
    if (sockfd < 0)
    {
        std::cerr << "open socket error" << std::endl;
        return 1;
    }
    int optval = 1;
    setsockopt(sockfd, SOL_SOCKET, SO_REUSEADDR, (const void
        *)&optval , sizeof(int));
```

3. We have to bind the socket we've created with a local address:

```
struct sockaddr_in serv_addr, cli_addr;
bzero((char *) &serv_addr, sizeof(serv_addr));
serv_addr.sin_family = AF_INET;
serv_addr.sin_addr.s_addr = INADDR_ANY;
serv_addr.sin_port = htons(SERVER_PORT);
if (bind(sockfd, (struct sockaddr *) &serv_addr, sizeof
    (serv_addr)) < 0)
{
    std::cerr << "bind error" << std::endl;
    return 2;
}
```

4. We're now ready to receive packets from the clients, this time using the `recvfrom` API:

```
std::string buffer (MAX_BUFFER, 0);
unsigned int len;
if (recvfrom(sockfd, &buffer[0],
            MAX_BUFFER, 0,
            (struct sockaddr*)& cli_addr, &len) < 0)
{
    std::cerr << "recvfrom failed" << std::endl;
    return 3;
}
std::cout << "Got the message:" << buffer << std::endl;
```

5. We want to send an *ACK* message to the client with the `sendto` API:

```
std::string outBuffer ("Message received!");
if (sendto(sockfd, outBuffer.c_str(),
          outBuffer.length(), 0,
          (struct sockaddr*)& cli_addr, len) < 0)
{
    std::cerr << "sendto failed" << std::endl;
    return 4;
}
```

6. Finally, we can close the socket:

```
        close(sockfd);
        return 0;
    }
```

7. Let's now create the client program. On another shell, create the
   file `clientUDP.cpp`:

```
#include <stdio.h>
#include <stdlib.h>
#include <unistd.h>
#include <string.h>
#include <sys/types.h>
#include <sys/socket.h>
#include <netinet/in.h>
#include <netdb.h>
#include <iostream>

constexpr unsigned int SERVER_PORT = 50544;
constexpr unsigned int MAX_BUFFER = 128;
```

8. We have to instantiate the socket of the `datagram` type:

```
    int main(int argc, char *argv[])
    {
        int sockfd = socket(AF_INET, SOCK_DGRAM, 0);
        if (sockfd < 0)
        {
            std::cerr << "socket error" << std::endl;
            return 1;
        }
```

9. We need to get the host information to be able to identify the server that we want to send the packet to, and we do this by calling the `gethostbyname` API:

```
struct hostent* server = gethostbyname(argv[1]);
if (server == NULL)
{
    std::cerr << "gethostbyname, no such host" << std::endl;
    return 2;
}
```

10. Let's copy the host information into the `sockaddr_in` struct to identify the server:

```
struct sockaddr_in serv_addr, cli_addr;
bzero((char *) &serv_addr, sizeof(serv_addr));
serv_addr.sin_family = AF_INET;
bcopy((char *)server->h_addr,
        (char *)&serv_addr.sin_addr.s_addr,
        server->h_length);
serv_addr.sin_port = htons(SERVER_PORT);
```

11. We can finally send a message to the server using the socket descriptor, the message from the user, and the server address:

```
std::string outBuffer (MAX_BUFFER, 0);
std::cout << "What message for the server? : ";
getline(std::cin, outBuffer);
unsigned int len = sizeof(serv_addr);
if (sendto(sockfd, outBuffer.c_str(), MAX_BUFFER, 0,
            (struct sockaddr *) &serv_addr, len) < 0)
{
    std::cerr << "sendto failed" << std::endl;
    return 3;
}
```

12. We know that the server will reply with an *ACK*, so let's receive it with the `recvfrom` method:

```
std::string inBuffer (MAX_BUFFER, 0);
unsigned int len_cli_add;
if (recvfrom(sockfd, &inBuffer[0], MAX_BUFFER, 0,
            (struct sockaddr *) &cli_addr, &len_cli_add) < 0)
{
    std::cerr << "recvfrom failed" << std::endl;
    return 4;
```

```
        }
        std::cout << inBuffer << std::endl;
```

13. Finally, as usual, we take care of closing and freeing all the structures used:

```
        close(sockfd);
        return 0;
    }
```

Let's go deeper into the code and see how all of this works.

How it works...

In the *Learning to use TCP/IP to communicate with processes on another machine* recipe, we learned the client's and server's TCP algorithms. The UDP algorithms are simpler and, as you can see, the connection part is missing:

The UDP client's algorithm:

```
    socket() ->  sendto() -> recvfrom()
```

The UDP server's algorithm:

```
    socket() -> bind() ->  recvfrom() -> sendto()
```

Note how much simpler they are now—for example, the server, in this case, does not `listen` for and `accept` incoming connections.

The server-side code analysis is as follows:

1. We just defined some headers and two constants that represent the port where the server will expose the service (SERVER_PORT) and the maximum size of the data (MAX_BUFFER).
2. In this step, we defined the socket (sockfd), just like we did in the TCP code, but this time we use the SOCK_DGRAM (UDP) type. In order to avoid the bind issue of Address already in use, we set the option to allow the socket to reuse the address.

3. Next is the `bind` call. It accepts the parameters of `int socket, const struct sockaddr *address,` and `socklen_t address_len,` which are basically the socket, the address to bind the socket at, and the length of the address struct. In the `address` variable, we specify that we are listening to all the available local network interfaces (`INADDR_ANY`) and we will use the Internet Protocol version 4 (`AF_INET`).

4. We can now start receiving data by using the `recvfrom` method. The method takes as input the socket descriptor (`sockfd`), the buffer to store the data in (`buffer`), the maximum size of data we can store, a flag (`0`, in this case) to set the specific properties on the received message, the address of the sender of the datagram (`cli_addr`), and the length of the address (`len`). These last two parameters are returned filled in, so we'd know who sent the datagram.

5. We can now send an *ACK* to the client. We use the `sendto` method. As the UDP is a connectionless protocol, we don't have a client connected, so we need to pass this information somehow. We do this by passing the `cli_addr`, which is returned filled in by the `recvfrom` method along with the length (`len`), to the `sendto` method. Other than this, we need to pass the socket descriptor (`sockfd`), the buffer to send (`outBuffer`), the length of the buffer (`outBuffer.length()`), and the flag (`0`, in this case).

6. Then, we just need to clean up at the end of the program. We have to close the socket descriptor with the `close()` method.

The client-side code analysis is as follows:

1. In this step, we find the same headers that we have on the `serverUDP.cpp` source file with `SERVER_PORT` and `MAX_BUFFER`.

2. We have to define the socket of the datagram type by calling the `socket` method, passing again as input `AF_INET` and `SOCK_DGRAM`.

3. As we need to know who to send the datagram to, the client application takes as input on the command line the address of the server (for example, `localhost`) that we pass as input to the `gethostbyname`, which returns the host address (`server`).

4. We use the `server` variable to fill the `serv_addr` structure used to identify the address of the server that we want to send the datagram to (`serv_addr.sin_addr.s_addr`), the port (`serv_addr.sin_port`), and the family of the protocol (`AF_INET`).

5. We can then use the `sendto` method to send the user message to the server by passing the parameters of `sockfd`, `outBuffer`, `MAX_BUFFER`, the flag set to `0`, the address of the server `serv_addr`, and its length (`len`). Again, the client does not know at this stage who is the receiver of the message as it is not connected to anybody, and that is why the `serv_addr` structure must be properly filled in so that it contains a valid address.

6. We know that the server will send back an application *ACK*, so we have to receive it. We call the `recvfrom` method that is passing the socket descriptor (`sockfd`) as input, the buffer to store the returned data in (`buffer`), the maximum size of the data we can get, and a flag set to `0`. `recvfrom` returns the address of the sender of the message with its length, which we store in `cli_addr` and `len` respectively.

Let's run the server, then the client.

Run the server as follows:

```
root@839836698e38:/BOOK/chapter7# g++ serverUDP.cpp -o serverUDP
root@839836698e38:/BOOK/chapter7# ./serverUDP
```

Run the client as follows:

```
root@839836698e38:/BOOK/chapter7# g++ clientUDP.cpp -o clientUDP
root@839836698e38:/BOOK/chapter7# ./clientUDP localhost
What message for the server? : hi
Message received!
root@839836698e38:/BOOK/chapter7#
```

This shows how UDP works.

There's more...

Another way of using the UDP protocol, as a type of connectionless communication, is to send a datagram in multicast or broadcast format. A multicast is a communication technique that is used to send the same datagram to multiple hosts. The code does not change; we just have to set the IP of the multicast group so it knows where to send the message. It is a convenient and efficient way of communicating *one-to-many*, saving a lot of bandwidth. Another alternative is to send a datagram in broadcast mode. We have to set the IP of the receiver with a subnet mask in the form of `172.30.255.255`. The message will be sent to all the hosts in the same subnet.

You're invited to improve the server code by going through the following steps:

1. Set up an infinite loop over `recvfrom()` so that you always have a server up and ready to serve clients.
2. Start a new thread for each accepted connection. You can do this by using `std::thread` or `std::async`.

See also

- `Chapter 3`, *Dealing with Processes and Threads*, to refresh how processes and threads work to improve the server solution described here
- The *Learning the basics of connectionless-oriented communication* recipe to learn how the UDP connection works
- The *Learning what a communication endpoint is* recipe to learn what an endpoint is and how it is related to a socket

Dealing with endianness

Writing code at system level might mean dealing with different processors' architectures. When doing this, there is one thing that programmers had to take care of by themselves before C++20, which is **endianness**. Endianness refers to the byte's order in the binary representation of a number. Fortunately, the last C++ standard helps us to enter endian information at compile time. This recipe will teach you how to be aware of endianness and write code that can run on both little- and big-endian architecture.

How to do it...

We'll develop a program that will query the machine at compile time, so that we can make a conscious decision as to how to deal with numbers represented in different formats:

1. We need to include the `<bit>` headers file; then we can use the `std::endian` enumerations:

```cpp
#include <iostream>
#include <bit>

int main()
{
    if (std::endian::native == std::endian::big)
        // prepare the program to read/write
        // in big endian ordering.
        std::cout << "big" << std::endl;
    else if (std::endian::native == std::endian::little)
        // prepare the program to read/write
        // in little endian ordering.
        std::cout << "little" << std::endl;

    return 0;
}
```

Let's take a closer look at what implications this has in the next section.

How it works...

Big-endian and little-endian are the two dominant types of data representation. The little-endian ordering format means that the least significant byte (also known as **LSB**) is placed in the highest address, while in a big-endian machine, the most significant byte (also known as **MSB**) is placed in the lowest address. An example of the representation for the hexadecimal value `0x1234` would be as follows:

	Address	Address+1 (byte)
Big-endian	12	34
Little-endian	34	12

The main goal of the code snippet in step 1 is to answer the question: how do I know what machine architecture I'm dealing with? The new C++20 enumeration `std::endian` helps us solve this problem perfectly. How? Well, first in terms of *endian awareness*. Having `std::endian` as part of the C++ standard library helps the programmer to query at any time the endian architecture of the underlying machine. Second: for shared resources, the two programs have to agree on a format (like the TCP protocol does, that is, sending the info in *network order*) so that the reader (or receiver, if exchanging data over the network) can make the appropriate conversions.

The other question is: what should I do? There are two things that you should do: one is related to the application point of view and the second is related to networking. In both cases, if your application exchanges data with another machine with a different endian format (a file exchanged, or a filesystem shared, among many others) or sends data over the internet to a machine with a different architecture, then you have to make sure that your data will be understood. To do this, you can use the `hton`, `ntoh` macro and friends; this makes sure that the number is converted from host to network (for `hton`) and from network to host (for `ntoh`). We have to mention that most of the internet protocols use the big-endian format, which is the reason why, if you call `hton` from a big-endian machine, the function will not perform any conversion.

The Intel x86 family and the AMD64 series of processors use all the little-endian format, while the IBM z/Architecture, Freescale, and all the Motorola 68000 heritage processers use the big-endian format. There are some processors (such as the PowerPC) that can switch endianness.

There's more...

In theory, data representation formats other than little- and big-endian do exist. An example is the middle-endian format used by the Honeywell 316 minicomputer.

See also

- The *Learning to use TCP/IP to communicate with processes on another machine* recipe
- The *Learning to use UDP/IP to communicate with processes on another machine* recipe

Dealing with Console I/O and Files

8

This chapter covers recipes based on the console, streaming, and file I/O using the C++ Standard Library. We've been reading parameters into the programs we've written in other chapters but there are several other ways to do this. We'll deep dive into these topics and we will learn the alternatives, tips, and best practices for each with specific and dedicated hands-on recipes.

Once again, our main focus is to try to write system programming software by using C++ (and its standard library) as much as we can, so the code will have very limited C and POSIX solutions.

This chapter will cover the following topics:

- Implementing I/O to and from the console
- Manipulating I/O strings
- Working with files

Technical requirements

In order to let you try the programs right from the start, we've set up a Docker image that has all the tools and libraries we'll need throughout the book. It is based on Ubuntu 19.04.

In order to set it up, follow these steps:

1. Download and install the Docker Engine from `www.docker.com`.
2. Pull the image from Docker Hub: `docker pull kasperondocker/system_programming_cookbook:latest`

3. The image should now be available. Type in the following command to view the image: `docker images`

4. You should have this image now: `kasperondocker/system_programming_cookbook`

5. Run the Docker image with an interactive shell with the help of the following command: `docker run -it --cap-add sys_ptrace kasperondocker/system_programming_cookbook:latest /bin/bash`

6. The shell on the running container is now available. Use `root@39a5a8934370/#` `cd /BOOK/` to get all the programs that we develop throughout the book, organized by chapter.

The `--cap-add sys_ptrace` argument is needed to allow GDB in the Docker container to set breakpoints, which Docker does not allow by default.

Implementing I/O to and from the console

This recipe focuses on console I/O. Most programs we write need some kind of interaction with the user: we need to get inputs, do some processing, and return the output. Think, for example, about user inputs you could collect in an application that you'll build. In this recipe, we'll write code that shows different ways to get input from the console and return the output.

How to do it...

Let's write some code:

1. With the Docker image running, let's create a new file named `console_01.cpp` and type this code into it:

```cpp
#include <iostream>
#include <string>
int main ()
{
    std::string name;
    std::cout << "name: ";
    std::cin >> name;
    std::string surname;
    std::cout << "surname: ";
    std::cin >> surname;
```

```
    int age;
    std::cout << "age: ";
    std::cin >> age;
    std::cout << "Hello " << name << ", "
            << surname << ": " << age << std::endl;
    return 0;
}
```

2. Create another file now called `console_02.cpp` and type this code in to see the limitation of this approach:

```
#include <iostream>
#include <string>
int main ()
{
    std::string fullNameWithCin;
    std::cout << "full Name got with cin: ";
    std::cin >> fullNameWithCin;

    std::cout << "hello " << fullNameWithCin << std::endl;
    return 0;
}
```

3. Finally, let's create a new file and name it `console_03.cpp`; let's see how `std::getline` and `std::cin` can overcome this previous limitation:

```
#include <iostream>
#include <string>

int main ()
{
    std::string fullName;
    std::cout << "full Name: ";
    std::getline (std::cin, fullName);
    std::cout << "Hello " << fullName << std::endl;
    return 0;
}
```

Although these are very simple examples, they show the C++ way of interacting with the console standard input and output.

How it works...

In the first step, the `console_01.cpp` program just uses `std::cin` and `std::cout` to get the `name` and the `surname` information of the user and save it in the `std::string` variables. These are the first things to use when a simple interaction with the standard input and output is needed. By building and running the `console_01.cpp` file, we'll get the following output:

```
root@5bc267efc0dd:/BOOK/chapter8# g++ console_01.cpp
root@5bc267efc0dd:/BOOK/chapter8# ./a.out
name: ono
surname: vaticone
age: 43
Hello ono, vaticone: 43
root@5bc267efc0dd:/BOOK/chapter8#
```

The second step of the recipe shows the limitation of `std::cin` and `std::cout`. The user gives `name` and `surname` in the command line to the running process as programmed, but strangely enough, just the name is stored in the `fullNameWithCin` variable, completely skipping the surname. How come? The reason is simple: `std:cin` always considers spaces, tabs, or newlines as delimiters of the value captured from the standard input. How can we get the full line from the standard input, then? By compiling and running `console_02.cpp`, we get the following:

```
root@5bc267efc0dd:/BOOK/chapter8# g++ console_02.cpp
root@5bc267efc0dd:/BOOK/chapter8# ./a.out
full Name got with cin: ono vaticone
hello ono
root@5bc267efc0dd:/BOOK/chapter8#
```

The third step shows the use of the `getline` function in conjunction with `std::cin` to get the full line from the standard input. `std::getline` gets the line from `std::cin` and stores it in the `fullName` variable. In general, `std::getline` accepts any `std::istream` as input with the possibility of specifying the delimiter. The available prototypes in the standard library are as follows:

```
istream& getline (istream& is, string& str, char delim);
istream& getline (istream&& is, string& str, char delim);
istream& getline (istream& is, string& str);
istream& getline (istream&& is, string& str);
```

These make `getline` a very flexible method. By building and running `console_03.cpp`, we get the following output:

```
root@5bc267efc0dd:/BOOK/chapter8# g++ console_03.cpp
root@5bc267efc0dd:/BOOK/chapter8# ./a.out
full Name: ono vaticone
Hello ono vaticone
root@5bc267efc0dd:/BOOK/chapter8#
```

Let's have a look at the following example, where we pass a stream to the method, the variable to store the extracted piece of information, and the delimiter:

```cpp
#include <iostream>
#include <string>
#include <sstream>

int main ()
{
    std::istringstream ss("ono, vaticone, 43");

    std::string token;
    while(std::getline(ss, token, ','))
    {
        std::cout << token << '\n';
    }

    return 0;
}
```

The output of the preceding method is as follows:

```
root@5bc267efc0dd:/BOOK/chapter8# ./a.out
ono
vaticone
43
```

This can form the foundation for building your own tokenizer method.

There's more...

`std::cin` and `std::cout` allow chain requests, which makes the code more readable and concise:

```
std::cin >> name >> surname;
std::cout << name << ", " << surname << std::endl;
```

`std::cin` expects the user to pass their name, and then their surname. They have to be separated by a space, tab, or newline character.

See also

- The *Learning how to manipulate I/O strings* recipe covers how to manipulate strings as a complement of console I/O.

Learning how to manipulate I/O strings

String manipulation is a very important aspect of almost any software. Being able to manipulate strings simply and effectively is a key aspect of software development. How would you read the configuration file of your application or parse it? This recipe will teach you what tools C++ offers to make this an enjoyable task with the `std::stringstream` class.

How to do it...

In this section, we'll develop a program by using `std::stringstream` to parse streams, which can actually come from any source: files, strings, input arguments, and so on.

1. Let's develop a program that prints all the entries of a file. Type the following code into a new CPP file, `console_05.cpp`:

```
#include <iostream>
#include <string>
#include <fstream>

int main ()
{
    std::ifstream inFile ("file_console_05.txt",
```

```
std::ifstream::in);
    std::string line;
    while( std::getline(inFile, line) )
        std::cout << line << std::endl;

    return 0;
}
```

2. `std::stringstream` is very handy when we have to parse strings into variables. Let's see this in action by writing the following code in a new file, `console_06.cpp`:

```cpp
#include <iostream>
#include <string>
#include <fstream>
#include <sstream>

int main ()
{
    std::ifstream inFile ("file_console_05.txt",
        std::ifstream::in);
    std::string line;
    while( std::getline(inFile, line) )
    {
        std::stringstream sline(line);
        std::string name, surname;
        int age{};
        sline >> name >> surname >> age;
        std::cout << name << "-" << surname << "-"<< age <<
            std::endl;
    }
    return 0;
}
```

3. And, to complement the second step, parsing and creating string streams is easy too. Let's do this in `console_07.cpp`:

```cpp
#include <iostream>
#include <string>
#include <fstream>
#include <sstream>

int main ()
{
    std::stringstream sline;
    for (int i = 0; i < 10; ++i)
```

```
        sline << "name = name_" << i << ", age = " << i*7 <<
            std::endl;

    std::cout << sline.str();
    return 0;
}
```

The preceding three programs show how simple it is parsing a string in C++. The next section will explain them step by step.

How it works...

Step 1 shows that `std::getline` accepts any stream as input, not just the standard input (that is, `std::cin`). In this case, it gets the stream coming from a file. We include `iostream` for `std::cout`, `string` to be able to use strings, and `fstream` to be able to read the file.

Then, we open the `file_console_05.txt` file by using `std::fstream` (file stream). In its constructor, we pass the filename and the flags (in this case, just the information that is an input file with `std::ifstream::in`). We pass the file stream to `std::getline`, which will take care of copying each line from the stream and storing it in the `std::string` variable `line`, which is just printed. The output of this program is as follows:

```
root@5bc267efc0dd:/BOOK/chapter8# g++ console_05.cpp
root@5bc267efc0dd:/BOOK/chapter8# ./a.out
firstName01, secondName01, 43
firstName02, secondName02, 22
firstName03, secondName03, 12
firstName04, secondName04, 56
firstName05, secondName05, 26
firstName06, secondName06, 76
firstName07, secondName07, 41
firstName08, secondName08, 62
firstName09, secondName09, 31
firstName10, secondName10, 36
firstName11, secondName11, 19
root@5bc267efc0dd:/BOOK/chapter8#
```

Step 2 shows the same program reading the `file_console_05.txt` file, but, this time we want to parse each line of the file. We do this by passing the `line` string variable to the `sline std::stringstream` variable. `std::stringstream` offers convenient and easy-to-use parsing capabilities.

By just writing the line `sline >> name >> surname >> age`, the `operator>>` of
the `std::stringstream` class will save the `name`, `surname`, and `age` into the respective
variables, taking care of the type conversion (that is, for the `age` variable, from `string` to
`int`), assuming these variables appear in that order in the file. The `operator>>` will parse
the string and, by skipping leading **whitespaces**, for each token will call the appropriate
method (for example, `basic_istream& operator>>( short& value );` or
`basic_istream& operator>>( long long& value );`, among many others). The
output of this program is as follows:

```
root@5bc267efc0dd:/BOOK/chapter8# g++ console_06.cpp
root@5bc267efc0dd:/BOOK/chapter8# ./a.out
firstName01,-secondName01,-43
firstName02,-secondName02,-22
firstName03,-secondName03,-12
firstName04,-secondName04,-56
firstName05,-secondName05,-26
firstName06,-secondName06,-76
firstName07,-secondName07,-41
firstName08,-secondName08,-62
firstName09,-secondName09,-31
firstName10,-secondName10,-36
firstName11,-secondName11,-19
root@5bc267efc0dd:/BOOK/chapter8#
```

Step 3 shows that the same simplicity of parsing a stream into variables applies when
building a stream too. The same `std::stringstream` variable `sline` is used with the `<<`
operators, representing that the stream of data now flows in the direction of the `string
stream` variable, which is printed to the standard output in two lines in the following
screenshot. The output of this program is, as expected, as follows:

```
root@5bc267efc0dd:/BOOK/chapter8# g++ console_07.cpp
root@5bc267efc0dd:/BOOK/chapter8# ./a.out
name = name_0, age = 0
name = name_1, age = 7
name = name_2, age = 14
name = name_3, age = 21
name = name_4, age = 28
name = name_5, age = 35
name = name_6, age = 42
name = name_7, age = 49
name = name_8, age = 56
name = name_9, age = 63
root@5bc267efc0dd:/BOOK/chapter8#
```

`std::stringstream` makes it really easy to parse strings and streams, wherever they come from.

There's more...

If you're looking for low latency, streams manipulation with `std::stringstream` might not be your first choice. We always suggest that you measure the performance and make a decision based on data. If that's the case, you have different solutions you can try:

- Just focus on the low-latency part of the code to optimize, if you can.
- Write your layer using a standard C or C++ method to parse data, for example, the typical `atoi()` method.
- Use any open source low-latency framework.

See also

- The *Implementing I/O to and from the console* recipe covers how to deal with I/O from the console.

Working with files

This recipe will teach you the fundamental knowledge needed to deal with files. The C++ Standard Library historically offers a very good interface, but C++ 17 added a namespace called `std::filesystem`, which further enriches the offer. We'll not take advantage of the C++17 `std::filesystem` namespace, though, as it was already introduced in *Chapter ?, Revisiting C++*. Think about a concrete use case of creating a configuration file, or where you'd need to make a copy of that configuration file. This recipe will teach you how C++ makes this task easy.

How to do it...

In this section, we'll write three programs to learn how to work with files by using `std::fstream`, `std::ofstream`, and `std::ifstream`:

1. Let's develop a program that opens and writes into a new file, `file_01.cpp`, by using `std::ofstream`:

```cpp
#include <iostream>
#include <fstream>

int main ()
{
    std::ofstream fout;
    fout.open("file_01.txt");

    for (int i = 0; i < 10; ++i)
        fout << "User " << i << " => name_" << i << " surname_"
            << i << std::endl;

    fout.close();
}
```

2. In a new source file, `file_02.cpp`, let's read from a file and print to standard output:

```cpp
#include <iostream>
#include <fstream>

int main ()
{
    std::ifstream fiut;
    fiut.open("file_01.txt");

    std::string line;
    while (std::getline(fiut, line))
        std::cout << line << std::endl;

    fiut.close();
}
```

3. Now we want to combine the flexibility of opening a file for both reading and writing. We'll use `std::fstream` to copy the contents of `file_01.txt` into `file_03.txt` and then print its content. In another source file, `file_03.cpp`, type the following code:

```cpp
#include <iostream>
#include <fstream>

int main ()
{
    std::fstream fstr;
    fstr.open ("file_03.txt", std::ios::trunc | std::ios::out
        | std::ios::in);

    std::ifstream fiut;
    fiut.open ("file_01.txt");
    std::string line;
    while (std::getline(fiut, line))
        fstr << line << std::endl;
    fiut.close();

    fstr.seekg(0, std::ios::beg);
    while (std::getline(fstr, line))
        std::cout << line << std::endl;
    fstr.close();
}
```

Let's see how this recipe works.

How it works...

Before getting deep into the preceding three programs, we have to clarify how the standard library is structured with regards to file streams. Let's have a look at this following table:

		<fstream>
<ios>	<--<ostream>	<--ofstream
<ios>	<-- <istream>	<--ifstream

Let's break it down as follows:

- `<ostream>`: The streams class responsible for output streams.
- `<istream>`: The streams class responsible for input streams.
- `ofstream`: The streams class for writing to files. Present in the `fstream` header file.
- `ifstream`: The streams class for reading from files. Present in the `fstream` header file.

Both `std::ofstream` and `std::ifstream` inherit from the generic stream classes of `std::ostream` and `std::istream`, respectively. As you can imagine, `std::cin` and `std::cout` also inherit from `std::istream` and `std::ostream` (not shown in the preceding table).

Step 1: The first thing we do is include `<iostream>` and `<fstream>` in order to use `std::cout` and `std::ofstream` to read the `file_01.txt` file. Then we call the `open` method, which, in this case opens the file in writing mode, as we're using the `std::ofstream` class. We are now ready to write our strings into the `fout` file stream with the `<<` operator. Finally, we have to close the stream, which will end up closing the file. By compiling and running the program, we'll get the following output:

```
root@5bc267efc0dd:/BOOK/chapter8# g++ file_01.cpp
root@5bc267efc0dd:/BOOK/chapter8# ./a.out
root@5bc267efc0dd:/BOOK/chapter8# cat file_01.txt
User 0 => name_0 surname_0
User 1 => name_1 surname_1
User 2 => name_2 surname_2
User 3 => name_3 surname_3
User 4 => name_4 surname_4
User 5 => name_5 surname_5
User 6 => name_6 surname_6
User 7 => name_7 surname_7
User 8 => name_8 surname_8
User 9 => name_9 surname_9
root@5bc267efc0dd:/BOOK/chapter8#
```

Step 2: We do the opposite in this case: we read from the `file_01.txt` file and print to the standard output. The only difference, in this case, is that we use the `std::ifstream` class, which represents a reading file stream. By calling the `open()` method, the file is opened in reading mode (`std::ios::in`). By using the `std::getline` method, we can print to the standard output all the rows of the file. The output is shown as follows:

```
root@5bc267efc0dd:/BOOK/chapter8# g++ file_02.cpp
root@5bc267efc0dd:/BOOK/chapter8# ./a.out
User 0 => name_0 surname_0
User 1 => name_1 surname_1
User 2 => name_2 surname_2
User 3 => name_3 surname_3
User 4 => name_4 surname_4
User 5 => name_5 surname_5
User 6 => name_6 surname_6
User 7 => name_7 surname_7
User 8 => name_8 surname_8
User 9 => name_9 surname_9
root@5bc267efc0dd:/BOOK/chapter8#
```

The final third step shows the usage of the `std::fstream` class, which gives us more freedom by allowing us to open a file in both reading and writing mode (`std::ios::out | std::ios::in`). We also want to truncate the file if it exists (`std::ios::trunc`). There are many more options available to pass to the `std::fstream` constructor.

There's more...

C++17 made a huge improvement by adding the `std::filesystem` to the standard library. It is not completely new it is hugely inspired by the Boost library. The main public members exposed are as follows:

Method Name	Description
path	Represents a path
filesystem_error	An exception on filesystem errors
directory_iterator	An iterator to the content of the directory (the recursive version is available too)
space_info	Information about free and available space on the filesystem
perms	Identifies file system permissions system

In the `std::filesystem` namespace, there are also helper functions that give information about the file, such as `is_directory()`, `is_fifo()`, `is_regular_file()`, `is_socket()`, and so on.

See also

- The *Understanding the filesystem* recipe in `Chapter 2`, *Revisiting C++*, gives a refresher on the topic.

Dealing with Time Interfaces 9

Time is used in several forms in operating systems and applications. Typically, applications need to deal with the following **categories** of time:

- **Clock**: The actual time and date, as you would read on your watch
- **Time point**: Processing time taken to profile, monitor, and troubleshoot an application's usage (for example, a processor or resource in general)
- **Duration**: Monotonic time, that is, the elapsed time for a certain event

In this chapter, we'll deal with all these aspects from both a C++ and POSIX point of view in order so that you have more tools available in your toolbox. The recipes in this chapter will teach you how to measure an event by using time points and why you should use a steady clock for that, as well as when the time overruns and how to mitigate it. You'll learn how to implement these concepts with both POSIX and C++ `std::chrono`.

This chapter will cover the following recipes:

- Learning about the C++ time interface
- Using the C++20 calendar and time zone
- Learning about Linux timing
- Dealing with time sleep and overruns

Technical requirements

To try out the programs in this chapter immediately, we've set up a Docker image that contains all the tools and libraries we'll need throughout this book. It is based on Ubuntu 19.04.

In order to set it up, follow these steps:

1. Download and install Docker Engine from `www.docker.com`.
2. Pull the image from Docker Hub: `docker pull kasperondocker/system_programming_cookbook:latest`.
3. The image should now be available. Type in the following command to view the image: `docker images`.
4. You should have the following image: `kasperondocker/system_programming_cookbook`.
5. Run the Docker image with an interactive shell with the help of the `docker run -it --cap-add sys_ptrace kasperondocker/system_programming_cookbook:latest /bin/bash` command.
6. The shell on the running container is now available. Go to `root@39a5a8934370/# cd /BOOK/` to get all the programs that will be developed in this book.

The `--cap-add sys_ptrace` argument is needed to allow **GDB** (short for **GNU Project Debugger**) to set breakpoints, which Docker doesn't allow by default.

 Disclaimer: The C++20 standard has been approved (that is, technically finalized) by WG21 in a meeting in Prague at the end of February. This means that the GCC compiler version that this book uses, 8.3.0, does not include (or has very, very limited support for) the new and cool C++20 features. For this reason, the Docker image does not include the C++20 recipe code. GCC keeps the development of the newest features in branches (you have to use appropriate flags for that, for example, -std=c++2a); therefore, you are encouraged to experiment with them by yourself. So, clone and explore the GCC contracts and module branches and have fun.

Learning about the C++ time interface

The C++11 standard really marks an important step regarding time. Before that (C++ standard 98 and before), system and application developers had to rely on implementation-specific APIs (that is, POSIX) or external libraries (for example, `boost`) to manipulate **time**, which means less portable code. This recipe will teach you how to write C++ code by using the standard time manipulation library.

How to do it...

Let's write a program to learn about the concepts of **clock**, **time point**, and **duration**, as supported in the C++ standards:

1. Create a new file and call it `chrono_01.cpp`. We need a few includes first:

```
#include <iostream>
#include <vector>
#include <chrono>
```

2. In the `main` part, we need something to measure, so let's populate an `std::vector` with some integers:

```
int main ()
{
    std::cout << "Starting ... " << std::endl;
    std::vector <int> elements;
    auto start = std::chrono::system_clock::now();

    for (auto i = 0; i < 100'000'000; ++i)
        elements.push_back(i);

    auto end = std::chrono::system_clock::now();
```

3. Now that we have the two time points, `start` and `end`, let's calculate the difference (that is, duration) and print it to see how long it took:

```
// default seconds
std::chrono::duration<double, std::milli> diff = end - start;
std::cout << "Time Spent for populating a vector with
    100M of integer ..."
            << diff.count() << "msec" << std::endl;
```

4. Now, we want to print the `start` variable in another format; for example, in the format of calendar local time with `ctime`:

```
auto tpStart = std::chrono::system_clock::to_time_t(start);
std::cout << "Start: " << std::ctime(&tpStart) << std::endl;

auto tpEnd = std::chrono::system_clock::to_time_t(end);
std::cout << "End: " << std::ctime(&tpEnd) << std::endl;
std::cout << "Ended ... " << std::endl;
}
```

This program uses a few of the `std::chrono` features, such as `system_clock`, `time_point`, and duration available in the Standard Library, and has done since version 11 of the C++ standard.

How it works...

Step 1 takes care of including the headers we'll need later: `<iostream>` for the standard output and `<vector>` and `<chrono>` for the time.

Step 2 defines a vector of **int called elements**. Due to this, we can call the `now()` method on the `system_clock` class in the `chrono` namespace to get the current time. Although we used `auto`, this method returns a `time_point` object representing a point in time. Then, we looped over 100 million times to populate the `elements` array in order to highlight that we used the new C++14 feature to represent *100,000,000*, which improves the readability of the code. At the end, we took another point in time by calling the `now()` method and storing the `time_point` object in the `end` variable.

In *step 3*, we looked at how long it took to execute the loop. To calculate this, we instantiated a `duration` object, which is a template class that needs two parameters:

- **The representation**: A type representing the number of ticks.
- **The period**: This can be (among other things) `std::nano`, `std:micro`, `std::milli`, and so on.

The default value for the period is `std::seconds`. Then, we just write `diff.cout()` on the standard output, which represents the number of milliseconds between `start` and `end`. An alternative way of calculating this difference is by using `duration_cast`; for example, `std::chrono::duration_cast<std::chrono::milliseconds> (end-start) count()`.

In *step 4*, we print the `start` and `end` `time_point` variables in calendar `localtime` representation (note that the container time might not be in sync with the host container). To do this, we need to convert them into `time_t` by using the `to_time_t()` static variable of the `system_clock` class and then pass them to the `std::ctime` method.

Now, let's build and run this:

```
root@6a506094952c:/BOOK/chapter8# g++ clock.cpp
root@6a506094952c:/BOOK/chapter8# ./a.out
Starting ...

Time Spent for populating a vector with 100M of integer ...1646.96msec
Start: Sun Dec 15 21:52:47 2019

End: Sun Dec 15 21:52:49 2019

Ended ...
root@6a506094952c:/BOOK/chapter8#
```

We'll learn a bit more about this recipe in the next section.

There's more...

The program we developed uses the `system_clock` class. There are three clock classes in the `chrono` namespace:

- `system_clock`: This represents the so-called **wall clock time**. It can be adjusted at any moment, such as when an additional imprecision is introduced through a leap second or the user has just set it. Its epoch (that is, its starting point), in most implementations, uses UNIX time, which means the start counts from 1st January 1970.
- `steady_clock`: This represents the so-called **monotonic clock**. It'll never be adjusted. It remains steady. In most implementations, its starting point is the time when the machine boots. For calculating the elapsed time of a certain event, you should consider using this type of clock.
- `high_resolution_clock`: This is the clock with the shortest tick available. It might just be an alias for the `system_clock` or `steady_clock` or a completely different implementation. It is implementation-defined.

A second aspect to keep in mind is that the C++20 standard includes `time_of_day`, calendar, and time zone.

See also

- The *Learning the Linux timing* recipe for a brief comparison
- *A Tour of C++, Second Edition,* by Bjarne Stroustrup

Using the C++20 calendar and time zone

The C++20 standard has enriched the `std::chrono` namespace with calendar features. They include all the typical features you would expect, plus a more idiomatic and intuitive way of playing with it. This recipe will teach you about some of the most important features and how simple it is to interact with the calendar section of the `std::chrono` namespace.

How to do it...

Let's look at some code:

1. Create a new file, ensuring that you include `<chrono>` and `<iostream>`. We have a date and we want to know what day of the week `bday` will fall on:

```
#include <chrono>
#include <iostream>

using namespace std;
using namespace std::chrono;

int main ()
{
    auto bday = January/30/2021;
    cout << weekday(bday) << endl;

    auto anotherDay = December/25/2020;
    if (bday == anotherDay)
        cout << "the two date represent the same day" << endl;
    else
        cout << "the two dates represent two different days"
            << endl;
}
```

2. There's a whole set of classes that allow you to play with the calendar. Let's take a look at some of them:

```
#include <chrono>
#include <iostream>

using namespace std;
using namespace std::chrono;

int main ()
{
```

```
    auto today = year_month_day{ floor<days>(system_clock::now())
};
    auto ymdl = year_month_day_last(today.year(), monthday
        last{ month{ 2 } });
    auto last_day_feb = year_month_day{ ymdl };
    std::cout << "last day of Feb is: " << last_day_feb
        << std::endl;

    return 0;
}
```

3. Let's play with the time zone and print a list of times for different time zones:

```
#include <chrono>
#include <iostream>

using namespace std;
using namespace std::chrono;

int main()
{
    auto zone_names = {
       "Asia/Tokyo",
       "Europe/Berlin",
       "Europe/London",
       "America/New_York",
    };

    auto localtime = zoned_time<milliseconds>(date::current_zone(),
                                               system_clock::now());
    for(auto const& name : zone_names)
        cout << name
             << zoned_time<milliseconds>(name, localtime)
             << std::endl;

    return 0;
}
```

4. One feature that's used often is used to find the difference between two time zones:

```
#include <chrono>
#include <iostream>

using namespace std;
using namespace std::chrono;
```

```
int main()
{
    auto current = system_clock::now();
    auto lon = zoned_time{"Europe/London", current_time};
    auto newYork = zoned_time{"America/New_York", current_time};
    cout <<"Time Difference between London and New York:"
        << (lon.get_local_time() - newYork.get_local_time())
            << endl;

    return 0;
}
```

Let's go a little deeper into the `std::chrono` calendar section to learn more about this recipe.

How it works...

There are a lot of calendar and time zone helper functions available in the new C++20 standard. This recipe just scratched the surface, but still gives us an understanding of how easy it is to deal with time. A reference for all the `std::chrono` calendar and time zone capabilities can be found at `https://en.cppreference.com/w/cpp/chrono`.

Step 1 uses the `weekday` method to get the day of the week (using the Gregorian calendar). Before calling the `weekday` method, we need to get a specific day and with C++20, we can just set `auto bday = January/30/2021`, which represents a date. Now, we can pass it to the `weekday` method to get the specific day of the week, which in our case is Saturday. One useful property is that we can compare dates, just like we can compare between the `bday` and `anotherDay` variables. `weekday`, as well as all the other `std::chrono` calendar methods, handles leap seconds.

Step 2 shows the use of the `year_month_day` and `year_month_day_last` methods. The library contains a whole set of classes similar to these two, for example, `month_day` and `month_day_lat`, and so on. They clearly have a different scope, but their principles remain the same. In this step, we're interested in knowing the last day of February. We set the current date in the `today` variable with the `year_month_day{ floor<days>(system_clock::now()) }` and then we pass `today` to the `year_month_day_last` method, which will return something like `2020/02/last`, which we store in the `ymdl` variable. We can use the `year_month_day` method again to get the last day of February. We can skip a few steps and call the `year_month_day_last` method directly. We performed this step for educational purposes.

Step 3 moves into the scope of time zones. The snippet of code in this step prints a list of time zones by iterating over the `zone_names` array. Here, we got the `localtime` first by looping over each time zone identified by a string. Then, we converted the `localtime` into the time zone that was identified by the `name` variable using the `zoned_time` method.

In *step 4*, we covered an interesting and recurrent problem: finding the time difference between two time zones. The principle doesn't change; we still use the `zoned_time` method to get the local time of the two time zones, which in this case are `"America/New_York"` and `"Europe/London"`. Then, we subtract the two local times to get the difference.

There's more...

The `std::chrono` calendar offers a wide variety of methods that you are invited to explore. A complete list is available at `https://en.cppreference.com/w/cpp/chrono`.

See also

- *A Tour of C++, Second Edition*, by Bjarne Stroustrup, *Chapter 13.7, Time*

Learning the Linux timing

Before C++11, the Standard Library did not contain any direct time-management support, so system developers had to use *external* sources. By external, we mean either an external library (for example, Boost (`https://www.boost.org/`)) or OS-specific APIs. We believe it's necessary that a system developer understands the concept of time in terms of Linux. This recipe will help you master concepts such as **clock**, **time point**, and **duration** by using the POSIX standard.

How to do it...

In this recipe, we'll write a program so that we can learn about the concepts of **clock**, **time point**, and **duration** in terms of Linux. Let's get started:

1. In a shell, create a new file named `linux_time_01.cpp` and add the following includes and function prototype:

```
#include <iostream>
#include <time.h>
#include <vector>

void timespec_diff(struct timespec* start, struct timespec* stop,
struct timespec* result);
```

2. Now, we want to see the difference between `CLOCK_REALTIME` and `CLOCK_MONOTONIC` on the `clock_gettime` call. We need to define two `struct timespec` variables:

```
int main ()
{
    std::cout << "Starting ..." << std::endl;
    struct timespec tsRealTime, tsMonotonicStart;
    clock_gettime(CLOCK_REALTIME, &tsRealTime);
    clock_gettime(CLOCK_MONOTONIC, &tsMonotonicStart);
```

3. Next, we need to print the contents of the `tsRealTime` and `tsMonoliticStart` variables to see the difference:

```
    std::cout << "Real Time clock (i.e.: wall clock):"
        << std::endl;
    std::cout << " sec :" << tsRealTime.tv_sec << std::endl;
    std::cout << " nanosec :" << tsRealTime.tv_nsec << std::endl;

    std::cout << "Monotonic clock:" << std::endl;
    std::cout << " sec :" << tsMonotonicStart.tv_sec << std::endl;
    std::cout << " nanosec :" << tsMonotonicStart.tv_nsec+
        << std::endl;
```

4. We need a task to monitor, so we'll use a `for` loop to populate an `std::vector`. After that, we immediately get a time point in the `tsMonotonicEnd` variable:

```
std::vector <int> elements;
for (int i = 0; i < 100'000'000; ++i)
    elements.push_back(i);
```

```
struct timespec tsMonotonicEnd;
clock_gettime(CLOCK_MONOTONIC, &tsMonotonicEnd);
```

5. Now, we want to print the task's duration. To do this, we call `timespec_diff` (helper method) to calculate the difference between `tsMonotonicEnd` and `tsMonotonicStart`:

```
struct timespec duration;
timespec_diff (&tsMonotonicStart, &tsMonotonicEnd, &duration);

std::cout << "Time elapsed to populate a vector with
    100M elements:" << std::endl;
std::cout << " sec :" << duration.tv_sec << std::endl;
std::cout << " nanosec :" << duration.tv_nsec << std::endl;
std::cout << "Finished ..." << std::endl;
}
```

6. Finally, we need to implement a helper method to calculate the time difference (that is, duration) between the times represented by the `start` and `stop` variables:

```
// helper method
void timespec_diff(struct timespec* start, struct timespec* stop,
struct timespec* result)
{
    if ((stop->tv_nsec - start->tv_nsec) < 0)
    {
        result->tv_sec = stop->tv_sec - start->tv_sec - 1;
        result->tv_nsec = stop->tv_nsec - start->tv_nsec
            + 100'000'0000;
    }
    else
    {
        result->tv_sec = stop->tv_sec - start->tv_sec;
        result->tv_nsec = stop->tv_nsec - start->tv_nsec;
    }
    return;
}
```

The preceding program shows how to gather time points to calculate the duration of an event. Now, let's deep dive into the details of this program.

How it works...

First of all, let's compile and execute the program:

```
root@6a506094952c:/BOOK/chapter8# g++ linux_time_01.cpp
root@6a506094952c:/BOOK/chapter8# ./a.out
Starting ...
Real Time clock (i.e.: wall clock):
    sec    :1576505344
    nanosec :539574300
Monotonic clock:
    sec    :44266
    nanosec :816071174
Time elapsed to populate a vector with 100M elements:
    sec    :1
    nanosec :644348500
Finished ...
root@6a506094952c:/BOOK/chapter8#
```

We can immediately notice that the real-time clock (seconds) is way bigger than the monotonic clock (seconds). By doing some math, you'll notice that the first is about 49 years and the latter is about 12 hours. Why is that? The second observation is that our code took 1 `second` and `644348500` nanoseconds to populate a vector of 100 million items. Let's gather some insights to explain this.

Step 1 just adds some includes and the prototype we've written to calculate the time difference.

Step 2 defined two variables, `struct timespec tsRealTime` and `struct timespec tsMonotonicStart`, that will be used to store the two time points. Then, we called the `clock_gettime()` method twice by passing `CLOCK_REALTIME` and the `tsRealTime` variable. We did this a second time by passing `CLOCK_MONOTONIC` with the `tsMonotonicStart` variable. `CLOCK_REALTIME` and `CLOCK_MONOTONIC` are both of the `clockid_t` type. When `clock_gettime()` is called with `CLOCK_REALTIME`, the time that we get will be the `wall-clock` time (or real time).

This time point has the same issues that `std::chrono::SYSTEM_CLOCK` does, which we looked at in the *Learning about the C++ time interface* recipe. It can be adjusted (for example, if the system clock is synced with NTP), so this isn't suitable for calculating the elapsed time (or the duration) of an event. When `clock_gettime()` is called with the `CLOCK_MONOTONIC` parameter, the time does not adjust and most implementations make it start right from the boot of the system (that is, by counting the clock tick from the start of the machine). This is very suitable for event duration calculations.

Step 3 just prints the results of the time points, that is, `tsRealTime` and `tsMonotonicStart`. We can see that the first one contains the seconds since 1st January 1970 (about 49 years), while the latter contains the seconds since my machine has booted (about 12 hours).

Step 4 just adds 100 million items in an `std::vector` and then gets another time point in `tsMonotonicEnd`, which will be used to calculate the duration of this event.

Step 5 calculates the difference between `tsMonotonicStart` and `tsMonotonicEnd` and stores the result in the `duration` variable by calling the `timespec_diff()` helper method.

Step 6 implements the `timespec_diff()` method, which logically calculates (`tsMonotonicEnd` - `tsMonotonicStart`).

There's more...

For the `clock_gettime()` method, we used POSIX as the counterpart set method: `clock_settime()`. The same is valid for `gettimeofday()`: `settimeofday()`.

It's worth highlighting that `gettimeofday()` is an extension of `time()` that returns a `struct timeval` (that is, seconds and microseconds). The issue with this method is that it can be adjusted. What does this mean? Let's imagine you use `usegettimeofday()` to get a time point before the event to measure, and then you get another time point after the event to measure. Here, you would calculate the difference between the two time points thinking everything is fine. What issues may occur here? Imagine that, between the two time points you've taken, the **Network Time Protocol** (**NTP**) server demands the local machine to adjust the local clock to get it in sync with the time server. The duration that's calculated won't be accurate since the time point that's taken after the event is affected by the NTP sync. NTP is just an example of this. The local clock can be adjusted in other ways too.

See also

- The *Learning about the C++ time interface* recipe for comparison with C++
- *Linux System Programming, Second Edition, by* Robert Love

Dealing with time sleep and overruns

Time, in a system programming context, doesn't only involve the act of measuring the duration of an event or reading the clock. It's also possible to put a process to sleep for a certain amount of time. This recipe will teach you how to put a process to sleep by using the seconds-based API, the microseconds-based API, and the clock_nanosleep() method, which has nanosecond resolution. Furthermore, we'll see what time overruns are and how we can minimize them.

How to do it...

In this section, we'll write a program to learn how to put a program to sleep by using the different POSIX APIs that are available. We'll also look at the C++ alternative:

1. Open a shell and create a new file called sleep.cpp. We need to add some headers that we'll need later:

```
#include <iostream>
#include <chrono>
#include <thread>      // sleep_for
#include <unistd.h>    // for sleep
#include <time.h>      // for nanosleep and clock_nanosleep
```

2. We'll put the program to sleep for 1 second by using the sleep() method and the std::chrono::steady_clock class as time points to calculate the duration at the end:

```
int main ()
{
    std::cout << "Starting ... " << std::endl;

    auto start = std::chrono::steady_clock::now();
    sleep (1);
    auto end = std::chrono::steady_clock::now();
    std::cout << "sleep() call cause me to sleep for: "
            << std::chrono::duration_cast<std::chrono::
               milliseconds> (end-start).count()
            << " millisec" <<     std::endl;
```

3. Let's look at how `nanosleep()` works. We still use `std::chrono::steady_clock` to calculate the duration, but we need a `struct timespec`. We'll make the process sleep for about `100` milliseconds:

```
struct timespec reqSleep = {.tv_sec = 0, .tv_nsec = 99999999};
start = std::chrono::steady_clock::now();
int ret = nanosleep (&reqSleep, NULL);
if (ret)
    std::cerr << "nanosleep issue" << std::endl;
end = std::chrono::steady_clock::now();
std::cout << "nanosleep() call cause me to sleep for: "
          << std::chrono::duration_cast<std::
             chrono::milliseconds> (end-start).count()
          << " millisec" << std::endl;
```

4. A more advanced way of putting a process to sleep is by using `clock_nanosleep()`, which allows us to specify some interesting parameters (see the next section for more details):

```
struct timespec reqClockSleep = {.tv_sec = 1,
    .tv_nsec = 99999999};
start = std::chrono::steady_clock::now();
ret = clock_nanosleep (CLOCK_MONOTONIC, 0,
    &reqClockSleep, NULL);
if (ret)
    std::cerr << "clock_nanosleep issue" << std::endl;
end = std::chrono::steady_clock::now();
std::cout << "clock_nanosleep() call cause me to sleep for: "
          << std::chrono::duration_cast<std::chrono::
             milliseconds> (end-start).count()
          << " millisec" << std::endl;
```

5. Now, let's look at how we can put the current thread to sleep by using the C++ Standard Library (through the `std::this_thread::sleep_for` template method):

```
start = std::chrono::steady_clock::now();
std::this_thread::sleep_for(std::chrono::milliseconds(1500));
end = std::chrono::steady_clock::now();
std::cout << "std::this_thread::sleep_for() call
  cause me to sleep for: "
          << std::chrono::duration_cast<std::chrono::
             milliseconds> (end-start).count()
          << " millisec" << std::endl;
std::cout << "End ... " << std::endl;
}
```

Now, let's go over these steps in more detail.

How it works...

The program will be put to sleep in four different ways. Let's take a look at the runtime:

```
root@6a506094952c:/BOOK/chapter8# g++ sleep.cpp
root@6a506094952c:/BOOK/chapter8# ./a.out
Starting ...
sleep() call cause me to sleep for: 1000 millisec
nanosleep() call cause me to sleep for: 103 millisec
clock_nanosleep() call cause me to sleep for: 1102 millisec
std::this_thread::sleep_for() call cause me to sleep for: 1504 millisec
End ...
root@6a506094952c:/BOOK/chapter8#
```

Step 1 just contains the headers we need: <iostream> for the standard output and standard error (cout and cerr), <chrono> for the time points that will be used to measure the actual sleep, <thread> for the sleep_for method, <unistd> for sleep(), and <time.h> for nanosleep() and clock_nanosleep().

Step 2 puts the process to sleep for 1 second by using the sleep() method. We use steady_clock::now() to get the time points and duration_cast to cast the difference and get the actual duration. To be precise, sleep() returns 0 if the process has successfully slept for at least the amount of time specified, but it can return a value between 0 and the seconds specified, which would represent the time **not** slept.

Step 3 shows how to put a process to sleep by using nanosleep(). We decided to use this method since usleep() has been deprecated on Linux. nanosleep() has an advantage over sleep() since it has nanosecond resolution and POSIX.1b standardized. nanosleep() returns 0 on success and -1 in the case of an error. It does this by setting the errno global variable to the specific error that occurred. The struct timespec variable contains tv_sec and tv_nsec (seconds and nanoseconds).

Step 4 uses a more sophisticated clock_nanosleep(). This method contains two parameters we haven't looked at yet. The first parameter is clock_id and accepts, among other things, CLOCK_REALTIME and CLOCK_MONOTONIC, which we looked at in the previous recipes. As a rule of thumb, you want to use the first if you're sleeping until an absolute time (wall-clock time) and the second if you're sleeping until a relative time value. This makes sense based on what we saw in the previous recipe.

The second parameter is a flag; it can be `TIME_ABSTIME` or `0`. If the first one is passed, the `reqClockSleep` variable will be treated as absolute, but if `0` is passed, then it'll be treated as relative. To clarify the concept of absolute time further, it might come from a previous call of `clock_gettime()` that stores an absolute time point in a variable, say `ts`. By adding 2 seconds to it, we can pass `&ts` (that is, the address of the variable `ts`) to `clock_nanosleep()`, which will wait until that specific absolute time.

Step 5 puts the current thread of the process to sleep (in this case, the current thread is the main thread, so the whole process will sleep) for 1.5 seconds (1,500 milliseconds = 1.5 seconds). `std::this_thread::sleep_for` is simple and effective. It is a template method that takes in one parameter as input; that is, the `duration`, which needs the representation type and the period (`_Rep` and `_Period`), as we saw in the *Learning the C++ time interface* recipe. In this case, we only passed the period in milliseconds and left the representation in its default state.

There is an issue we should be aware of here: the **time overrun**. All the interfaces we've used in this recipe guarantee that the process will sleep *at least as long as requested*. They'll return an error otherwise. They might sleep for a time slightly longer than the time we requested for different reasons. One reason might be due to the scheduler that selects a different task to run. This problem occurs when the granularity of the timer is greater than the time that was requested. Think, for example, about the time that's shown by the timer (`10msec`) and that the sleep time is `5 msec`. We might have a case where the process has to wait 5 milliseconds more than expected, which is 100% longer. Time overrun can be mitigated by using methods that support high-precision time sources, such as `clock_nanosleep()`, `nanosleep()`, and `std::this_thread::sleep_for()`.

There's more...

We didn't explicitly mention the thread implications for `nanosleep()` and `clock_nanosleep()`. Both methods cause the current thread to sleep. Sleep on Linux means that the thread (or the process, if it is a single-threaded application) will enter a **Not Runnable** state so that the CPU can continue with other tasks (remember that Linux does not differentiate between threads and processes).

See also

- *The Learning the C++ time interface* recipe for a review of the `std::chrono::duration<>` template class
- The *Learning the Linux timing* recipe for a review of the concepts of **REALTIME** and **MONOTONIC**

10
Managing Signals

Signals are software interrupts. They provide a way of managing asynchronous events, for example, a user from the terminal typing the interrupt key or another process sending a signal that must be managed. Every signal has a name that starts with `SIG` (for example, `SIGABRT`). This chapter will teach you how to write code to properly manage software interrupts, what the default actions defined by Linux for each signal are, and how to override them.

This chapter will cover the following recipes:

- Learning all of the signals and their default actions
- Learning how to ignore a signal
- Learning how to trap a signal
- Learning how to send a signal to another process

Technical requirements

In order to let you try the programs in this chapter immediately, we've set up a Docker image that has all the tools and libraries we'll need throughout the book, it is based on Ubuntu 19.04.

In order to set it up, follow these steps:

1. Download and install the Docker Engine from `www.docker.com`.
2. Pull the image from Docker Hub: `docker pull kasperondocker/system_programming_cookbook:latest`.
3. The image should now be available. Type in the following command to view the image: `docker images`.
4. You should have at least this image now: `kasperondocker/system_programming_cookbook`.

5. Run the Docker image with an interactive shell with the help of the following command: `docker run -it --cap-add sys_ptrace kasperondocker/system_programming_cookbook:latest /bin/bash`.

6. The shell on the running container is now available. Use `root@39a5a8934370/# cd /BOOK/` to get all the programs developed, by chapters.

The `--cap-add sys_ptrace` argument is necessary to allow GDB in the Docker container to set breakpoints, which, by default, Docker does not allow.

Learning all of the signals and their default actions

This recipe will show you all the signals and related default actions supported by Linux. We'll also learn why signals are an important concept and what Linux does for a software interrupt.

How to do it...

In this section, we'll list all the signals supported by our Linux distribution in order to be able to describe the most common ones in the *How it works...* section.

On a shell, type the following command:

```
root@fefe04587d4e:/# kill -l
```

If you run this command on the Docker image of the book, which is based on the Ubuntu version 19.04 distribution, you'll get this output:

```
 1) SIGHUP  2) SIGINT  3) SIGQUIT  4) SIGILL  5) SIGTRAP
 6) SIGABRT  7) SIGBUS  8) SIGFPE  9) SIGKILL 10) SIGUSR1
11) SIGSEGV 12) SIGUSR2 13) SIGPIPE 14) SIGALRM 15) SIGTERM
16) SIGSTKFLT 17) SIGCHLD 18) SIGCONT 19) SIGSTOP 20) SIGTSTP
21) SIGTTIN 22) SIGTTOU 23) SIGURG 24) SIGXCPU 25) SIGXFSZ
26) SIGVTALRM 27) SIGPROF 28) SIGWINCH 29) SIGIO 30) SIGPWR
31) SIGSYS 34) SIGRTMIN 35) SIGRTMIN+1 36) SIGRTMIN+2 37) SIGRTMIN+3
38) SIGRTMIN+4 39) SIGRTMIN+5 40) SIGRTMIN+6 41) SIGRTMIN+7 42) SIGRTMIN+8
43) SIGRTMIN+9 44) SIGRTMIN+10 45) SIGRTMIN+11 46) SIGRTMIN+12 47)
SIGRTMIN+13
48) SIGRTMIN+14 49) SIGRTMIN+15 50) SIGRTMAX-14 51) SIGRTMAX-13 52)
SIGRTMAX-12
```

```
53) SIGRTMAX-11 54) SIGRTMAX-10 55) SIGRTMAX-9 56) SIGRTMAX-8 57)
SIGRTMAX-7
58) SIGRTMAX-6 59) SIGRTMAX-5 60) SIGRTMAX-4 61) SIGRTMAX-3 62) SIGRTMAX-2
63) SIGRTMAX-1 64) SIGRTMAX
```

In the next section, we'll learn what the default actions of the most common signals a process can receive are, a description for each, and how Linux manages these software interrupts.

How it works...

In *step 1*, we executed the `kill -l` command to get all the signals the current Linux distribution supports. The following table provides a list of the most common signals with the default action and description:

Signal	Description	Default Action
SIGHUP	The Terminal controlling the process was closed (for example, the user logged out?)	Terminate
SIGABRT	Signal sent by `abort()`	Terminate (with a core dump, if possible)
SIGSEGV	Invalid memory reference	Terminate (with a core dump, if possible)
SIGSYS	Bad system call or process tried to execute an invalid system call.	Terminate (with a core dump, if possible)
SIGINT	Interrupt generated from the keyboard (for example *Ctrl + C*)	Terminate
SIGQUIT	Quit generated from the keyboard (for example: *Ctrl + /*)	Terminate (with a core dump, if possible)
SIGPIPE	A process tried to write to a pipe but with no reader	Terminate
SIGILL	A process tried to execute an illegal instruction	Terminate (with a core dump, if possible)
SIGALRM	Signal sent by `alarm()`	Terminate
SIGSTOP	Stop a process	Stop the process
SIGIO	Async I/O event	Terminate
SIGTRAP	Breakpoint trapped	Terminate
SIGTERM	Termination signal (catchable)	Terminate
SIGKILL	Process termination (un-catchable)	Terminate

For each signal sent to a process, Linux applies its default action. The system developer can, of course, override this action by implementing the desired one on within the process, as we'll see in the *Learning how to trap a signal* recipe.

Signals are defined in the `<signal.h>` header file and are simply positive integers with a meaningful name always prefixed by the `SIG` word. What does Linux do when a signal (that is, a software interrupt) is raised? Simply put, it always applies the same sequential life cycle, which is as follows:

1. The signal is raised by a user of another process, or by Linux itself.
2. The signal is stored until Linux is able to deliver it.
3. Once delivered, Linux performs one of these specific actions:
    1. Ignore the signal: we've seen that there are signals that cannot be ignored (for example, `SIGKILL`).
    2. Perform the default action: you can refer to column 3 of the preceding table.
    3. Handle the signal with the registered function (which the system developer implemented).

There's more...

All the signals, described and defined in the `<signal.h>` header file are POSIX compliant. This means that each identifier, their names, and the default actions are defined by the POSIX.1-2003 standard, which Linux adheres to. This guarantees the portability of the `signals` implementation or support in the applications.

See also

- The *Learning how to trap a signal* recipe
- The *Learning how to ignore a signal* recipe
- The *Learning how to send a signal to another process* recipe
- `Chapter 3`, *Dealing with Processes and Threads* for a refresh on processes and threads.

Learning how to ignore a signal

There might be cases where we just need to ignore a specific signal. However, rest assured, there are few signals that cannot be ignored, for example, `SIGKILL` (uncatchable). This recipe will teach you how to ignore a catchable signal.

How to do it...

To ignore a catchable signal, follow these steps:

1. On a shell, open a new source file called `signal_ignore.cpp` and start by adding the following code:

```cpp
#include<stdio.h>
#include<signal.h>
#include <iostream>

int main()
{
    std::cout << "Starting ..." << std::endl;
    signal(SIGTERM, SIG_IGN);
    while (true) ;
    std::cout << "Ending ..." << std::endl;
    return 0;
}
```

2. In this second program (`signal_uncatchable.cpp`), we want to see that an *uncatchable* signal cannot be *ignored*. To do this, we'll use the SIGKILL signal that we've seen in the *Learning all of the signals and their default actions* recipe, which is not catchable (that is, the program cannot ignore it):

```cpp
#include<stdio.h>
#include<signal.h>
#include <iostream>

int main()
{
    std::cout << "Starting ..." << std::endl;
    signal(SIGKILL, SIG_IGN);
    while (true) ;
    std::cout << "Ending ..." << std::endl;
    return 0;
}
```

The next section will explain the details of the preceding two programs.

How it works...

Step 1 contains the program to ignore the SIGTERM signal. We do this by calling the signal(); system call by passing the specific signal as the first parameter (SIGTERM) and the action to follow as the second parameter, which, in this case, is SIG_IGN, is to ignore.

Step 2 has the same code as *step 1*. We just used the signal(); method passing the SIGKILL parameter and SIG_IGN. In other words, we asked Linux to ignore the SIGKILL signal for this process (signal_uncatchable.cpp will become a process once built and executed). As we learned in the *Learning all of the signals and their default actions* recipe, SIGKILL is an uncatchable signal.

Let's build and run the two programs now. What we expect to see is the SIGTERM signal ignored in the first program and SIGKILL signal, which cannot be ignored in the second one, respectively. The output of the first program is as follows:

```
root@43b71a833c8f:/# ps aux                                 root@43b71a833c8f:/BOOK/chapter10# g++ signal_ignore.cpp
USER       PID %CPU %MEM    VSZ   RSS TTY      STAT START   TIME COMMAND    root@43b71a833c8f:/BOOK/chapter10# ./a.out
root         1  0.0  0.1   4180  3448 pts/0    Ss   17:10   0:00 /bin/bash  Starting ...
root        40  0.0  0.1   4180  3416 pts/1    Ss   17:19   0:00 bash
root       115 82.8  0.0   5832  1640 pts/0    R+   20:06   0:04 ./a.out
root       116  0.0  0.1   5832  2916 pts/1    R+   20:06   0:00 ps aux
root@43b71a833c8f:/# kill -15 115
root@43b71a833c8f:/#
```

Here, we retrieved the PID of the process, using ps aux, and sent the SIGTERM signal by running the command: kill -15 115 (where 15 represents SIGKILL). As you can see, the process keeps running by completely ignoring the signal to terminate it.

The second program, signal_uncatchable.cpp, shows that even if we specified to catch the SIGKILL signal, Linux ignored this and killed our process anyway. We can see this in the following screenshot:

```
root@43b71a833c8f:/# ps aux                                 root@43b71a833c8f:/BOOK/chapter10# g++ signal_uncathable.cpp
USER       PID %CPU %MEM    VSZ   RSS TTY      STAT START   TIME COMMAND    root@43b71a833c8f:/BOOK/chapter10# ./a.out
root         1  0.0  0.1   4180  3448 pts/0    Ss   17:10   0:00 /bin/bash  Starting ...
root        40  0.0  0.1   4180  3416 pts/1    Ss   17:19   0:00 bash       Killed
root       126 96.0  0.0   5832  1704 pts/0    R+   20:18   0:03 ./a.out    root@43b71a833c8f:/BOOK/chapter10#
root       127  0.0  0.1   5832  2792 pts/1    R+   20:18   0:00 ps aux
root@43b71a833c8f:/# kill -9 126
root@43b71a833c8f:/#
```

There's more...

To have a list of all the signals supported on a Linux machine, the `kill -l` command is of great help and `man signal` contains all the details you need to successfully integrate the signal in your program.

See also

- The *Learning the Linux fundamentals – shell* recipe in `Chapter 1`, *Getting Started with System Programming,* for a refresh on how to run programs on the shell
- *Learning how to trap a signal* recipe
- *Learning how to send a signal to another process* recipe
- *Learning all of the signals and their default actions* recipe
- `Chapter 3`, *Dealing with Processes and Threads,* for a refresh on processes and threads

Learning how to trap a signal

This recipe will teach you how to catch (or trap) a signal in a program. There might be a need to perform some actions for a specific signal. An example of this is when an application receives the signal to terminate (`SIGTERM`) but we are required to clean up some used resources before quitting.

How to do it...

Let's write an application where we'll catch the `SIGTERM` signal, print a string, and terminate the application:

1. On a shell, create a new file called `signal_trap.cpp`. We need to include, among other headers, `<signal.h>` to be able to handle signals. We also have to add the prototype needed to manage the signal we want to trap. In the `main` method then, we call the `signal()` system call by passing `SIGTERM` that we want to catch and the method used to manage it:

   ```
   #include<stdio.h>
   #include<signal.h>
   #include <iostream>
   ```

```
void handleSigTerm (int sig);

int main()
{
    std::cout << "Starting ..." << std::endl;
    signal(SIGTERM, handleSigTerm);
    while (true);
    std::cout << "Ending ..." << std::endl;
    return 0;
}
```

2. We need to define the `handleSigTerm()` method (which can be named whatever we want):

```
void handleSigTerm (int sig)
{
    std::cout << "Just got " << sig << " signal" << std::endl;
    std::cout << "cleaning up some used resources ..."
        << std::endl;
    abort();
}
```

The next section will describe the program in detail.

How it works...

Step 1 essentially defines the `main` method. First, we require the `<signal.h>` header. In the definition of the `main` method, the central part is the `signal()` system call where we pass the `SIGTERM` signal we want to trap and the method we want to get called by Linux. This is an important aspect worth highlighting. The `signal()` system call accepts (as a second parameter) a pointer to a function that the system developer has to define, as we did. In the kernel, when a software interrupt is raised, Linux sends it to the specific process and the method will be called (in the form of a callback). The prototype of the `signal()` method looks like this:

```
void(*signal(int, void (*)(int)))(int);
```

Step 2 has the definition of the method that will manage the `SIGTERM` signal we want to trap. This method, in its simplicity, shows a couple of interesting things. First, this method is a callback invoked from the `signal()` system call. Second, we necessarily have to define its prototype as `void (*)(int)`, that is, return void and accept an integer in the input (it represents the signal that the application actually receives). Anything different from this prototype will result in a compilation error.

Let's now build and execute the program we've developed in the previous section:

```
root@d1624cb42f2f:/BOOK/chapter10# g++ signal_trap.cpp     root@d1624cb42f2f:/BOOK/chapter10# ps aux
root@d1624cb42f2f:/BOOK/chapter10# ./a.out                 USER      PID %CPU %MEM   VSZ  RSS TTY    STAT START  TIME COMMA
Starting ...                                               ND
Just got 15 signal                                         root        1  0.0  0.1  4184 3404 pts/0  Ss  18:49  0:00 /bin/
cleaning up some used resources ...                        root       28  0.0  0.1  4184 3416 pts/1  Ss  18:59  0:00 bash
Aborted                                                    root       46  103  0.0  5836 1760 pts/0  R+  19:00  0:08 ./a.o
root@d1624cb42f2f:/BOOK/chapter10#                         root       47  0.0  0.1  5836 2844 pts/1  R+  19:00  0:00 ps au
                                                           root@d1624cb42f2f:/BOOK/chapter10# kill -15 46
                                                           root@d1624cb42f2f:/BOOK/chapter10#
```

We built and linked the `signal_trap.cpp` program and generated the `a.out` executable. We run it; the PID associated with the process is `46`. On the right shell, we send the `SIGTERM` signal (with identifier = `15`) to the process with PID `46`. As you can see on the standard output (the shell on the left), the process caught the signal and called the method we defined `handleSigTerm()`. This method printed some logs in the standard output and called the `abort()` system call, which sends the `SIGABORT` signal to the running process. As you can see in the *Learning all of the signals and their default actions* recipe, the default action of `SIGABORT` is to terminate the process (and generate the core dump). You can, of course, play with it and terminate the process in another, more suitable, way, depending on the requirements you have (for example, `exit()`).

There's more...

So, what does happen to signals when a process forks (or executes) another one? The following table will help you to understand how to deal with signals with a process-child relationship:

Signal Behavior	Process Fork	Process Exec
Default	Inherited	Inherited
Ignored	Inherited	Inherited
Handled	Inherited	Not inherited

At this stage, you should not be surprised that, when a process forks another process, the child essentially inherits all the behaviors of the parent. When a process executes another task (with `exec`), it inherits the **default behavior** and the **ignored behavior**, but it does not inherit the handled method that is implemented.

See also

- The *Learning how to ignore a signal* recipe
- The *Learning all of the signals and their default actions* recipe
- The *Learning how to send a signal to another process* recipe
- Chapter 3, *Dealing with Processes and Threads,* for a refresh on processes and threads

Learning how to send a signal to another process

There could be scenarios where a process needs to send a signal to other processes. This recipe will teach you how to achieve that using a hands-on approach.

How to do it...

We'll write a program that will send the SIGTERM signal to a running process. We'll see the process terminating as expected. On a shell, open a new source file called signal_send.cpp. We'll be using the system call, kill(), which sends a signal sig to a process specified by pid. The program accepts an input parameter, which is pid of the program to terminate:

```cpp
#include<stdio.h>
#include<signal.h>
#include <iostream>

int main(int argc, char* argv[])
{
    std::cout << "Starting ..." << std::endl;
    if (argc <= 1)
    {
        std::cout << "Process pid missing ..." << std::endl;
        return 1;
    }
    int pid = std::atoi(argv[1]);
    kill (pid, SIGTERM);

    std::cout << "Ending ..." << std::endl;
    return 0;
}
```

We'll be using the `signal_trap.cpp` program developed in the *Learning how to trap a signal* recipe as the process to terminate. The next section will go deep in the detail of the code seen here.

How it works...

In order to see the correct behavior, we need to run a process we intend to terminate. We'll run the `signal_trap.cpp` program. Let's build and run the `signal_send.cpp` program as follows:

```
root@cc8a9a1c5cf0:/BOOK/chapter10# ps aux
USER        PID %CPU %MEM    VSZ   RSS TTY      STAT START   TIME COMMAND
root          1  0.0  0.1   4180  3428 pts/0    Ss   11:45   0:00 /bin/bash
root         15  0.0  0.1   4180  3392 pts/1    Ss   11:47   0:00 bash
root        133  101  0.0   5832  1768 pts/1    R+   13:39   0:27 ./a.out
root        136  0.0  0.1   5832  2908 pts/0    R+   13:39   0:00 ps aux
root@cc8a9a1c5cf0:/BOOK/chapter10# g++ signal_send.cpp -o terminate
root@cc8a9a1c5cf0:/BOOK/chapter10# ./terminate 133
Starting ...
Ending ...
root@cc8a9a1c5cf0:/BOOK/chapter10#
```

```
root@cc8a9a1c5cf0: /BOOK/chapter10 (dock...  ⌘1
root@cc8a9a1c5cf0:/BOOK/chapter10# g++ signal_trap.cpp
root@cc8a9a1c5cf0:/BOOK/chapter10# ./a.out
Starting ...
Just got 15 signal
cleaning up some used resources ...
Aborted
root@cc8a9a1c5cf0:/BOOK/chapter10#
```

Here, we performed a couple of things, as follows:

1. We've built the `signal_trap.cpp` program and generated the `a.out` executable.
2. Run `./a.out`.
3. On the shell on the left, we took `pid` of the `a.out` process, which was `133`.
4. We've built the `signal_send.cpp` program to the `terminate` executable.
5. We run `./terminate` with the `pid` variable of the process `a.out` we wanted to terminate: `./terminate 133`.
6. On the shell on the right, we could see the `a.out` process terminating correctly.

Step 1 has a couple of things we have to explain. First, we parsed the `pid` variable from the command-line parameter, converted to an integer, and then saved it into the `pid` variable. Second, we called the `kill()` system call by passing the `pid` variable and the `SIGTERM` signal we have to send to the running process.

man 2 kill: int kill(pid_t pid, int sig);
The kill() function sends the signal specified by sig to pid.
For System V compatibility, if the PID is negative (but not −1), the signal is sent to all of the processes whose process group IDs are equal to the absolute value of the process number. However, if the pid is 0, sig is sent to every process in the **invoking process's** process group.

There's more...

In order to send a signal to another process (or processes), the sending process must have appropriate privileges. Put simply, a process can send signals to another process if the current user owns it.

There might be cases where a process has to send a signal to itself. In this case, the system call, raise(), does the job:

```
int raise (int signo);
```

Note one final, yet very important, thing: the handler code that manages the signal raised must be reentrant. The rationale behind that is that the process might be in the middle of any processing, so the handler must be very careful in modifying any static or global data. A function is **reentrant** if the data manipulated is allocated on the stack or passed in the input.

See also

- The *Learning how to trap a signal* recipe
- The *Learning how to ignore a signal* recipe
- The *Learning all of the signals and their default actions* recipe

11
Scheduling

System programming is about interacting with the underlying OS. The scheduler is one of the core components of every OS and impacts the way processes are allocated on CPUs. Ultimately, this is what the end user is concerned about: processes running smoothly and with correct priority over other processes. This chapter will teach you the practical skills you need in order to interact with the scheduler by changing the process' policy, its `nice` value, the real-time priority, processor affinity, and how real-time processes can **yield** the processor.

This chapter will cover the following recipes:

- Learning to set and get a scheduler policy
- Learning to get the timeslice value
- Learning how to set a nice value
- Learning how to yield the processor
- Learning about processor affinity

Technical requirements

To try out the programs in this chapter, we've set up a Docker image that contains all the tools and libraries we'll need throughout this book. It is based on Ubuntu 19.04.

To set it up, follow these steps:

1. Download and install Docker Engine from `www.docker.com`.
2. Pull the image from Docker Hub: `docker pull kasperondocker/system_programming_cookbook:latest`.
3. The image should now be available. Type in the following command to view the image: `docker images`.

4. You should have the following image:
   `kasperondocker/system_programming_cookbook`.

5. Run the Docker image with an interactive shell with the help of the `docker run -it --cpu-rt-runtime=95000 --ulimit rtprio=99 --cap add=sys_nice kasperondocker/system_programming_cookbook:latest /bin/bash` command.

6. The shell on the running container is now available. Use `root@39a5a8934370/# cd /BOOK/` to get all the programs that have been developed for this book.

The `--cpu-rt-runtime=95000`, `--ulimit rtprio=99`, and `--cap add=sys_nice` arguments are needed to allow the software written in Docker to set the scheduler parameters. If the host machine has been configured correctly, the software won't have any issues.

Disclaimer: The C++20 standard has been approved (that is, technically finalized) by WG21 in a meeting in Prague at the end of February. This means that the GCC compiler version that this book uses, 8.3.0, does not include (or has very, very limited support for) the new and cool C++20 features. For this reason, the Docker image does not include the C++20 recipe code. GCC keeps the development of the newest features in branches (you have to use appropriate flags for that, for example, `-std=c++2a`); therefore, you are encouraged to experiment with them by yourself. So, clone and explore the GCC contracts and module branches and have fun.

Learning to set and get a scheduler policy

In a system programming context, there are cases where some processes must be handled differently than others. By differently, we mean the different ways a process gets a processor time or a different priority. A system programmer must be aware of this and learn how to interact with the scheduler's API. This recipe will show you how to change the **policy** of a process to meet different scheduling requirements.

How to do it...

This recipe will show you how to get and set the *policy* of a process alongside the limits that can be assigned to it. Let's get started:

1. On a shell, let's open a new source file called `schedParameters.cpp`. We need to check what the current (default) process policy is. To do this, we'll use the `sched_getscheduler()` system call:

```cpp
#include <sched.h>
#include <iostream>
#include <string.h>
#include <sys/types.h>
#include <unistd.h>

int main ()
{
    int policy = sched_getscheduler(getpid());
    switch(policy)
    {
        case SCHED_OTHER: std::cout << "process' policy =
            SCHED_OTHER"
                                    << std::endl ; break;
        case SCHED_RR: std::cout << "process' policy = SCHED_RR"
                                 << std::endl; break;
        case SCHED_FIFO: std::cout << "process' policy =
SCHED_FIFO"
                                    << std::endl; break;
        default: std::cout << "Unknown policy" << std::endl;
    }
```

2. Now, we want to assign the `SCHED_FIFO` policy with a real-time (`rt`) priority. To make the code portable, we get the min and max from the `sched_get_priority_min` and `sched_get_priority_max` APIs:

```cpp
int fifoMin = sched_get_priority_min(SCHED_FIFO);
int fifoMax = sched_get_priority_max(SCHED_FIFO);
std::cout << "MIN Priority for SCHED_FIFO = " << fifoMin
    << std::endl;
std::cout << "MAX Priority for SCHED_FIFO = " << fifoMax
    << std::endl;

struct sched_param sched;
sched.sched_priority = (fifoMax - fifoMin) / 2;
if (sched_setscheduler(getpid(), SCHED_FIFO, &sched) < 0)
    std::cout << "sched_setscheduler failed = "
```

```
                        << strerror(errno) << std::endl;
    else
        std::cout << "sched_setscheduler has set priority to = "
                    << sched.sched_priority << std::endl;
```

3. We should be able to check the new `SCHED_FIFO` policy that was assigned with the `sched_getscheduler()` function:

```
policy = sched_getscheduler(getpid());
std::cout << "current process' policy = " << policy << std
    ::endl ;
return 0;
}
```

The next section will describe the preceding code in detail.

How it works...

The POSIX standard defines the following policies:

- `SCHED_OTHER`: The normal scheduler policy (that is, not for real-time processes)
- `SCHED_FIFO`: First-in/first-out
- `SCHED_RR`: Round-robin

Here, `SCHED_OTHER` is the default one and `SCHED_FIFO` and `SCHED_RR` are the real-time ones. Actually, Linux defines `SCHED_NORMAL`, `SCHED_BATCH`, and `SCHED_IDLE` as other real-time policies. These are defined in the `sched.h` header file.

Step 1 calls `sched_getscheduler()` to check the current policy of the process. As expected, the default is `SCHED_OTHER`. We passed the input to the `getpid()` function (`<unistd.h>`), which returns the PID of the current process. `sched_getscheduler()` also accepts 0, which in this case represents the current process.

Step 2 has the goal of setting a real-time policy and giving priority to the current process with the `sched_setscheduler()` function. We want this process to have a higher priority over the normal processes running on the machine. Think, for example, of a (soft) real-time application where the computation cannot be interrupted or if a software interrupt is received and its processing cannot be postponed. These Linux boxes usually run very few processes for a dedicated purpose. To achieve this, the policy to set is `SCHED_FIFO` and the priority we set is the middle value between the min and max that can be set on the current system. It is always suggested to check these values with the `sched_get_priority_max()` and `sched_get_priority_min()` functions in order to write portable code. One thing to highlight is that the `sched_setscheduler()` function internally sets the `rt_priority` field of `struct task_struct`.

Step 3 checks that `SCHED_FIFO` has been correctly set by calling the `sched_getscheduler()` function, similar to what happened in *step 1*.

There's more...

`SCHED_FIFO` and `SCHED_RR` are the two policies that are defined by POSIX and implemented on Linux that allocate tasks on processors that are more suitable for real-time software. Let's go over how they work:

- `SCHED_FIFO`: When a task is returned by this policy, it continues to run until it blocks (for example, I/O requests), it yields the processor, or a higher priority task preempts it.
- `SCHED_RR`: This has the exact same logic as `SCHED_FIFO` but with one difference: the tasks that are scheduled with this policy have a timeslice assigned so that a task continues to run until the time slice expires or a higher task preempts it or yields the processor.

Note that when `SCHED_OTHER` (or `SCHED_NORMAL`) implements a preemptive form of multitasking, `SCHED_FIFO` and `SCHED_RR` are cooperative (they are not preempted).

The Linux main scheduler function loops over all the policies and for each one, it asks the next task to run. It does this with the `pick_next_task()` function, which is implemented by each policy. The main scheduler is defined in `kernel/sched.c`, which defines the `sched_class` struct. This states that each policy must be defined and implemented so that all the different policies are working properly. Let's take a look at this at a graphical level:

- `kernel/sched.c`: Defines `struct sched_class` and loops over the following policies:
  - `kernel/rt.c` (for `SCHED_FIFO` and `SCHED_RR`) sets `const struct sched_class rt_sched_class` with the specific real-time policy functions.
  - `kernel/fair.c` (for `SCHED_NORMAL` or `SCHED_OTHER`) sets `const struct sched_class fair_sched_class` with the fair scheduler-specific functions.

One way of looking at the Linux scheduler design is this: `kernel/sched.c` defines the interface and the specific policies beneath the interface. The interface is represented by the `struct sched_class` structure. The following is the interface implementation for `SCHED_OTHER`/`SCHED_NORMAL` (the CFS fair scheduler policy):

```
static const struct sched_class fair_sched_class = {
 .next = &idle_sched_class,
 .enqueue_task = enqueue_task_fair,
 .dequeue_task = dequeue_task_fair,
 .yield_task = yield_task_fair,
 .check_preempt_curr = check_preempt_wakeup,
 .pick_next_task = pick_next_task_fair,
 .put_prev_task = put_prev_task_fair,

#ifdef CONFIG_SMP
 .select_task_rq = select_task_rq_fair,
 .load_balance = load_balance_fair,
 .move_one_task = move_one_task_fair,
 .rq_online = rq_online_fair,
 .rq_offline = rq_offline_fair,
 .task_waking = task_waking_fair,
#endif
 .set_curr_task = set_curr_task_fair,
 .task_tick = task_tick_fair,
 .task_fork = task_fork_fair,
 .prio_changed = prio_changed_fair,
 .switched_to = switched_to_fair,
 .get_rr_interval = get_rr_interval_fair,
```

```
#ifdef CONFIG_FAIR_GROUP_SCHED
  .task_move_group = task_move_group_fair,
#endif
};
```

The real-time priority range of the `SCHED_FIFO` and `SCHED_RR` policies is `[1, 99]`, while the `SCHED_OTHER` priority (called `nice`) is `[-20, 10]`.

See also

- The *Learning how to set a nice value* recipe to see how the real-time priority is related to the nice priority
- The *Learning how to yield the processor* recipe to learn how to yield a running real-time task
- *Linux Kernel Development, Third Edition,* by Robert Love

Learning to get the timeslice value

The Linux scheduler offers different policies for allocating processor time to tasks. The *Learning to set and get a scheduler policy* recipe shows what policies are available and how to change them. The `SCHED_RR` policy, that is, the round-robin policy, is the one that's used on real-time tasks (with `SCHED_FIFO`). The `SCHED_RR` policy assigns a timeslice to each process. This recipe will show you how to configure the timeslice.

How to do it...

In this recipe, we'll be writing a small program to get the round-robin timeslice by using the `sched_rr_get_interval()` function:

1. On a new shell, open a new file called `schedGetInterval.cpp`. We have to include `<sched.h>` for the scheduler capabilities, `<iostream.h>` to log to the standard output, and `<string.h>` to use the `strerror` function and translate the `errno` integer into a readable string:

   ```
   #include <sched.h>
   #include <iostream>
   #include <string.h>

   int main ()
   ```

```
    {
        std::cout << "Starting ..." << std::endl;
```

2. To get the round-robin interval, we have to set the scheduler policy for our process:

```
struct sched_param sched;
sched.sched_priority = 8;
if (sched_setscheduler(0, SCHED_RR, &sched) == -1)
    std::cout << "sched_setscheduler failed = "
        << strerror(errno)
            << std::endl;
else
    std::cout << "sched_setscheduler, priority set to = "
        << sched.sched_priority << std::endl;
```

3. Now, we can get the interval with the `sched_rr_get_interval()` function:

```
struct timespec tp;
int retCode = sched_rr_get_interval(0, &tp);
if (retCode == -1)
{
    std::cout << "sched_rr_get_interval failed = "
            << strerror(errno) << std::endl;
    return 1;
}

std::cout << "timespec sec = " << tp.tv_sec
        << " nanosec = " << tp.tv_nsec << std::endl;
std::cout << "End ..." << std::endl;
return 0;
}
```

Let's see how this works under the hood.

How it works...

When a task gets the processor with the SCHED_RR policy, it has priority over the SCHED_OTHER and SCHED_NORMAL tasks and gets allocated a defined timeslice that continues to run until the timeslice expires. Higher priority tasks run until they explicitly yield the processor or block. An important factor for a system programmer is to know the timeslice for the SCHED_RR policy. This is quite important. If the time slice is too large, other processes might wait a long time before getting CPU time, while if it is too small, the system might spend a significant amount of time context switching.

Step 1 shows the includes that are needed for the rest of the program. `<iostream>` is for the standard output, `<sched.h>` is used to get access to the scheduler features, and `<string.h>` is used for the `strerror()` function.

Step 2 is very important as it sets the SCHED_RR policy for the current process. As you may have noticed, we passed 0 as the first parameter. This is perfectly fine since the man page of the `sched_setscheduler()` function says, *If pid equals zero, the policy of the calling thread will be set.*

Step 3 calls the `sched_rr_get_interval()` function. It accepts two parameters: the PID and `struct timespec`. The first is an input parameter, while the latter is an output parameter that contains the timeslice in the form of `{sec, nanoseconds}`. For the first parameter, we could have passed the `getpid()` function, which returns the PID of the current process. Then, we simply log the standard output to the timeslice that's returned.

There's more...

Where does the SCHED_RR timeslice come from? The Linux scheduler, as we already know, has different policies. All of them are implemented in different modules: `kernel/sched_fair.c` for SCHED_NORMAL or SCHED_OTHER and `kernel/rt.c` for SCHED_RR and SCHED_FIFO. By looking at `kernel/rt.c`, we can see that the `sched_rr_get_interval()` function returns the `sched_rr_timeslice()` variable, which is defined on top of the module. We can also see that if `sched_rr_timeslice()` is called for the SCHED_FIFO policy, it returns 0.

See also

- The *Learning how to yield the processor* recipe as an alternative to stopping the running task instead of waiting for the timeslice
- The *Learning to set and get a scheduler policy* recipe
- *Linux Kernel Development, Third Edition*, by Robert Love

Learning how to set a nice value

The SCHED_OTHER/SCHED_NORMAL policy implements the so-called completely fair scheduler (CFS). This recipe will show you how to set the nice value for normal processes in order to increase their priority. We'll see that the nice value is used to weigh the timeslice that a process has. Priority must not be confused with the real-time priority, which is specific to the SCHED_FIFO and SCHED_RR policies.

How to do it...

In this recipe, we'll implement a program that will increase the nice value of a process:

1. On a shell, open a new source file called schedNice.cpp. We need to add some includes and call the nice() system call by passing the value we want to set for the current process:

```
#include <string.h>
#include <iostream>
#include <unistd.h>

int main ()
{
    std::cout << "Starting ..." << std::endl;

    if (nice(5) == -1)
        std::cout << "nice failed = " << strerror(errno)
            << std::endl;
    else
        std::cout << "nice value successfully set = " << std::endl;
    while (1) ;

    std::cout << "End ..." << std::endl;
    return 0;
}
```

In the next section, we'll see how this program works and how the nice value is used to influence the time a task gets on a processor.

How it works...

Step 1 basically calls the `nice()` system call, which increments the static priority of the task by the given amount. Just to be clear, assuming a process starts with a priority of `0` (which is the default value for the `SCHED_OTHER` and `SCHED_NORMAL` policies), two consecutive calls of `nice(5)` will set its static priority to `10`.

Let's build and run the `schedNice.cpp` program:

```
root@d8e2d9e717f1:/BOOK/chapter11# ./a.out    root@d8e2d9e717f1:/# ps -el
Starting ...                                  F S   UID   PID  PPID  C PRI  NI ADDR SZ WCHAN   TTY          TIME CMD
nice value succesfully set =                  4 S     0     1     0  0  80   0 -  1045 -      pts/0    00:00:00 bash
                                              4 S     0   150     0  0  80   0 -  1045 -      pts/1    00:00:00 bash
                                              0 R     0   169     1 97  85   5 -  1458 -      pts/0    00:00:03 a.out
                                              0 R     0   170   150  0  80   0 -  1438 -      pts/1    00:00:00 ps
                                              root@d8e2d9e717f1:/#
```

Here, we can see that, on the left, we have our process running and on the right, we've run the `ps -el` command to get the nice values of the running processes. We can see that the `./a.out` process now has a `nice` value of 5. To give a task a higher priority (and then a lower value of `nice`), the process needs to run as root.

There's more...

The `struct task_struct` structure has three values to represent a task priority: `rt_prio`, `static_prio`, and `prio`. We discussed `rt_prio` in the *Learning to set and get a scheduler policy* recipe and defined that this field represents the priority for real-time tasks. `static_prio` is the `struct task_struct` field that's used to store the `nice` value, while `prio` contains the actual task priority. The lower `static_prio` is, the higher the `prio` value of the task.

There may be cases where we need to set the `nice` value of a process at runtime. The command we should use in this situation is `renice value -p pid`; for example, `renice 10 -p 186`.

See also

- The *Learning how to yield the processor* recipe as an alternative to stopping the running task instead of waiting for the timeslice
- The *Learning to set and get a scheduler policy* recipe

Learning how to yield the processor

When a task is scheduled with one of the real-time scheduling policies (that is, SCHED_RR or SCHED_FIFO), you may need to yield the task from the processor (yielding the task means to relinquish the CPU, making it available to other tasks). As we described in the *Learning to set and get a scheduler policy* recipe, when a task is scheduled with the SCHED_FIFO policy, it does not leave the processor until a certain event occurs; that is, there is no concept of a timeslice. This recipe will show you how to yield a process with the sched_yield() function.

How to do it...

In this recipe, we'll develop a program that will yield the current process:

1. On a shell, open a new source file called schedYield.cpp and type in the following code:

```cpp
#include <string.h>
#include <iostream>
#include <sched.h>

int main ()
{
    std::cout << "Starting ..." << std::endl;

    // set policy to SCHED_RR.
    struct sched_param sched;
    sched.sched_priority = 8;
    if (sched_setscheduler(0, SCHED_RR, &sched) == -1)
        std::cout << "sched_setscheduler failed = "
                        << strerror(errno)
                        << std::endl;

    for( ;; )
    {
        int counter = 0;
        for(int i = 0 ; i < 10000 ; ++i)
            counter += i;

        if (sched_yield() == -1)
        {
            std::cout << "sched_yield failed = "
                        << strerror(errno) << std::endl;
            return 1;
```

```
        }
    }

    // we should never get here ...
    std::cout << "End ..." << std::endl;
    return 0;
}
```

In the next section, we'll describe how our program and `sched_yield()` work.

How it works...

When `sched_yield()` is called on a task scheduled with `SCHED_FIFO` or `SCHED_RR`, it is moved to the end of a queue with the same priority and another task is run. Yields cause a context switch, so it should be used carefully and when strictly needed.

Step 1 defines the program that shows us how to use `sched_yield()`. We simulated a CPU-bound type of process where we check periodically in order to yield the processor. Before doing that, we had to set the policy type for this process to `SCHED_RR` and the priority to 8. As you can see, there is no information about the process (PID) to yield, so it assumes that the current task will be yielded.

There's more...

`sched_yield()` is a system call that can be used by userspace applications. Linux usually calls the `yield()` system call, which has the advantage of keeping the process in a `RUNNABLE` state.

See also

- The *Learning to set and get a scheduler policy* recipe to review how to change a policy's type
- *Linux Kernel Development, Third Edition*, by Robert Love

Learning about processor affinity

In a multi-processor environment, the scheduler has to deal with task allocation on multiple processors or cores. From a Linux perspective, processes and threads are the same thing; both are represented by the `struct task_struct` kernel structure. There may be the need to force two or more tasks (that is, threads or processes) to run on the same processor to leverage, for example, the cache by avoiding the cache invalidation. This recipe will teach you how to set a *hard affinity* on a task.

How to do it...

In this recipe, we'll develop a small piece of software in which we'll force it to run on a CPU:

1. On a shell, open a new source file called `schedAffinity.cpp`. What we want is to check the affinity mask for the newly created process. Then, we need to prepare the `cpu_set_t` mask to set the affinity on the CPU to 3:

```cpp
#include <iostream>
#include <sched.h>
#include <unistd.h>

void current_affinity();
int main ()
{
    std::cout << "Before sched_setaffinity => ";
    current_affinity();

    cpu_set_t cpuset;
    CPU_ZERO(&cpuset);
    int cpu_id = 3;
    CPU_SET(cpu_id, &cpuset);
```

2. Now, we are ready to call the `sched_setaffinity()` method and force the hard affinity for the current task on CPU number 3. To check whether the affinity has been set correctly, we'll also print the mask:

```cpp
int set_result = sched_setaffinity(getpid(),
                                   sizeof(cpu_set_t),
                                   &cpuset);
if (set_result != 0)
{
    std::cerr << "Error on sched_setaffinity" << std::endl;
```

```
        }

        std::cout << "After sched_setaffinity => ";
        current_affinity();
        return 0;
    }
```

3. Now, we have to develop the `current_affinity()` method, which will just print the mask for the processors:

```
// Helper function
void current_affinity()
{
    cpu_set_t mask;
    if (sched_getaffinity(0, sizeof(cpu_set_t), &mask) == -1)
    {
        std::cerr << "error on sched_getaffinity";
        return;
    }
    else
    {
        long nproc = sysconf(_SC_NPROCESSORS_ONLN);
        for (int i = 0; i < nproc; i++)
        {
            std::cout << CPU_ISSET(i, &mask);
        }
        std::cout << std::endl;
    }
}
```

What would happen if we set the affinity on a nonexistent CPU (for example, `cpu_id = 12`)? Where in the kernel is the affinity mask information stored? We'll answer these and other questions in the next section.

How it works...

Step 1 does two things. First, it prints the default affinity mask. We can see that the process is scheduled to run on all the processors. Second, it prepares `cpu_set_t`, which represents a set of CPUs, by initializing it with the `CPU_ZERO` macro and setting the affinity on CPU 3 with the `CPU_SET` macro. Note that the `cpu_set_t` object must be manipulated directly but only via the macro provided. A full list of macros is documented on the man page: `man cpu_set`.

Step 2 calls the `sched_setaffinity()` system call to set the affinity (specified in the `mask` variable, that is, `cpu_set_t`) on the process with the PID returned by the `getpid()` function. We could have passed `0` instead of `getpid()`, meaning the current process. After the `setaffinity` function, we printed the CPU's mask to verify the correct new value.

Step 3 contains the definition of the helper function we used to print the standard output onto the mask for the CPUs. Note that we get the number of available processors through the `sysconf()` system call and by passing `_SC_NPROCESSORS_ONLN`. This function checks the system information that's present in the `/sys/` folder. Then, we loop over each processor and call the `CPU_ISSET` macro while passing `i-th`. The `CPU_ISSET` macro will set the respective bit for the `i-th` CPU.

If you try to modify `int cpu_id = 3` and pass a different processor, that is, a nonexisting one (for example, `15`), the `sched_setaffinity()` function will obviously fail, returning `EINVAL` and leaving the affinity mask untouched.

Let's take a look at the program now:

```
root@d8e2d9e717f1:/BOOK/chapter11# g++ schedAffinity.cpp
root@d8e2d9e717f1:/BOOK/chapter11# ./a.out
Before sched_setaffinity => 1111
After sched_setaffinity => 0001
root@d8e2d9e717f1:/BOOK/chapter11#
```

As we can see, the CPUs mask is set to 1 for each processor. This means that the process, at this stage, can be scheduled on each CPU. Now, we set the mask, asking the scheduler to run the process (**hard affinity**) only on CPU 3. When we call `sched_getaffinity()`, the mask reflects this.

There's more...

When we call the `sched_setaffinity()` system call, we ask the scheduler to run a task on a specific processor. We call this hard affinity. There is also a soft affinity. This is automatically managed by the scheduler. Linux always tries to optimize resources and avoids cache invalidation in order to speed up the performance of the whole system.

When we set the affinity mask through the macro, we are basically setting `cpus_allowed` in the `task_struct` structure. This makes a lot of sense since we're setting the affinity of a process or thread on one or more CPUs.

If you want to set the affinity of a task to more than one CPU, the `CPU_SET` macro must be called for the CPUs you want to set.

See also

- The *Learning how to yield the processor* recipe
- The *Learning to get the timeslice value* recipe
- The *Learning to set and get a scheduler policy* recipe

Other Books You May Enjoy

If you enjoyed this book, you may be interested in these other books by Packt:

Hands-On Embedded Programming with C++17
Maya Posch

ISBN: 978-1-78862-930-0

- Choose the correct type of embedded platform to use for a project
- Develop drivers for OS-based embedded systems
- Use concurrency and memory management with various microcontroller units (MCUs)
- Debug and test cross-platform code with Linux
- Implement an infotainment system using a Linux-based single board computer
- Extend an existing embedded system with a Qt-based GUI
- Communicate with the FPGA side of a hybrid FPGA/SoC system

Advanced C++ Programming Cookbook
Dr. Rian Quinn

ISBN: 978-1-83855-991-5

- Solve common C++ development problems by implementing solutions in a more generic and reusable way
- Achieve different levels of exception safety guarantees by introducing precise declarations
- Write library-quality code that meets professional standards
- Practice writing reliable, performant code that exposes consistent behavior in programs
- Understand why you need to implement design patterns and how it's done
- Work with complex examples to understand various aspects of good library design

Leave a review - let other readers know what you think

Please share your thoughts on this book with others by leaving a review on the site that you bought it from. If you purchased the book from Amazon, please leave us an honest review on this book's Amazon page. This is vital so that other potential readers can see and use your unbiased opinion to make purchasing decisions, we can understand what our customers think about our products, and our authors can see your feedback on the title that they have worked with Packt to create. It will only take a few minutes of your time, but is valuable to other potential customers, our authors, and Packt. Thank you!

Index

using 51, 52, 53
span
  using 72, 73
standard de facto tool 24
Standard Template Library (STL) 119
static memory 93
synchronization building blocks 137, 139, 140, 142

T

task-based threading 60, 63
TCP/IP
  used, for communicating with processes on another machine 184, 186, 188, 190, 192
template class, parameters
  period 222
  representation 222
thread
  creating 91, 92, 93
three-way handshake 176
time overrun
  about 235
  dealing with 232, 233
  working 234, 235
timeslice value

obtaining 255, 256, 257
  working 256
trailing-return-type 44
Translation Units (TUs) 79
Transport Control Protocol (TCP) 175

U

UDP/IP
  used, for communicating with processes on another machine 192, 194, 195, 197, 199
unique_ptr
  about 51
  using 53, 103, 104, 105
universal reference 58
User Data Protocol (UDP) 179
users
  commands for administration activities, setting up 17, 19, 21

V

variables 24
Voice over Internet Protocol (VoIP) 192

W

wall clock time 223

www.ingramcontent.com/pod-product-compliance
Lightning Source LLC
LaVergne TN
LVHW081519050326
832903LV00025B/1543